THE
GLORY OF
SPURS

A FAN'S GUIDE TO THE
ALL-TIME HIGHS AND LOWS OF
TOTTENHAM HOTSPUR

JIM DUGGAN

For my parents, who started me on the Spurs path, and Mary, for joining me on it.

The Glory of Spurs: A fan's guide to the all-time highs and lows of Tottenham Hotspur

This first edition published in 2012 by
Crimson Publishing Ltd., Westminster House, Kew Road, Richmond, Surrey
TW9 2ND

© Crimson Publishing 2012

Author: Jim Duggan

British Library Cataloguing in Publication Data
A catalogue record for this book is available from the British Library

ISBN 978 1 78059 112 4

Typeset by IDSUK (DataConnection) Ltd
Printed and bound in the UK by TJ International Ltd, Padstow, Cornwall

CONTENTS

INTRODUCTION

I was sipping a quick livener on Brighton Pier before an afternoon at the races back in May 2011 when I got a call to write a book about Spurs. It seemed like a good idea on that balmy afternoon, but the reality was a lot of long miserable nights with writer's block during the subsequent winter. The researching and re-reading of Spurs' fine history was fun, but it's an altogether different proposition turning it into something readable, vaguely witty and interesting.

The backdrop to writing the book was the fascinating 2011/12 season, when Spurs went from early disasters to one of the best runs in their history, only to then collapse before a final late rally taking them to the precipice of Champions League qualification, which they only missed out on when a German team lost a penalty shoot-out.

No medals, but for me a season to remember, and something in keeping with the triumphs and disasters that have marked the club's history since 1882. Give me a season where something happens over one of those terrible seasons between 1991 and 2005, when Spurs failed to finish inside the top or bottom six on any occasion.

Football – or more accurately, being a supporter – changed immeasurably over those years. The self-effacing terrace fun of the early fanzine era is often now replaced by a humourless cult of angry faces in expensive all-seater stadia, as the marketing of modern football ramps up the faux-importance of the game, and creates the illusion that all the worthwhile prizes are out of the reach of most of the fans most of the time.

Structured in a series of lists, this book takes a step back and remembers it's all a bit of fun. It remembers the triumphs and disasters along the way for the famous Lilywhites, and treats those two impostors just the same. The very best and the very worst of Spurs and, I hope, some of the fun that makes it all worthwhile.

An allegiance to a football club is a journey, a shared experience with pals over time. This book is for those who travel hopefully and don't take it too seriously.

ACKNOWLEDGEMENTS

Firstly, I'd like to thank Hugh Brune at Crimson Publishing for giving me the opportunity to write this book.

I'd also like to thank my Spurs pals over the years, including (from the wonderful FTL messageboard): Lynford, Scooby, Noodles, Naylor, Bazzer, Griot, Berti's, Geordie, Meatloaf, GlenS, Crackers, Langley, JPF, RobbyBoy, Ranger, Amarillo S, Shane, Shelfside, CAPSLOCK Ben, Alex, Rosie, Kiop and RichardP, SanJoaquin, Clives49, Woodo, Hazardman, Colston, Lauren, Eric M, Jim O'N, 'Jacob G', Stockport Si, UBB, Andy V, Bizzness, Logan, Carsie, McKeano, Hans M, Godders, DarrenA, DanielW, Antony G and Jurgen B.

Pat, Frank, Cockney and the rest of the lads from Cork Spurs. Mally, Paul D and all the Cumbrian Spurs. My music man Danny Keane. Lee, Will and the rest of the Block20 contingent, Winky, Jocky, Leader and everyone at the Brickies, Oystein, Langis and Vidar up in Norway, Grahame and Annamarie in Hungary, Boris in Macedonia, Martin and Adam in authors' corner, Mario, Wyart and Bernie from the fanzine days, Chris Leadbetter, Greg at the Kent Pub, the exiles Sean, Mat and Richard, Wendy and Dan from the new family, StephenE in Mexico and all the chaps on TOPSPURS Facebook and Twitter. And last but not least, club historian Andy Porter, who knows everything.

THE HISTORY

BRIEF TIMELINE: THE KEY DATES OF TOTTENHAM HOTSPUR

- **1882:** Hotspur FC formed under a street lamp on Tottenham High Street near the current ground by local schoolboys from St John's Presbyterian Grammar School looking for a winter pastime.

- **1884:** Renamed 'Tottenham Hotspur Football and Athletic Club'.

- **1888:** Spurs move to play home matches at Northumberland Park and the ever-canny owners introduce an admission fee of 3d.

- **1898:** After a few kit changes, the club adopt the lilywhite shirts of the leading northern side Preston North End, but retain their navy blue shorts.

- **1899:** Spurs move to a new ground, which eventually became known as White Hart Lane, with a capacity of 35,000 – ironically, around the same as the current ground. The inaugural match saw a 4-1 win for Spurs against Notts County, and generated £115 in gross receipts, which would just about buy a seat and a half-time bagel in the West Stand these days.

- **1901:** In a never-to-be-repeated feat, non-League Spurs lift the FA Cup after beating Fatty Foulke's Sheffield United 3-1 in a replay at Burnden Park, Bolton.

- **1908:** After consistent displays in the Southern League, Spurs are elected to the Second Division of the Football League.

- **1909:** Spurs win their first ever Football League match 3-0 against Wolves and take the division by storm, finishing runners-up and gaining promotion to First Division at the first attempt.

- **1919:** A fixed match between Liverpool and Manchester United and some shady shenanigans at a Football League meeting see Spurs relegated and replaced by Arsenal, who'd finished a miserable sixth in Division Two but leapfrog a host of better teams finishing ahead of them.

- **1920:** The relegation is a blessing in disguise, as Spurs storm to their first League title, the Second Division championship, with a record 70 points.

- **1921:** Jimmy Dimmock is the goal-scoring hero as Spurs lift the FA Cup after beating Wolves on a very wet Stamford Bridge pitch.

- **1922:** Spurs finish runners-up in the top flight for the first time, behind Liverpool.

- **1928:** Spurs end the decade on a low, with relegation to the Second Division — despite achieving a points total which would guarantee safety in most seasons.

- **1933:** Promotion again, this time as Division Two runners-up.

- **1935:** Despite finishing third the year before, Spurs are relegated to Division Two again.

- **1938:** Although it may affect some teams' fanbase, relegation does not stop the Tottenham faithful, and a White Hart Lane record of 75,038 turn up for the visit of Sunderland in the sixth round of the FA Cup. Typically, Spurs spoil the show by losing 1-0.

- **1950:** Led by football visionary Arthur Rowe, Spurs win the Second Division championship for the second time.

- **1951:** The revolutionary 'push and run' Spurs team claim the top flight title for the first time. It takes another two years and England's 6-3 home defeat to Hungary — the international equivalent of Spurs – before the rest of the country embraces the new footballing realities.

- **1952:** The 'push and run' team finish runners-up to Manchester United.

- **1957:** Spurs are runners-up once more to Manchester United.

- **1958:** Spurs beat Everton 10-4 in the first match of newly appointed manager Bill Nicholson.

- **1961:** Bill Nicholson's Spurs are crowned champions of the Football League and win the FA Cup final to become the first team to do the double in the 20th century.

- **1962:** Spurs retain the FA Cup with a 3-1 win against Burnley, new signing Jimmy Greaves scoring one of his record 266 Spurs goals in the final.

- **1963:** Spurs become the first British club to win a major European competition with a 5-1 win over Atlético Madrid in the Cup Winners' Cup Final in Rotterdam. At home, Spurs are runners up to Everton in Division One.

- **1967:** A 2-1 win over Chelsea gives Spurs the FA Cup for the fifth time.

- **1971:** Two goals from Martin Chivers are enough to see off lowly Aston Villa in the League Cup final.

- **1972:** Spurs claim the first ever UEFA Cup, a forerunner of the modern Champions League, with a 3-2 aggregate win over Wolves.

- **1973:** A late goal from sub Ralph Coates against Norwich City is enough to win Spurs the League Cup for the second time.

- **1974:** Defeat and disgrace in Europe. Supporters go on the rampage after Spurs lose 4-2 on aggregate to Feyenoord in the UEFA Cup final as the Nicholson era comes to an end.

- **1977:** After a few close scrapes, Spurs finish bottom and are relegated to the Second Division.

- **1978:** In a memorable season, a controversial 0-0 draw at Southampton is enough to see Spurs scrape into the last promotion spot on goal difference, with their 9-0 hammering of Bristol Rovers proving particularly significant.

- **1978:** The same year, Spurs scoop the world by signing Argentine World Cup winners Ossie Ardiles and Ricky Villa, but it's a struggle for the team to acclimatise to the top flight without any top-flight forwards.

- **1981:** Crooks and Archie signed, the year ends in one . . . and Spurs are back to win the 100th cup final against Manchester City with Ricky Villa's famous goal.

- **1982:** After losing the League Cup final in extra time to Liverpool, Spurs reach the semi-final of the Cup Winners' Cup, finish a creditable fourth in the League, and win the FA Cup for a then-record seventh time in the 66th game of a memorable season – after a less than memorable replay against QPR – in the club's centenary year.

- **1983:** Spurs are the first football club to float shares on the London Stock Exchange.

- **1984:** Spurs are winners of the UEFA Cup for the second time, after a penalty shoot-out with Anderlecht.

- **1987:** Clive Allen sets a new club record with 49 goals in a single season; yet it's close but no cigar as Spurs finish third in the League, make the semi-finals of the League Cup, but suffer a shock defeat to Coventry City in the FA Cup final.

- **1991:** Spurs conquer champions-elect Arsenal 3-1 in the FA Cup semi-final and return to Wembley the following month to beat Notts Forest 2-1 in the final.

- **1992:** Spurs are founder members of the new FA Premier League.

- **1993:** Chairman Alan Sugar removes Terry Venables and promises a League title within three seasons. Jason Dozzell signs for Spurs.

- **1994:** Ossie's famous five briefly dazzle the footballing world.

- **1999:** Spurs win the League Cup for a third time, with a last-minute winner from Allan Nielsen against Leicester, despite being down to 10 men after Justin Edinburgh's sending-off.

- **2002:** A wet weekend in Wales is made more miserable by Spurs being beaten 2-1 by Blackburn Rovers in the League Cup final.

- **2004:** After a high turnover of unsuccessful managers, Spurs eventually stumble upon Martin Jol.

- **2006:** A poisoned Spurs narrowly miss out on fourth place and Champions League football, but qualify for the UEFA Cup by a League placing for the first time in a generation.

- **2007:** Another fifth-place finish sees Spurs embark on successive European campaigns for the first time since the 1980s.

- **2008:** Spurs are winners of the League Cup for the fourth time, coming from a goal down to beat Chelsea 2-1 after extra time.

- **2009:** Spurs reach the League Cup final again but fail to retain the trophy, losing 4-1 on penalties to Manchester United after a goalless 120 minutes.

- **2010:** A win at Man City sees Spurs finish fourth in the Premier League and qualify for the Champions League for the first time.

- **2011:** A memorable first Champions League campaign sees Spurs progress to the last eight in Europe, with victories over both Milan giants along the way.

- **2012:** Spurs enter 2012 challenging for the League title for the first time in years, but a dip in form coinciding with the manager getting linked with the vacant England job sees the season go into a tailspin, before they eventually recover for a creditable fourth place. The fall-out sees Redknapp miss out on England then lose his Spurs job, while fourth place turns out not to be enough for Champions League qualification thanks to Chelsea winning the competition.

FIRST SPURS: FOURTEEN INSTANCES OF BLAZING THE TRAIL

1 There have been many 'Cities', 'Uniteds', 'Albions' etc. – but there is only one Hotspur.

2 First and only team to win the FA Cup as a non-League team in 1901, and in doing so becoming the first club to receive the Cup adorned by a set of ribbons in team colours.

3 First team to embrace continental techniques, as Arthur Rowe put his time in Hungary to good effect to change English football forever with 'push and run' football.

4 First team to win Division Two and Division One titles in consecutive seasons in 1950 and 1951.

5 First team to achieve the 20th century FA Cup and League Championship double with a record number of wins, including a record number of consecutive wins at the start of the season in 1960/61.

6 First team to sign a £99,999 player, as Jimmy Greaves put pen to paper for the iconic fee in 1961 to avoid being the first £100,000 player.

7 First British team to win a European trophy, with a 5-1 defeat of Atlético Madrid in the European Cup Winners' Cup final in 1963. This also remains the highest one-game score for a British side in a European final.

8 First team to win the UEFA Cup in 1972, with a 3-2 aggregate win over Wolves in the inaugural competition.

9 First team to float on the Stock Exchange in 1983.

10 First British team to win the UEFA Cup twice, in 1984, and by doing so becoming the first British team to win European trophies in three consecutive decades.

11 First team to engage in non-football branding, unfortunately with Hummel, in the late 1980s.

12 First team to nearly bankrupt itself twice by single-stand ground redevelopments in the 1980s and 1990s.

13 Founder (and ever-present) member of English Premier League, the most successful football franchise in the world.

14 First team to blast through the group stage of the Champions League with an average of three goals a game, to top a group containing reigning Champions Inter Milan in 2010.

SPURS FIRSTS: FORTY PIONEERING PEOPLE AND EVENTS

1 **First captain:** Bobby Buckle

2 **First chairman:** John Ripsher

3 **First colours:** Navy blue

4 **First ground:** Tottenham Marshes

5 **First match:** A two-goal defeat to Radicals on 30 September 1882

6 **First goal:** Scorer not recorded, in a 1-8 defeat to Latymer in October 1882

7 **First win:** 6 October 1883, a 9-0 home win over Brownlow Rovers

8 **First (recorded) goal scorer:** Bobby Buckle in the 1-3 defeat by Grange Park in October 1883

9 **First hat-trick:** Jack Jull scoring all three in a 3-0 home win against Albion in 1884

10 **First competitive match:** A 5-2 home win against St Albans in the London Association Cup in 1885

11 **First FA Cup match:** Beating West Herts, later to become Watford, 3-2 in 1894

12 **First international:** Jack Jones, for Wales against Ireland in 1898

13 **First England player (and scorer):** Two goals for Vivian Woodward v Ireland in 1903

14 **First manager:** Frank Brettell in 1898

15 **First game at White Hart Lane:** Beating Notts County 4-1 in front of more than 5000 supporters, thanks to a hat-trick from David Copeland, in September 1899

16 **First major trophy:** Spurs crowned Southern League champions in 1900

17 **First FA Cup:** Winning 3-1 against Sheffield United in a replay at Burnden Park in 1901

18 **First sending off:** Joe Walton, against Brighton and Hove Albion in the Southern League in 1904

19 **First League goal:** Vivian Woodward, in a 3-0 win against Wolves in 1908 – also the first League goal at White Hart Lane

20 **First promotion:** Second in Division Two 1908/09

21 **First relegation:** 20th in Division One 1914/15

22 **First four-goal scorer:** Bert Bliss, in a 6-1 win on Boxing Day 1914 over Sheffield Wednesday

23 **First League championship:** Division Two in 1919/20

24 **First topped the League:** Winning first four matches and topping the League for the first eight of the 1925/26 season, before the traditional fall away to finish 15th

25 **First five-goal scorer:** Ted Harper, in a 7-1 opening-day win over Reading in August 1930

26 **First top-flight championship:** Division One in 1950/51

27 **First floodlit game:** A 5-3 win over Racing Club de Paris in September 1953

28 **First Wembley appearance:** FA Cup final in 1961, with a 2-0 win over Leicester

29 **First double:** League champions and FA Cup winners in 1960/61

30 **First European game:** A 4-2 defeat at Górnik Zabrze, which turned into a 10-5 aggregate win back at White Hart Lane in the second leg

31 **First European trophy:** Winning European Cup Winners' Cup in Rotterdam in 1963, beating Atlético Madrid 5-1

32 **First substitute:** Roy Low coming on for Derek Posse in 1965, in a draw against Arsenal

33 **First League Cup:** Two goals from Chivers to beat Aston Villa in the 1971 final

34 **First PLC:** Became the first football club to float on the London Stock Exchange, in 1983

35 **First million-pound signing:** Subsequent cup final hero Paul Stewart from Manchester City for £1.7 million

36 **First Premier League win:** 2-0 home win over Sheffield United in the sixth Premier League game in 1992

37 **First £10 million signing:** Sergei Rebrov signing for a reported £11 million in summer 2000 from Dynamo Kiev

38 **First goal of the new millennium:** Chris Armstrong, in the 1-0 home win over Liverpool

39 **First World Cup final player:** Christian Ziege becoming the first current Spurs player to appear in a World Cup final when he came on as substitute for Germany in their defeat to Brazil in 2002

40 **First Champions League game:** Losing 4-2 away in the first leg (as they had in the former European Cup), before winning the tie back at White Hart Lane against Young Boys Berne in 2010

SPURS' COMPLETE HONOURS

MAJOR TROPHIES

- Football League championships 1950/51 and 1960/61; runners-up 1921/22, 1951/52, 1956/57, 1962/63

- FA Cup winners 1900/01, 1920/21, 1960/61, 1961/62, 1966/67, 1980/81, 1981/82, 1990/91; runners-up 1986/87
- Football League Cup winners 1970/71, 1972/73, 1998/99, 2007/08; runners-up 1981/82, 2001/02, 2008/09
- European Cup Winners' Cup winners 1962/63
- UEFA Cup winners 1971/72, 1983/84; runners-up 1973/74
- Football League Division Two champions 1919/20, 1949/50
- FA Charity Shield winners 1920/21, 1951/52, 1961/62, 1962/63, 1967/68 (joint), 1981/82 (joint), 1991/92 (joint)
- Anglo-Italian League Cup winners 1971/72

PRE-LEAGUE TROPHIES

- Southern League champions 1899/1900
- Western League champions 1903/04
- London League Premier Division champions 1902/03
- Southern District Charity Cup winners 1901/02, 1904/05 (joint), 1906/07

WARTIME TROPHIES

- Football League South, C Division champions 1939/40
- Football League South champions 1943/44, 1944/45

TOUR TROPHIES

- Costa Del Sol Tournament winners 1965 (Standard Liege 1-0), 1966 (Benfica 2-1)
- Nolia Cup (Sweden) winners 1977 (Leicester City 2-1)
- Japan Cup winners 1979 (Dundee United 2-0)
- Sun International Challenge Trophy (Swaziland) winners 1983 (Manchester United on penalties)
- Peace Cup (Korea) winners 2005 (beating French Champions Lyon 3-1 in the final)

- Vodacom Challenge Trophy (South Africa) winners 2007 (Orlando Pirates 3-0)

- Jubileum Toernooi (Holland) winners 2008 (beating Celtic and Borussia Dortmund)

- Asia Cup (China) Winners 2009 (Hull City 3-0)

OTHER TROPHIES

- London Challenge Cup winners 1910/11, 1928/29
- Dewar Shield winners 1901/02, 1933/34, 1934/35
- Norwich Charity Cup winners 1919/20
- Norwich Hospital Charity Cup winners 1946/47, 1949/50 (joint)
- Ipswich Hospital Charity Cup winners 1951/52 (joint)

THIRTY-TWO SPURS MANAGERS

1 **Frank Brettell (1898–1899):** Spurs' first manager lasted only a year in the job before being poached by big-money Pompey! The clubs with money may change, but the motivations of those in football do not.

2 **John Cameron (1899–1907):** Signed by Brettell as a player, the dashing Scotsman took on managerial duties with great aplomb while still playing, winning the Southern League before landing the FA Cup the following season.

3 **Fred Kirkham (1907–1908):** Commercial traveller and some-time referee, Kirkham's appointment was unpopular and short-lived.

4 **The directors (1908–1913):** Not for the first time, Spurs' owners thought they knew best, but a series of bottom-half finishes eventually convinced them otherwise.

5 **Peter McWilliam (1913–1927):** A club legend who steered Spurs through the difficult wartime period and on to the Second Division title, an FA Cup final win and the club's highest League finish when they were runners-up in

Division One in consecutive seasons. A miserly Spurs boardroom, who not for the last time failed to appreciate a good thing, forced him to move on after a contract dispute.

6 **Billy Minter (1927–1929):** Minter was a member of the elite '100 goals for Spurs' club during a long and distinguished playing career, but despite his best efforts was less successful from the touchline. His passion for Spurs was such that he offered to resign when he could not bring the results he felt a club of Spurs' stature deserved.

7 **Percy Smith (1929–1935):** The promise of promotion and a third-place finish soon evaporated and Smith left as Spurs were relegated amid accusations of boardroom interference.

8 **Jack Tresadern (1935–1938):** Unhappy ex-Hammer Tresadern was unpopular, unsuccessful and undermined. Efforts to re-recruit McWilliam were stepped up as Spurs' fortunes continued to slide.

9 **Peter McWilliam (1938–1942):** Like most things, it wasn't as good second time round, and McWilliam lasted little over a year before the outbreak of war, during which he retired.

10 **Arthur Turner (1942–1946):** Although never officially named as manager, club stalwart Turner steered Spurs during the wartime years, picking up a couple of titles along the way. This was one of a number of roles he had during his near-50-year association with the club.

11 **Joe Hulme (1946–1949):** Ex-Arsenal Hulme failed to get Spurs out of the Second Division, but did the groundwork for the glory to come with Rowe's team.

12 **Arthur Rowe (1949–1955):** Tottenham-born, and a former Spurs centre half, Rowe revolutionised British football with 'push and run' football, which saw Spurs win Division Two and Division One titles in consecutive seasons, with a runners-up place the season after. Further success eluded Rowe as he failed to replace ageing players, but fullback Sir Alf Ramsey and right half Bill Nicholson picked up plenty about the art of football management.

13 **Jimmy Anderson (1955–1958):** Anderson was another Spurs stalwart, whose last job at the club he joined in 1908 was to keep things ticking over until Bill Nicholson, his first team coach, was ready to take over.

14 **Bill Nicholson (1958–1974):** Mr Tottenham Hotspur started with a 10-4 win against Everton, managed Spurs' record 13-2 win over Crewe, but most importantly produced Spurs' greatest side, who achieved immortality by landing the double in 1961. Managed Spurs for 832 matches over 16 years and landed eight major trophies, which defined 'the Tottenham Hotspur way'.

15 **Terry Neill (1974–1976):** Former Gooner, whose unpopular period of 'Terry Nihilism' lasted only a couple of seasons before he buggered off back to Arsenal.

16 **Keith Burkinshaw (1976–1984):** Spurs went back to promoting from within the club and struck gold, eventually, with another dour Yorkshireman. General Burkinshaw endured relegation in his first season but achieved promotion at the first attempt and delivered a golden era of two FA Cups, the UEFA Cup and two consecutive fourth-place finishes during arduous Cup campaigns. Quoted as saying 'There used to be a football club over there,' after resigning due to a change of direction in the boardroom.

17 **Peter Shreeve (1984–1986):** Nearly won the League in his first season, but his understated manner counted against him in the flash yuppie era of the share floatation.

18 **David Pleat (1986–1987):** Based his Spurs side on the good-to-watch but unsuccessful Belgian World Cup team of 1986, and like the Belgians, Spurs won more plaudits than trophies. Walked the plank after just over a year in charge following tabloid allegations about his private life.

19 **Terry Venables (1987–1991):** Like Fergie at United, Venables took four years to win a trophy, but landed the FA Cup in his fourth season after a top-three finish in the League in the previous years. Unlike Fergie, who was spared a Michael Knighton takeover, Venables' stint at

Spurs was cut off in its prime due to financial troubles and boardroom reshuffles.

20 **Peter Shreeve (1991–1992):** 'Omar' was even less popular second time round as a stop-gap manager in a post-Gazza season of struggle.

21 **Livermore and Clemence (1992–1993):** There were two names above the door, but Venables was pulling the strings from the boardroom. It looked like it was all coming together with a superb end of season run in 1993, but an unlucky semi-final defeat, and Sugar's summer inquisition, put an end to all hope for a generation.

22 **Ossie Ardiles (1993–1994):** Tried to reinvent football without defenders and eventually failed, but not quite as bad as the stats make him look.

23 **Gerry Francis (1994–1997):** Like Dorian Gray, Spurs maintained a semblance of respectability in terms of League position while decaying internally as good players were replaced with bad ones, before it all collapsed in a relegation struggle in autumn 1997.

24 **Christian Gross (1997–1998):** Came with a train ticket dream, but struggled to control big dressing room egos. Achieved his objective of keeping Spurs up but was not allowed to build on it before Sugar killed him off three games into the next season.

25 **George Graham (1998–2001):** Sugar's increasing antagonism with the Spurs faithful culminated in the appointment of the anti-football messiah, who crowned his career by making the club – which had given English football 'push and run' and the double team – play out four consecutive 0-0s with Andy Booth leading the line in 2000.

26 **Glenn Hoddle (2001–2003):** The great one returned to lead Spurs to the brink of a trophy in his first season. However a luckless display in the final, inconsistent League form and the unsettling presence of a director of football with a grudge saw it end before it really began.

27 **David Pleat (2003–2004):** With Hoddle gone after six games, this was the longest end of a season ever, and season tickets rained down on the pitch as Spurs reached a modern low.

28 **Jacques Santini (2004):** A bizarre reign of few goals lasted only half the nine months the directors had taken to appoint him after sacking Hoddle.

29 **Martin Jol (2004–2007):** Gradually started to restore Spurs' long-lost pride with consecutive fifth place finishes and European football. Sometimes his sides could be over-cautious, but importantly Jol stopped the rot and prepared the ground for later success. If there is any justice he will be remembered with affection rather than for the undignified end, which came at half time during a televised match.

30 **Juande Ramos (2007–2008):** Spurs may have landed the League cup with a famous win over Chelsea in the first visit to the New Wembley, but 'Wendy Random' soon sent Spurs into a tailspin with his bizarre mix of tactics and substitutions.

31 **Harry Redknapp (2008–2012):** In an astonishing transformation, Redknapp took Spurs from two points in eight games in 2008 to three top five finishes for the first time since 1965, two of which were Premier League highs for the team, as well as the last eight of the Champions League. And yet Redknapp remained largely unappreciated by the masses, and was eventually sacked in summer 2012 despite the team's fourth place finish and a record League-points-per-game ratio for a Spurs manager.

32 **Andre Villas-Boas (2012–):** Spurs continue the alternation between simple (Jol and Redknapp) and complex (Santini and Ramos) in the manager's seat by appointing AVB within the dreaded Director of Football system.

THE HIGHS AND LOWS
OF SPURS

Spurs are mostly known, and sometimes loved, as a cup team, but they have had a good deal of League success, with two championships, four runners-up spots and a further nine third-place finishes. In statistical terms, this averages out at a podium finish once every five years and a top-six spot every three years in the top flight. The current run of 35 seasons in the top flight, and only one of the last 63 seasons outside it, is also the envy of many.

THE HIGHS

When Spurs do hit the summit, it is a cause for a paradigm shift in English football, as the table below shows.

Spurs' highs

	P	W	D	L	F	A	Pts
1950/51 Division I Champions	42	25	10	7	82	44	60
1960/61 Division I Champions	42	31	4	7	115	55	66

The first title in 1951 came under the astute tutelage of the often-overlooked football genius Arthur Rowe, who pioneered 'push and run' football – which ran rings around the traditional 'hit and hope' tactics of the era.

Spurs' next title was delivered under Bill Nicholson, who had earlier been an ever-present player in the 'push and run' side. Billy Nick's astute leadership off the field was matched by Danny Blanchflower's inspiration on it, and after winning the first 11 games of the season, Spurs stormed to the title with a 2-1 win over Sheffield Wednesday with four games to spare. By coincidence, the 1951 title was also secured with a narrow win over the Owls at White Hart Lane.

Another coincidence was that both managers who have led Spurs to the League title have done so on the back of long, distinguished playing careers with Spurs but only one England cap. With that in mind, did Spurs miss a trick in not appointing Steve Perryman, after his one game in charge as caretaker manager against Blackburn in 1994? He also had one cap for England after a long, distinguished career.

THE LOWS

At the other end of the scale, the worst Spurs have done in more than 100 years in the Football League is a 12th-place finish in the second tier in 1930. When you think of how some of the larger clubs have struggled from time to time, this is hardly a disaster.

Spurs have suffered four exits from the top flight in 112 years of League football (as shown in the table below), about the average West Ham manage in a decade.

Spurs' lows

	Position	P	W	D	L	F	A	Pts
1914/15 Division 1	20th	38	8	12	18	57	90	28
1927/28 Division 1	21st	42	15	8	19	74	86	38
1934/35 Division 1	22nd	42	10	10	22	54	93	30
1976/77 Division 1	22nd	42	12	9	21	48	72	33

The relegation in 1977 was overdue after the end of the great Bill Nicholson era, but the relegation in 1935 must have come as a bit of a shock. Spurs had finished third the season before under Percy Smith, but a disastrous run of only two wins in 20 games, including a 0-6 home defeat to Arsenal, sealed Spurs' fate.

The top-flight exit in 1928 was as bizarre and unlucky as a team could get. A 2-0 win over Arsenal at the start of April took Spurs to eighth and seven points off the summit. However, a failure to win any of the last four games, culminating in the customary defeat at Anfield, saw Spurs relegated. This was despite winning more home games than champions Everton and being only three wins away from fourth place, as an extraordinary sequence of events saw 18 of the 22 teams separated by six points at the end of the top flight's strangest season, as the table below shows.

Division One League table 1927/28

		P	W	D	L	F	A	Pts
1	Everton	42	20	13	9	102	66	53
2	Huddersfield Town	42	22	7	13	91	68	51
3	Leicester City	42	18	12	12	96	72	48
4	Derby County	42	17	10	15	96	83	44
5	Bury	42	20	4	18	80	80	44
6	Cardiff City	42	17	10	15	70	80	44
7	Bolton Wanderers	42	16	11	15	81	66	43
8	Aston Villa	42	17	9	16	78	73	43

		P	W	D	L	F	A	Pts
9	Newcastle United	42	15	13	14	79	81	43
10	Arsenal	42	13	15	14	82	86	41
11	Birmingham	42	13	15	14	70	75	41
12	Blackburn Rovers	42	16	9	17	66	78	41
13	Sheffield United	42	15	10	17	79	86	40
14	Sheffield Wednesday	42	13	13	16	81	78	39
15	Sunderland	42	15	9	18	74	76	39
16	Liverpool	42	13	13	16	84	87	39
17	West Ham United	42	14	11	17	81	88	39
18	Manchester United	42	16	7	19	72	80	39
19	Burnley	42	16	7	19	82	98	39
20	Portsmouth	42	16	7	19	66	90	39
21	Tottenham Hotspur	42	15	8	19	74	86	38
22	Middlesbrough	42	11	15	16	81	88	37

The relegation of 1915 was probably deserved, with a struggling team and minds turned towards Europe, but was not helped by a reputedly fixed result in Manchester United's match with Liverpool, which ensured safety for both.

THE BEST AND WORST OF THE SPURS KITS

The familiar lilywhite shirts are an homage to early frontrunners in English football Preston North End, while the navy blue shorts are retained from Spurs' original 1882 colours. Nothing much changed up to the 1970s, but increasing commercialism first saw an Umbro badge appear on the shirt, then an Admiral logo advance down the sleeves, before finally in the early 1980s the front of the shirt was adorned with the name of club sponsors Holsten. These days, there are at least three kits per season, and they change each campaign to encourage those who feel obliged to dress like the players on match day to part with their money.

Here are the best and worst of the Spurs kits over the years.

BEST HOME KITS

1 **European: pure lilywhite** With the special atmosphere generated by continental opposition under the lights of White Hart Lane, a Spurs team from any era always looks

something special in the all lilywhite strip enhancing the wonderful home record in Europe.

2 **Le Coq Sportif:** *magnifique* A great commercial match between a club and company with a shared cockerel motif, and our *copains Français* did not let us down, providing a fine kit with the badge moved to the middle and cool 3D numbers on the back. Best appreciated on Steve Perryman with the FA Cup held above his head in 1981.

3 **1991 FA Cup final: long shorts** The 1991 FA Cup final offered plenty of surprises, one of which was Spurs wearing a smart new kit that represented a break from the sad association with Hummel. It was also the first kit anywhere in the world to signal the return to longer shorts after a decade or more of them getting shorter and shorter.

4 **1970s home: pure and simple** A plain white shirt with a navy blue cockerel-on-ball badge. Simple and perfect, and the last of the line before commercial intrusion.

5 **2011/12 home: back to basics** Most modern kits have too much going on, with tweaks to colours and over-designed patterns to make them look sufficiently different from the year before to keep the fans buying. But Puma got it just right by going back to a simple lilywhite shirt and navy blue shorts with the minimum of fuss.

6 **And the worst ...** Aside from some of Ian Walker's colourful keeper's jerseys from the early 1990s, it has to be the unnecessary blue sleeves of the 2005/06 home kit. Blue sleeves meant it just wasn't a Spurs kit, and it also used terrible clingy material that made the average fat bloke wearing one look even more in need of a salad. The silly red Thomson logo, in the era of 'never red', compounded the impropriety.

BEST AWAY KITS

1 **2006/07 away: chocolate** It is quite rare that something gains instant iconic status, but it was obvious very early on that the club had stumbled upon a commercial success with

the chocolate third kit, which traced its lineage back to a chocolate and gold forerunner in the 1890s. It was simple and stylish, and in one of its first outings Spurs won away on their belated return to European competition in Prague.

2 **1977/78 away: epaulettes** In yellow, the traditional 'away' colour of the 1970s, and made by Admiral, it had two distinctive navy blue epaulettes that set it apart from the numerous yellow shirts of the era and those which followed for Spurs. Its iconic status was assured when it featured in many of the memorable moments of the 1977/78 promotion season.

3 **1995/96 away: purple** Spurs' first move away from blue or yellow produced a two-tone striped purple kit that even looked good when Dozzell was wearing it. Best appreciated with Sheringham, Armstrong, Fox and Howells doing the Vic Reeves *Shooting Stars*-style thigh-rubbing goal celebration at Coventry.

4 **Early 1970s away: vicar** Gained its clerical nickname because of its distinctive white collar at the top of a plain navy blue jersey with a white cockerel-on-ball badge. Like the home equivalent, simple and perfect.

5 **1993/94 away: pale blue** A kit with the word 'SPURS' written in very large letters over the shoulders was about as bold as it got in the era that taste forgot in the early 1990s.

6 **And the worst . . .** Come to think of it, it was probably that selfsame 1993 away kit. But in the darkest era for kit design, at least it was not as bad as the infamous Arsenal away shirt of the era, which remains the worst football shirt of all time.

The Spurs alphabet

A is for the Allens, Les, Clive and Paul.

B is for Blanchflower, defined the genius of Spurs.

C is for Cyril: nice one, son.

D is for Debut, Dominguez dazzling Derby.

E is for Europe, which is 'magnificent to be in', according to Bill Nicholson.

F is for Faithful; the Spurs fans who turn up in large numbers home and away, good or bad, rain or shine, year after year.

G is for Greaves, genius goalscorer.

H is for Hoddle, born the king of White Hart Lane.

I is for Ireland: Jennings, Blanchflower, Keane, Hughton, Galvin, Kinnear, Armstrong, Kirwan, Holmes and McGrath.

J is for Jones: Cliff, the Welsh wing wizard.

K is for Klinsmann, the most adored German ever.

L is for Lineker, '. . . uses him by not using him . . .'

M is for Mabbutt, the last in the tradition of the great club servants.

N is for Nicholson: Mr Tottenham Hotspur.

O is for Ossie, 'in de cup for Tottingham'.

P is for Perryman: the skipper.

Q is for Qu Bo. What was that all about?

R is for Ripsher and Rowe, the men who wrote the gospels according to Spurs.

S is for Scotland: Mackay, Archibald, White, Gilzean, Brown, Conn, Gough, Durie and Brazil.

T is for Tottenham, super Tottenham from the Lane.

U is for Ugly: some of the freaks down the road in N5.

V is for Villa: 'And it's still Ricky Villa!'

W is for Willie Morgan, and welcome to White Hart Lane, the world-famous home of the Spurs.

X is for X-rated, one of Graham Roberts' ferocious tackles.

Y is for Yeast, as in 'Why do Spurs fans sing "yeast"?' from the archive of misheard terrace lyrics.

Z is for Ziege, gifted wide man who was Spurs' first World Cup final representative.

IF ONLY . . . SEVENTEEN
EVENTS IN A PARALLEL
SPURS UNIVERSE

1   The schoolboys from St John's Presbyterian Grammar
    School are not given *Henry IV* but another Shakespeare play
    to study during the summer of 1882. Consequently, when
    they meet their pals from the cricket club, it's not Harry
    Hotspur but one of the Bard's other characters who is at
    the forefront of their minds when they come to choose a
    name for their newly formed association football club.
    'Tottenham Romeo', 'Tottenham Othello' or even
    'Tottenham Shylock' fail to encapsulate the same aura of
    glory associated with the derring-do of the Hotspur. After
    all, look what happened to Dulwich Hamlet.

2   After looking into Spurs' payment to Ernie Payne for his new
    boots in 1895, the FA for once decide not to bend Spurs
    over, and declare that nothing untoward has occurred. Spurs
    are not forced to become a professional club and remain
    amateurs, drifting around the base of the football pyramid
    for the next 100-plus years in the shadow of Enfield Town.

3   Arsenal move from Woolwich in 1913, but instead of
    heading to Islington they go just a few miles up the road
    to Abbey Wood. Chairman Henry Norris has his collar felt
    and spends the next couple of decades at His Majesty's
    pleasure, and Woolwich Arsenal drop down the League
    pyramid before finally being wound up when the ground
    is bulldozed for the new Thamesmead development in
    the 1960s.

4   Instead of losing 3-1 in the European Cup semi-final first leg
    in Benfica and at home to subsequent League Champions
    Ipswich in March 1962, Spurs are not victims of controver-
    sial decisions in Lisbon and repeat their 5-1 Charity Shield
    win over Alf Ramsey's Tractor Boys. Spurs go on to win the
    European Cup, as well as netting the domestic double for the
    second consecutive season, and are acknowledged as
    Europe's premier club for the rest of the century.

5 The Spurs board take Bill Nicholson's advice and appoint
Johnny Giles Spurs manager in 1974.

6 Southampton beat Spurs 1-0 in the last game of the season
in 1978 and are promoted as champions along with Bolton
and Brighton, while Spurs drop from League leaders to
fourth in the last week of the season. Keith Burkinshaw is
relieved of his duties and there is no Spurs presence in
Argentina to sign any of the World Cup-winning team.
Hoddle accepts an offer to play in Italy and Perryman signs
for League champions Liverpool. Daines, Pratt, Lacy and
Jones all commit themselves to the club, which languishes
outside the top flight for decades.

7 People still talk about Neville Southall's save from Falco's
header; but its not enough to prevent Spurs from beating
Everton 3-2 to go clear in the title race in March 1985 and
later win the League. Manager Shreeve, a promotion from
the boot room like the manager of the other successful
team of the era, Liverpool, is forever a Spurs legend and
creates his own dynasty with assistant John Pratt.

8 With Spurs leading Arsenal 1-0 at half time in the second
leg of the League Cup semi-final in 1987, the club don't
prematurely announce details of how to get tickets for the
final over the tannoy. Ungoaded Goons lose the game, and
lose again in the following year's final to Luton Town,
which sees George Graham sacked after a trophyless
decade at Highbury, and further obscurity follows.

9 Robert Maxwell outbids Alan Sugar for control of Spurs
in 1991.

10 The referee awards Spurs a penalty and sends Lineghan off
after a foul on Anderton in the 1993 FA Cup semi-final.
Spurs win a thrilling final against Chris Waddle's Sheffield
Wednesday, and the FA Cup never loses its magic or prestige.

11 Bryan Robson falls and dislocates his collar bone while
attempting to foul Sheringham in the League game between
Manchester United and Spurs at Old Trafford in 1993. Ted

recovers and Spurs continue their impressive start under Ossie with a win against United to go second in the League. The winter transfer window is full of quality and Ossie eventually finds the right balance between attack and defence, and the North London challenge to Manchester United comes from the Lilywhites for the rest of the decade.

12 Gerry Francis laughs off suggestions that he thought Zidane was 'wooden' and welcomes the Frenchman as a new signing to Spurs in 1995. Suitably impressed, Klinsmann, Barmby and Sheringham all stay (and Anderton doesn't get injured) and Spurs retain the Premier League title as Zidane lifts the World Cup in 1998.

13 Any one of a host of chances against Blackburn is taken to win Spurs the League Cup in 2002. With a trophy in his first season, Hoddle has the money and influence to mould a Spurs team in his image, and follows his mentor Bill Nicholson's footsteps to win a host of trophies as player and manager.

14 Daniel Levy takes the call from Roman Abramovich in 2002 and the Russian never gets to speak to Chelsea, who go bankrupt soon after.

15 Despite the food poisoning scare, Spurs beat West Ham to qualify for the Champions League for the first time in 2006. Arsenal, who miss out, are forced to sell their best players by the crippling debt from the new stadium that they find difficult to fill, and are eventually relegated after declaring bankruptcy.

16 Redknapp is unavailable after the Ramos sacking in 2008 and the recalled David Pleat finally succeeds in relegating Spurs by the following Easter.

17 In the last minute of injury time, Jermain Defoe slides in to score, capping a remarkable comeback from 2-0 down to win the title six-pointer at Eastlands in January 2012. The victory lifts Spurs to within two points of the Manchester pair, and the start of February brings further good news with Redknapp's acquittal in court. Before the FA have a chance

to disrupt Spurs' season by allowing speculation to link Harry with the England job, fickle Gooners force Wenger to walk out of the Emirates and straight into the newly vacant national role. Later that month, Spurs stroll into a two-goal lead at Arsenal and see out the rest of the game without incident as newly appointed manager Tony Adams struggles to get to grips with his new job. Spurs gain revenge on Manchester United for the opening-day defeat to top the table for the first time at the start of March, and win the remaining four games in the month to go clear. In the FA Cup, Spurs barely break stride to reach the final, overcoming Chelsea in the semi. A comical Liverpool side put up little resistance in the final and a win on the last day against old boy Martin Jol's Fulham seals the League title and the double for Spurs.

THE BIBLE ACCORDING TO SPURS

- **The Holy Trinity:** the Father, Bill Nicholson; the Son, Glenn Hoddle; and the Holy Spirit, Danny Blanchflower.

- **John the Baptist: Arthur Rowe,** who laid the groundwork for the greatness to come.

- **St Peter: Steve Perryman,** the rock of the Spurs church.

- **St Paul: Gareth Bale,** who was on the road to a loan spell at Notts Forest when, injury-prone and out of form, he was blinded by a light from Heaven and returned to Spurs as world-class winger.

- **Judas Iscariot: Sol Campbell,** who betrayed the righteous for not quite 30 pieces of silverware.

- **Doubting Thomas: Teddy Sheringham,** who didn't believe that Sugar and Francis could bring glory to Spurs. Correctly, as it turned out.

- **Lazarus: Darren Anderton,** who came back from the dead just in time for international tournaments for England, not once but twice.

- **Joseph: Ian Walker** and his technicolour goalkeeper's jersey.

- **Samson: Stephen Carr.** While young Carr had his 1990s crop, he blossomed into just about the best right back in the Premier League. After his Delilah moment when he became a skinhead, he turned into a miserable git who'd lost most of his footballing powers.

- **Angel Gabriel: Batistuta,** who performed God's will by knocking Arsenal out of the Champions League.

- **Jonah: Darren Anderton.** When was not being Lazarus, Anderton's presence in an FA Cup semi-final meant an early start to the summer holidays for his teammates in 1992, 1993, 1995, 1999 and 2001.

- **Moses: Martin Jol,** who led Spurs out of a generation of Premier League wilderness.

- **St Hotspur Day: 14 April,** celebrating the triumph of good over evil annually since 1991.

- **The damned: Arsenal fans,** doomed to watch anti-football in silence for eternity.

- **The good Samaritan: Alan Sugar,** who crossed the road to help Spurs out of financial trouble.

2

THE PLAYERS

MOST SPURS APPEARANCES

Top appearances

Player	Appearances	Goals
Steve Perryman (1969–86)	851 (3)	39
Pat Jennings (1964–77)	590	0
Gary Mabbutt (1982–98)	585 (26)	38
Cyril Knowles (1964–75)	504 (2)	17
Glenn Hoddle (1975–87)	478 (12)	110
Ted Ditchburn (1946–58)	452	
Jimmy Dimmock (1919–31)	438	112
Alan Gilzean (1964–74)	429 (10)	133
Phil Beal (1963–75)	417 (3)	1
John Pratt (1969–80)	381 (34)	49
Maurice Norman (1955–65)	411	19
Chris Hughton (1979–90)	389 (9)	19
Mike England (1966–75)	397	19

Statistics from League, FA Cup, League Cup, European Cup, European Cup Winners' Cup and UEFA Cup games, with bracketed appearances being as substitutes

When you add in other representative appearances in friendlies and the like, Perryman played in an astonishing 1,023 matches for Spurs – more matches than the number of days modern players tend to commit to a club. Having been given the Spurs captaincy at 23, Perryman also has the record for most games in the role. Another record that is unlikely to be broken is that he scored at least one League goal in each of his 17 consecutive seasons with Spurs. A proper legend.

John Pratt sometimes looked a bit like Perryman from a distance, which may explain why successive managers kept picking him. JP was Spurs through and through, in passion if not always in ability, and never let Spurs down in his 400-plus appearances. Well, never intentionally.

Overlapping Perryman at the start of the 1980s, Gary Mabbutt had to earn his Spurs the hard way. Arriving unheralded from Bristol Rovers in an era of superstars, Mabbutt's quiet determination and effectiveness initially in midfield and then at centre back won him many admirers and helped define the Spurs way in the modern era. Mabbutt lifting the cup in 1991 with Princess Diana looking on is one of the enduring Spurs images.

Chris Hughton was another stalwart from the successful 1980s team who formed a formidable left-side partnership with fellow 'Irishman' Tony Galvin. His two goals against Arsenal in a 5–0 win during Easter 1983 are one of many great moments for a player Spurs never successfully replaced for nearly 20 years. For most of this time, Hughton was on the other side of the white line on the coaching staff.

Five of the top 13 players – Jennings, Knowles, Beal, England and Gilzean – played alongside each other as the spine of the successful post-double team for Bill Nicholson, with a collective total of 2,366 appearances. All provided the consistent quality demanded by Bill Nick over a long period of time in an era of cup wins and elevated League placings. No wonder Spurs found life hard without them, and were relegated as the last of them left in 1977.

Maurice Norman's already impressive total would have been higher but for suffering a career-finishing injury in a mid-season friendly. It was a sad end to a great career, which included being a mainstay of the double team's defence.

From an earlier era, Jimmy Seed, Tommy Clay, Arthur Grimsdell and Jimmy Dimmock were the first group of players to play more than 250 times for Spurs. They were regulars for most of the roaring 20s, picking up a Division Two championship medal and an FA Cup winners' medal each along the way.

And last but not least, Glenn Hoddle. From scoring 22 goals in midfield in 1979, through supplying Crooks and Archie in the early 1980s, to the mature player who excelled in the 1987 side, Hoddle was quite simply the most gifted footballer his country has ever produced, and tragically underappreciated in his own time outside his adoring Spurs audience.

ELEVEN CASES OF 'DID HE PLAY THAT OFTEN!'

1 **John Pratt (1969–80); appearances 381 (34), goals 49.** There was no-one quite like John Pratt, not before or after, or for any other club. Who else can claim to have been given his chance at Spurs by the great Bill Nicholson, make 415 appearances (the 10th highest), score 49 goals, and yet be booed at his own testimonial?

2 **Darren Anderton (1992–2004); appearances 329 (29), goals 48.** The pre-injuries Anderton was a crowd favourite and world-class winger who could not play often enough. However, his second coming, which seemed to last much longer, struggled to fulfil his early promise in the middle of midfield in Spurs sides that mirrored his own decline.

3 **Justin Edinburgh (1990–2000); appearances 246 (30), goals 1.** The real trouble with 'Ricky' was not that he wasn't very good (he wasn't), it was that Spurs kept trying to replace him with players who were even worse and he would eventually get back into the team.

4 **Mitchell Thomas (1986–91); appearances 176 (22), goals 8.** Known more for his YTS start and zany haircuts, Mad Mitch somehow negotiated the shifting sands from Pleat to Venables to notch up nearly 200 appearances for Spurs.

5 **Jermaine Jenas (2005–11) appearances 175 (26), goals 26.** As a £5 million teenager, Jenas had always been hailed as a player with great promise. Spurs fans watched

and waited for something special to happen, and despite his being part of a decent side, nothing happened. Jenas was eventually loaned to the place where nothing ever happens, Aston Villa.

6 **Chris Jones (1974–82); appearances 166 (19), goals 42.** Like another goal-scoring hero, Len Duquemin, Jones was a forward from the Channel Islands. However, the similarities ended there for the player who developed a comical bald spot towards the end of his career that made him resemble a monk.

7 **John Lacy (1978–83); appearances 126 (6), goals 3.** The fact that the giraffe-like Lacy started as many games as Ginola is just sad.

8 **Stefan Freund (1999–2003); appearances 121 (10), goals 0.** A midfielder who could not pass and managed to avoid scoring in 131 appearances for Spurs. This made him the epitome of the George Graham team. His tackling wasn't great either.

9 **Terry Fenwick (1988–93); appearances 115 (3), goals 10.** Fenwick must have possessed some voodoo power over Venables, who took him to each of his clubs (apart from Barcelona for some reason). He could take a decent penalty, but on the whole he was a bit of a donkey who never really clicked with the crowd, and had a profile more befitting an Arsenal player off the pitch.

10 **Jason Dozzell (1993–97); appearances 80 (19), goals 14.** There are some players who you watch and genuinely wonder how they became footballers. Dozy defined the type, lacking skill and athleticism in almost equal measure during his all-too-long stint with Spurs.

11 **Gordon Smith (1979–81); appearances 40 (5), goals 1.** A player so inconsequential he is unlikely to ever make any top ten Spurs lists.

BORN IS THE KING OF WHITE HART LANE: SEVENTEEN OF THE BEST FROM THE GREAT GLENN

1 The 18-year-old Hoddle announced himself to the football world by scoring the winning goal against Stoke City on his full debut in 1976, with a rasping shot from outside the box that was too good for England keeper Peter Shilton.

2 After a couple of seasons, Hoddle's skill made him a firm favourite with the fans. Every time Spurs won a free kick just outside the box, the fans would chant 'Hoddle, Hoddle, Hoddle!' One such instance was going into the last minute at Mansfield in 1978, when Spurs were staring down the barrel of an embarrassing and potentially costly defeat. Hoddle stepped up to perfectly curl home what would become a trademark free kick with a level of skill rarely associated with a British player, earning Spurs a point and enhancing his growing reputation.

3 With Spurs trailing 2-0 at Villa Park going into the final 15 minutes in 1979, Hoddle inspired an epic comeback that saw the Lilywhites score three goals in six minutes to win the match 3-2. He started the comeback with a low shot from the edge of the area, and then helped Chris Jones nab the equaliser, but saved the best to last. A stunned Villa allowed Hoddle to break through and he found himself one on one with keeper Jimmy Rimmer, but as the keeper advanced Hoddle executed the most perfect chip without breaking stride, which looped over Rimmer and into the net. Pure magic.

4 The opening months of the 1979/80 season saw Hoddle in magnificent goal-scoring mode. There was a goal after 30 seconds against Norwich, but the two most memorable were the iconic leaping volleys into the Park Lane net against Manchester United and Forest. The first came from a one-two after a short free kick, and the second from a headed-on goal kick. Both set-ups produced a pass a few feet off the ground that Hoddle jumped at, and with his left

leg tucked in, thrashed into the net, giving England goal-keepers Bailey and Shilton no chance.

5 Hoddle shows he is a man of many talents by taking the gloves in the first half at Elland Road against Leeds United after an injury to Barry Daines. Hoddle did his bit in a rare away win, and was similarly impressive later in the season when asked to reprise the keeper's role in an FA Cup replay at Old Trafford. Joe Jordan had smashed up Milija Aleksic's teeth and Hoddle stepped in to keep a clean sheet in a famous win.

6 Hoddle's only hat-trick for Spurs came in a 4-3 home win over Coventry, and was more remarkable not for containing two penalties but a rare headed goal as well.

7 Hoddle ends the 1979/80 season as Spurs' top scorer, with 22 goals from midfield, one of which, against Man U, won the goal of the season on *Match of the Day*, and another, against Notts Forest, the same gong on *The Big Match*. The season also saw a goal on his England debut against Bulgaria and the Professional Footballers' Association Young Player of the Year accolade.

8 The arrival of Crooks and Archibald in the summer of 1980 ensured that Spurs had forwards who could convert Hoddle's midfield brilliance into goals, and encouraged Hoddle to fashion even more chances with his incredible vision and technique.

9 With nine minutes to go in the 1981 FA Cup final, the pressure was on Hoddle as Spurs were awarded a free kick on the edge of the Manchester City penalty area. It wasn't his best, but it found Tommy Hutchison's shoulder and sailed into the net for the equaliser. Hoddle was also Spurs' saviour a year later when scoring what should have been the winner in extra time in the first match with a long-range shot, and then calmly putting away what proved to be the winning penalty in the replay.

10 The sixth-round cup win at Chelsea in 1982 displayed the early 1980s Spurs team at their best, with Hoddle and his Mini-Me, Hazard, in majestic form. Hazard set up Hoddle

for one of the great Spurs goals and later in the match, Hoddle made a fool of a Chelsea defender from a dropping ball, before setting up Hazard for his goal.

11 Spurs may have suffered yet another defeat to Liverpool in May 1982, but not before Anfield was treated to a moment of Hoddle magic in the form of a 40-yard screamer into the Kop net that gave Spurs the lead.

12 It was only the departure of Keith Osgood midway through the 1977/78 season that saw Glenn Hoddle take over penalty duty for Spurs. However, in the next 10 years Hoddle was deadly at 12 yards, only missing one spot kick, a thrice-taken affair that Shilton eventually saved for Forest. In all, Hoddle scored 30 penalties for Spurs, including a very famous one to win the 1982 FA Cup final replay against QPR.

13 The 3-2 win at Watford was memorable for many reasons. A returning Archibald scoring the winner would have created a few headlines had it not been for a moment of utter genius from Hoddle. A little pass was played into him inside the Watford box; he feinted right but flicked the ball the other way. Having left his defender behind and without looking up, he turned and chipped in one movement, giving the ball sufficient elevation to beat Steve Sherwood and enough dip to come in under the crossbar. It was the work of a football visionary, and a mainstay of the *Match of the Day* titles for years.

14 Hoddle's reputation was such that in 1983 when Spurs met Feyenoord in the UEFA Cup, world legend Johan Cruyff took it upon himself to man-mark Hoddle. It was a decision the Dutchman soon regretted, as Hoddle took him and Feyenoord apart in a brilliant first half, orchestrating all four Spurs goals. Hoddle's brilliance was such that Cruyff abandoned the tactic in the second half.

15 During his brilliant Spurs career and despite nearly leading England to World Cup glory in 1986, Hoddle never started more than three consecutive Internationals for his country, who mistrusted skill over industry at the time. A different

philosophy in France saw Michel Platini lead his side to win the European Championship in 1984. As Danny Blanchflower remarked when defending Hoddle as a 'luxury', 'It's bad players that are the luxury, not the skilful ones.'

16 The 1980s Wimbledon side were the antithesis of the good football played by Hoddle during his career. Hoddle used the FA Cup tie in 1987 to show skill prevail over brawn, with a brilliant long-range free kick, and along with the other scorer Chris Waddle he dedicated the win to Danny Thomas, who'd seen his playing career ended by a bad tackle in another London derby. 'This one's for you Danny.'

17 Hoddle saved one of the best for his last Spurs goal. Hoddle picked up the ball midway inside the Spurs half and quickly accelerated towards the Oxford United goal. He shimmied his way past the defenders on the halfway line and then used another subtle body swerve to dump Peter Hucker on his backside, before rolling the ball into an empty net.

TEAMS OF THE DECADES

TEAM OF THE DECADE: 1950S

 1 Ted Ditchburn

 2 Alf Ramsey

 3 Mel Hopkins

 4 Bill Nicholson

 5 Harry Clarke

 6 Ron Burgess

 7 Sonny Walters

 8 Tommy Harmer

 9 Len Duquemin

10 Eddie Bailey

11 George Robb

TEAM OF THE DECADE: 1960S

1   Bill Brown
2   Peter Baker
3   Ron Henry
4   Danny Blanchflower
5   Maurice Norman
6   Dave Mackay
7   Cliff Jones
8   John White
9   Bobby Smith
10 Jimmy Greaves
11 Terry Dyson

TEAM OF THE DECADE: 1970S

1   Pat Jennings
2   Terry Naylor
3   Cyril Knowles
4   Alan Mullery
5   Mike England
6   Phil Beal
7   Alan Gilzean
8   Steve Perryman
9   Martin Chivers
10 Martin Peters
11 Peter Taylor

TEAM OF THE DECADE: 1980S

1   Ray Clemence
2   Danny Thomas

3　Chris Hughton

4　Graham Roberts

5　Gary Stevens

6　Ossie Ardiles

7　Paul Gascoigne

8　Steve Archibald

9　Chris Waddle

10　Glenn Hoddle

11　Garth Crooks

TEAM OF THE DECADE: 1990S

1　Ian Walker

2　Stephen Carr

3　Justin Edinburgh

4　Paul Allen

5　Gary Mabbutt

6　Sol Campbell

7　Darren Anderton

8　Gary Lineker

9　Jürgen Klinsmann

10　Teddy Sheringham

11　David Ginola

TEAM OF THE DECADE: 2000S

1　Paul Robinson

2　Paul Stalteri

3　Christian Ziege

4　Michael Carrick

5 Ledley King

6 Michael Dawson

7 Jermaine Jenas

8 Dimitar Berbatov

9 Jermain Defoe

10 Robbie Keane

11 Aaron Lennon

TEN GREAT SPURS CAPTAINS

1 **Bobby Buckle (1882–83),** Spurs' first ever captain.

2 **Jack Jull (1884–96),** the longest-serving Spurs captain over the formative years of the club.

3 **Jack Jones (1897–1904),** the first Spurs captain to lift the FA Cup.

4 **Arthur Grimsdell (1920–29),** Captained the run-up to Spurs' first League title in 1920 and lifted the FA Cup the following season.

5 **Ron Burgess (1946–54).** The captain of the 'push and run' side, who won consecutive championships at the start of the 1950s, including Spurs' first ever top-flight title.

6 **Danny Blanchflower (1955–56 and 1959–64).** Initially stripped of the captaincy in the fallout from an FA Cup semi-final defeat, Nicholson restored the charismatic Ulsterman to the role soon after taking over to add the magic to his method. He was rewarded with the League and Cup double, followed by another FA Cup and the European Cup Winners' Cup in Spurs' greatest ever era.

7 **Dave Mackay (1965–68),** the ultimate lead-by-example captain, who lifted the FA Cup in 1967.

8 **Alan Mullery (1968–72).** Mullers captained the 'third' Nicholson side to UEFA and League Cup glory in the early 1970s.

9 **Steve Perryman (1975–86),** Spurs' youngest ever captain, endured relegation to lead Spurs back to the top flight at the first attempt and successive FA Cups in the early 1980s.

10 **Gary Mabbutt (1988–98).** Came back from the disappointment of the 1987 FA Cup final to lift the trophy in 1991. A great ambassador for the club, and a rock through some difficult times for Spurs both on and off the pitch

ELEVEN GREAT
DEBUTS FOR SPURS

1. JOSE DOMINGUEZ (1997)

With Spurs in the doldrums after the summer departure of Sheringham and losing the opening two games of the season, things seemed to be going from bad to worse when new signing David Ginola limped off early in the game against Derby County in August 2007. Little was expected of Ginola's replacement, a tiny Portuguese player who'd done next to nothing in the Second Division with Birmingham City earlier in his career. However, the mood of White Hart Lane lifted as Dominguez ran through his whole repertoire of dazzling skills to mesmerise the Derby defenders for the rest of the game, in what was a proper hammering despite the 1-0 scoreline. Dominguez's star never burned as brightly again, and it was a portent that his best game came as a substitute, since 42 of his 58 appearances were from the bench. The longer-lasting impact was on Ginola, who seemed to use the experience as a wake-up call to go on to great things after a low key start.

2. COLIN LEE (1977)

On 15 October, Colin Lee was part of a Torquay United side involved in a 0-0 at the old Shay stadium against Halifax. Another unremarkable game in an unremarkable career. One week later, Lee was lucky to have the *Match of the Day* cameras present as he scored four of the nine goals Spurs put past Bristol Rovers to become an instant household name. Lee had a solid season helping Spurs to promotion but had a reduced role, often in defence, once Spurs were back in the top flight, before moving on to Chelsea.

3. TERRY GIBSON (1979)

Spurs made the rare decision of giving a 17-year-old his debut in what was the last game of the 1970s, against Stoke City. The diminutive Gibson did not let anyone down and left the field with a torn and bloodied shirt to rapturous applause. Gibson's Spurs career never really took off, but as part of the Crazy Gang at Wimbledon he helped pull Liverpool's pants down to win the FA Cup in 1988.

4. MIDO (2005)

Martin Jol was just starting to resurrect Spurs in early 2005, but spirits were a bit low after an underwhelming transfer window had just closed, the most notable signing being the rotund Andy Reid who'd been plying his trade at the bottom of the Championship. Not much was known about the enigmatic Mido who'd arrived earlier in the window, but he announced himself in spectacular fashion with two goals and an outstanding debut display against Pompey. Strong in the air, good with the ball and with the presence about him of a star player, Mido seemed to have it all. But then again, there had to be *something* wrong with him otherwise he would have gone to a higher-profile club. And so it turned out: these proved to be his only League goals that season, and despite the occasional good performance, he slipped down the pecking order before moving on to Middlesbrough.

5. DAVID HOWELLS (1986)

Howells' first showing for Spurs, as an 18-year-old up at Hillsborough against Wednesday, came when Spurs were in a run of six games without a goal, including five defeats that March. Sporting a trendy mullet, Howells had the dream debut, scoring in a win for the Lilywhites, and he went on to become a Spurs stalwart – and occasional scapegoat – over the next 12 seasons, which included an FA Cup winners' medal for him in 1991.

6. JIMMY GREAVES (1961)

Every Jimmy Greaves debut contained a goal, including one *against* Spurs as a 17-year-old starting out for Chelsea. His hat-trick in a 5-2 win against Blackpool in December 1961 was very much a sign of things to come during his 266-goal career with Spurs.

7. JÜRGEN KLINSMANN (1994)

Until Sugar signed him on his yacht in Monaco, Klinsmann had been a bit of a hate figure in English football for his perceived cheating antics. The German lined up as one of Ossie's famous five alongside Sheringham, Anderton, Barmby and Dumistrescu for his debut at Hillsborough against Sheffield Wednesday. In a classic match, he wasted little time in showing his great talent by flashing home a header for Spurs' fourth goal and then won the hearts of fans and the nation with his now famous 'dive' goal celebration. Klinsmann recovered from being stretchered off with a head injury later in the game to score a further 29 goals and win the Football Writers' Association (FWA) Footballer of the Year accolade in his all-too-brief stay first time round.

8&9. RICKY VILLA AND OSSIE ARDILES (1978)

After all the fanfare of the signing and Spurs' return to the top flight, the team were given the hardest possible start with a trip to champions Notts Forest on the opening day. Both Argentinians had good matches, and the bearded one scored Spurs' goal in a creditable 1-1 draw. Things went downhill for a while, with a 1-4 home debut defeat to Villa followed by the 0-7 humiliation at Anfield, but both stayed the course to write themselves into Spurs folklore.

10. NOURREDINE NAYBET (2004)

In an era when Spurs were largely shambolic, Naybet flew in a day before the opening fixture against Liverpool, and without training with the team, slotted in alongside Ledley and earned Spurs a 1-1 draw against Liverpool. The consummate professional.

11. DEAN RICHARDS (2001)

Not so much a great debut as a great first half of a debut. Richards went off at half time in his first match after his £8 million move from Southampton, with Spurs leading Manchester United 3-0 after Richards had also scored the first of the three with a flick header from a corner. It would be an understatement to say the second half was not quite as good, as Spurs capitulated – prompting the joke 'Have you heard about Dean Richards' new house? It's a three up, five down.'

THREE OF THE WORST DEBUTS

1. PAOLO TRAMEZZANI (AWAY AT WIMBLEDON, 1998; SPURS LOST 3-1)

Hopes were high that new signing Paolo Tramezzani, a blond, blue-eyed Italian who looked like he was straight out of a spaghetti western, could solve the problematic fullback role after his £1.35 million summer move from Piacenza in 1998.

Throwing the ball over the bemused Ginola's head from a simple throw-in early in the game was the first evidence that Tramezzani may be more San Marino vintage rather than proper Italian. Things went from bad to worse for both Tramezzani and Spurs, as manager Christian Gross looked on helplessly. Tramezzani's Spurs career barely lasted a month, as did his manager's.

2. PAUL STEWART (AT HOME AGAINST MANCHESTER UNITED, 1988; SPURS DREW 2-2)

Spurs acquired Stewart for what was then a club-record fee of £1.7 million, after a decent season with Manchester City in Division Two. As a result of a previous suspension, his debut was delayed until October and could not come quick enough for Spurs, who'd made an indifferent start to the season.

Going into the closing minutes, Paul Walsh had just drawn Spurs level and the momentum was with the home team. With the 90 minutes nearly up, Stewart was bundled over and Spurs were awarded a penalty. Stewart himself grabbed the ball from normal spot kick taker Terry Fenwick, who'd scored one the week before in a Spurs 3-2 comeback win. All looked set for a dream debut, but it turned into a nightmare as the ball rattled off the crossbar and bounced to safety. Fenwick scored a penalty in the next match but Spurs went into a tailspin, losing four consecutive matches, and Stewart never took another spot kick for Spurs.

Stewart's redemption took a while coming, but arrived with a goal in a 'man of the match' performance in Spurs' Cup final win against Forest in 1991.

3. ERIK THORSTVEDT (AT HOME AGAINST NOTTS FOREST, 1989; SPURS LOST 2-1)

Venables signed the Norwegian keeper known to everyone as Erik the Viking for £400,000 from IFK Gothenburg. With gaffe-prone 'Booby' Mimms as competition, Spurs fans reckoned anyone had to be an improvement. The combination of a poor run of form and the game being the televised Sunday afternoon fixture saw fewer than 17,000 turn up at White Hart Lane. While his was not a terrible debut as such, Erik made one massive howler more befitting his predecessor to gift Forest a goal and set them up for a win.

Fortunately, Spurs stuck with Big Erik, and he was the foundation of the side that finished third in 1990 and won the Cup, along with Paul Stewart, the following season.

Spurs footballers of the year

1957/58 Danny Blanchflower	Football Writers' Association (FWA) Player of the Year
1960/61 Danny Blanchflower	FWA Player of the Year

1972/73 Pat Jennings	FWA Player of the Year
1975/76 Pat Jennings	Professional Footballers' Association (PFA) Player of the Year
1979/80 Glenn Hoddle	PFA Young Player of the Year
1981/82 Steve Perryman	FWA Player of the Year
1986/87 Clive Allen	FWA Player of the Year
	PFA Player of the Year
1991/92 Gary Lineker	FWA Player of the Year
1994/95 Jürgen Klinsmann	FWA Player of the Year
1998/99 David Ginola	FWA Player of the Year
	PFA Player of the Year
2010/11 Gareth Bale	PFA Player of the Year
2011/12 Kyle Walker	PFA Young Player of the Year

BEST VALUE SPURS PLAYERS

THE FIRST OF THE DOUBLE TEAM

- Danny Blanchflower, from Aston Villa, December 1954, £30,000
- Maurice Norman, from Norwich City, November 1955, £28,000
- Bobby Smith, from Chelsea, December 1955, £18,000.

In 1955, Spurs signed an inspirational captain, their second best scorer of all-time and the rock of their defence for a decade, for a total of about a week's wages for a modern professional.

FINAL PIECES OF THE DOUBLE TEAM

- Cliff Jones, from Swansea City, February 1958, £35,000

- John White, from Falkirk, October 1959, £20,000

- Dave Mackay, from Heart of Midlothian, March 1959, £30,000.

Bill Nicholson's first months in charge were more successful off the pitch in picking up the players who would complete the double-winning side.

GEORDIE SKILL

- Chris Waddle, from Newcastle United, July 1985, £590,000

- Paul Gascoigne, from Newcastle United, July 1988, £2,000,000

- David Ginola, from Newcastle United, August 1997, £2,500,000.

Three of the most gifted Spurs players of all time were picked up cheaply from Newcastle United, who tried to get their own back by providing Kevin Scott and Ruel Fox as well.

LOWER LEAGUES

- Tony Galvin, from Goole Town, January 1978, £30,000

- Graham Roberts, from Weymouth, May 1980, £35,000

- Gary Mabbutt, from Bristol Rovers, August 1982, £120,000.

With Bill Nick in the Spurs scouting system, the early 1980s were a golden era for bargains in the lower leagues.

WORLD STRIKERS

- Jürgen Klinsmann, from Monaco, July 1994, £2,000,000

- Gary Lineker, from Barcelona, June 1989, £1,200,000.

Two of the greatest strikers in the history of world football picked up for buttons.

KEEPERS

- Ray Clemence, from Liverpool, August 1981, £300,000
- Pat Jennings, from Watford, May 1963, £27,000.

Two legendary keepers acquired for combined fees less than that of Booby Mimms.

EARLY 1980S GOAL SCORERS

- Steve Archibald, from Aberdeen, May 1980, £800,000
- Garth Crooks, from Stoke City, July 1980, £650,000.

Both fees were fairly lumpy for the time, but Archibald and Crooks proved almost priceless as they were able to turn Hoddle's brilliance into goals and move Spurs on a level.

SPURS SCOOP THE WORLD

- Ricardo Villa, from Racing Club, June 1978, £375,000
- Osvaldo Ardiles, from Huracan, June 1978, £325,000.

Two World Cup winners, signed for (and remembered by) a song.

HAMMERS

- Martin Peters, from West Ham United, March 1970, £200,000
- Paul Allen, from West Ham United, June 1985, £400,000
- Michael Carrick, from West Ham United, August 2004, £2,500,000.

Unofficial feeder club West Ham have provided some gems over the years, and Carrick's subsequent £18.6 million sale to Manchester United pleased the bean counters as well.

EARLY 1990S

- Darren Anderton, Portsmouth, July 1992, £2,000,000
- Teddy Sheringham, Notts Forest, August 1992, £2,100,000.

With Venables identifying the targets, Sugar's first real spend as Spurs chairman was a good one, netting two players who excelled for both club and country over the next decade.

MODERN ERA

- Aaron Lennon, Leeds United, June 2005, £1,000,000
- Michael Dawson, Notts Forest, January 2005, £3,500,000.

They've been around for quite a while by modern standards, and provided Spurs with some great service in the recent revival.

WHAT A WASTE OF MONEY! TRANSFER MARKET TRAGEDIES

ARSENAL SIGNINGS

- David Jenkins, from Arsenal, October 1968, £55,000
- Laurie Brown, from Arsenal, February 1964, £40,000.

Bill Nick learns the hard way that no-good Gooners are just that.

FROM THE OSSIE ERA

- Colin Calderwood, from Swindon Town, July 1993, £1,250,000
- Jason Dozzell, from Ipswich Town, August 1993, £1,900,000
- Andy Gray, from Crystal Palace, June 1992, £900,000
- Ronnie Rosenthal, from Liverpool, January 1994, £250,000
- Kevin Scott, from Newcastle Utd, February 1994, £850,000
- David Kerslake, from Leeds United, September 1993, £450,000.

More than half a team of dross that weakened the attacking exploits of the famous five, and eventually sunk Ossie the manager.

FROM THE FRANCIS ERA

- Andy Sinton, from Sheffield Weds, January 1996, £1,500,000
- Ruel Fox, from Newcastle Utd, October 1995, £4,200,000
- Ramon Vega, from Cagliari, January 1997, £3,750,000
- John Scales, from Liverpool, December 1996, £2,500,000.

The shoegazer replaced some classy players with a mixture of bland and mostly rubbish ones.

ON THE DIRECTOR OF FOOTBALL'S ORDER

- Alan Hutton, from Rangers, January 2008, £8,000,000
- Darren Bent, from Charlton Athletic, June 2007, £16,500,000
- Andy Reid, from Notts Forest, January 2005, £4,500,000
- David Bentley, from Blackburn Rovers, July 2008, £15,000,000.

Bad value and not wanted by their respective managers. Record signing Darren Bent was only fourth choice after his move, Andy Reid didn't look like a modern footballer and the initials DB were the only similarities between Bentley and Beckham.

THE REDKNAPP RE-SIGNS

- Robbie Keane, from Liverpool, February 2009, £15,000,000
- Jermain Defoe, from Portsmouth, January 2009, £16,000,000
- Pascal Chimbonda, from Sunderland, January 2009, £3,000,000.

No returning Spur has ever been much good, and in the early Redknapp era, not very good value for money either.

AND THE 'OH DEAR' LIST

- Terry Venables, from Chelsea, May 1966, £80,000; as unpopular in his playing days as he later was in the boardroom.

- Paolo Tramezzani, from Piacenza, July 1998, £1,350,000; utterly abysmal.

- Bobby Mimms, from Everton, February 1988, £375,000; but he looked so good for Everton . . .

- Ben Thatcher, from Wimbledon, July 2000, £5,000,000; George Graham's cruel revenge on Spurs fans.

- Sergei Rebrov, from Dynamo Kiev, May 2000, £11,000,000; if they were Wham!, Shevchenko was the George Michael and we managed to sign the other one for a record fee. Within five months, he was looking on from the bench at Andy Booth's goalless loan spell at Spurs.

- Wilson Palacios, from Wigan Athletic, January 2009, £12,000,000; decent enough, but £12 million for a Honduran water carrier seemed a lot.

- Chris Armstrong, from Crystal Palace, June 1995, £4,500,000; Sugar's anti-'Carlos Kickaball' policy gave us a player whose left foot never touched the ball.

- Willem Korsten, from Vitesse Arnhem, July 1999, £1,500,000; another George Graham trick to replace Ginola with quite simply one of the worst players ever.

- Rodrigo Defendi, from Cruzeiro, July 2004, £600,000; prophetic parents, but Spurs fans were never quite sure if he existed or was some kind of April fool, as he never made the first team.

- Grzegorz Rasiak, from Derby County, July 2005, £2,200,000; the epitome of a rushed deal on the last day of the transfer window.

- Terry Fenwick, from QPR, December 1987, £550,000; followed Venables around but reassuringly unloved by the fans throughout his stay.

- Willie Young, from Aberdeen, September 1975, £100,000; plenty of love between Spurs and the Dons over the years, despite them selling us Young.

TEN TERRACE VILLAINS

There is a general dynamic that if a player does well they will be lauded, and if they struggle they will get abuse. The abuse is usually in proportion to the size of their transfer fee, with youth players getting a lot more leeway than expensive flops. But there are always players who get it no matter what they do.

1. JOHN PRATT

It's probably fair to say that John Pratt got more abuse than all other Spurs players in history combined. Pratt's legendary status won him a tribute site, 'the John Pratt shrine', at the TOPSPURS website, where the following anecdote was recounted by a 1970s Spurs fan.

> One of my favourite memories of Pratt was in the late '70s when, in the warm-up before kick-off, there was the usual chanting the names of those on the pitch. After the 'Hoddle, born is the king . . .' and 'Peter Taylor on the wing' stuff, out came 'Oh Johnny, Johnny, Johnny Pratt, Johnny Pratt . . .' . . . and Pratt turned to the shelf and gave us all a clap as it (apparently) came to an end. Then the shelf in their thousands burst into the second verse 'Oh wank, wank, wank, wank, wank.' Pratt's head dropped and he returned to his one-twos with Perryman while, high on the shelf, we wet ourselves laughing!

2. BARRY DAINES

Despite impressing in his rare opportunities while Pat Jennings was at the club, Daines proved consistently gaffe-prone after Jennings was released, and was caned by the supporters accordingly, especially when turning up with an unconvincing perm at the start of one season.

3. TIM SHERWOOD

There was something unlovable about Sherwood and he never really found favour with the fans. Rumours of an Arsenal tattoo under his always long-sleeved shirt and an uncelebrated winning goal against the Gunners further fuelled the antipathy.

Towards the end of his stay, his infuriating habit of just pointing gave his detractors further ammunition.

4. IAN MOORES

John Pratt must have enjoyed playing with Moores and Daines as it meant that some of the abuse was bound to be shared about. Moores never really found his form after his £75,000 move from Stoke, with his clumsy touch and lack of goals, and got predictably little leeway from the unforgiving crowd before drifting off to Leyton Orient.

5. GARY STEVENS

Shakey was a fine defender who after making the move to midfield won England recognition and was the heart of the Spurs midfield that nearly won the League title in 1985. Despite this, the fans never really forgave his slow start and the impression that he was signed on the back of one good performance in the 1983 Cup final for Brighton.

6. TERRY VENABLES

Not very well received as a player after failing to impress as a successor to double team heroes. Even less well received in the boardroom at the end of his Spurs association in the 1990s.

7. TERRY FENWICK

Primary focus for abuse when things were going wrong with the Venables team.

8. MARK KENDALL

Like most youth team players, Kendall was welcomed with an open mind, but goalkeeping errors combined with an expanding midriff drew the terrace venom as Spurs shipped goals on a regular basis in the late 1970s.

9. PAUL STEWART

A record transfer fee weighed heavily on Stewart, who displayed a lack of early goals and clumsy style, before reinventing himself as a midfielder.

10. GEORGE GRAHAM

The two worlds collided when one of the high priests of anti-football was invited to manage the home of good football. Fans sang 'Bloke in the raincoat's blue and white army,' while venting their less generous feelings more privately, at least until the sale of Ginola, the debacle at Kaiserslautern and the nil-nils brought it all to the surface.

History will honour those brave Lilywhites . . . the double team 1960/61

Spurs name as many people for a typical Premier League game as Bill Nick used in the whole of that season.

1 Bill Brown: 41 appearances (Johnny Hollowbread one appearance)
2 Peter Baker: 41 appearances (Ken Barton one appearance)
3 Ron Henry: ever present
4 Danny Blanchflower: ever present
5 Maurice Norman: 41 appearances (Tony Marchi one appearance)
6 Dave Mackay: 37 appearances (Tony Marchi five appearances)
7 Cliff Jones: 29 appearances (Terry Medwin 12 appearances, John Smith one appearance)
8 John White: ever present
9 Bobby Smith: 36 appearances (Frank Saul six appearances)
10 Les Allen: ever present
11 Terry Dyson: 40 appearances (Tony Marchi two appearances)

Goals

- Bobby Smith: 28
- Les Allen: 23
- Cliff Jones: 15
- John White: 13
- Terry Dyson: 12
- Others: 24

THE FOREIGN LEGION

FOREIGN DIAMONDS

1 **Erik Thorstvedt:** 'I love Erik the Viking, Erik the Viking loves me . . .'

2 **Benoit Assou-Ekotto:** charismatic fullback of the Redknapp era.

3 **Christian Ziege:** fantastic skill shone through a very un-Teutonic work ethic.

4 **Younes Kaboul:** improved to be a high-quality defender.

5 **Giga Popescu:** skilful Romanian who scored the winner against Arsenal and repeated the dose by putting away the decisive penalty for Galatasary to beat them in the UEFA Cup final.

6 **Ossie Ardiles:** a midfield artist who was good enough to play with Glenn Hoddle.

7 **Ricardo Villa:** played with his heart on his sleeve, and won the nation's heart in winning the 1981 FA Cup final for Spurs.

8 **David Ginola:** burned brightly with the Spurs spirit as George Graham tried to take us into the darkness.

9 **Nicola Berti:** aged around 30 when scoring vital goals to keep Spurs up in 1998, and somehow keeps Modric out of this line-up.

10 **Jürgen Klinsmann:** World Cup-winning legend who was just as good for Spurs.

11 **Dimitar Berbatov:** a fantastic player who unfortunately thought he was better off cleaning Danny Wellbeck's boots.

FOREIGN DOUGHNUTS

1 **Kasey Keller:** sounded like a clown and often played like one.

2 **Paolo Tramezzani:** one of a kind.

3 **Thimothee Atouba:** crazy name, crazy guy.

4 **Ramon Vega:** had the demeanour of a hero, but the actions of a fool.

5 **Ricardo Rocha:** a footballing clone of Vega, or should that be 'clown'?

6 **Stefan Freund:** badge-kissing midfielder who could not run, pass or tackle.

7 **Milenko Ačimović:** hailed as 'the Slovenian Trevor Brooking' . . .

8 **Kevin-Prince Boateng:** a shining career either side of being comically bad for Spurs.

9 **Kazuyuki Toda:** baffling signing and embarrassing to watch.

10 **Ronnie Rosenthal:** moments of brilliance, long periods of incompetence.

11 **Helder Postiga:** expensive, lightweight and mostly useless for Spurs, but popped up to knock England out of Euro 2004.

TEN GREAT GARETH BALE MOMENTS

1 A brilliant free kick in one of his first games for Spurs against Arsenal in 2007 was a hint of the great things to come, albeit it in a losing side.

2 After a run of injuries and poor form that nearly saw him sold in the January transfer window, Bale caps a return to form with the winner in a long-overdue win over Arsenal in April 2010.

3   A few days later, and Bale repeats the dose with the winner in a 2-1 win over Chelsea to put Spurs in the driving seat for Champions League qualification.

4   With Spurs trailing 4-2 from the first leg of the qualifier for the Champions League group stages, Bale sets up all four Spurs goals in a magnificent win against Young Boys Berne, setting the tone for the memorable Champions League run.

5   Bale scores a couple up at Stoke to help Spurs record the first win of the 2010/11 season, the second of which is a stunning Van Basten-esque volley.

6   With Spurs 0-4 down and reduced to 10 men against reigning European Champions Inter Milan in the San Siro, Bale instigated an unlikely and memorable fight back with one of the greatest individual performances of all time in a Spurs shirt. He destroyed Maicon, who was considered the best fullback in the world at the time, and scored a superb individual hat-trick, and although this was not enough to avoid defeat on the night, it turned the momentum back Spurs' way.

7   A couple of weeks after leading the great comeback in the San Siro, Bale produced a virtuoso performance to help Spurs to their most memorable win in Europe over Inter at White Hart Lane.

8   The nemesis of Arsenal once again, leading the Spurs comeback from 2-0 down to win 3-2 and record an away win at Arsenal for the first time in 17 years.

9   Bale scores both goals at Norwich in one of the most complete Spurs away performances of the Redknapp era.

10   No comeback is complete without a Gareth Bale goal, and after going 2-0 down against Manchester City in a title six-pointer in January 2012, Bale completed the comeback with another brilliant finish to bring Spurs level, only for a cruel turn of events at the end of the game to rob Spurs.

Because they're worth it: ten Spurs haircuts

1 **Mitchell Thomas:** *the pioneer of many crazy looks in the late 1980s.*
2 **Benoit Assou-Ekotto:** *'Disco Benny' is the natural successor to Mad Mitch in the modern era.*
3 **Chris Waddle:** *iconic 1980s mullet.*
4 **Ian Walker:** *famously foppish haircuts of the early 1990s.*
5 **Paul Walsh:** *a Michael Bolton Mini-Me.*
6 **Ralph Coates:** *the finest exponent of the comb-over.*
7 **Antony Gardner:** *unexpectedly selected for one game when his hair was in between styles, for the most bizarre look.*
8 **Gazza's perm:** *just terrible.*
9 **Gerry Francis:** *kept the legend of the mullet going well into the 1990s.*
10 **David Ginola:** *no list mentioning both Spurs players and hair would be complete without our favourite Frenchman, who gave the impression his locks were his hobby.*

JIMMY GREAVES' SPURS LEAGUE GOALS

- 1961/62: 22 appearances, 21 League goals; Spurs finished 3rd

- 1962/63: 41 appearances, 37 League goals; Spurs finished 2nd

- 1963/64: 41 appearances, 35 League goals; Spurs finished 4th

- 1964/65: 41 appearances, 29 League goals; Spurs finished 6th

- 1965/66: 29 appearances, 15 League goals; Spurs finished 8th

- 1966/67: 38 appearances, 25 League goals; Spurs finished 3rd
- 1967/68: 39 appearances, 23 League goals; Spurs finished 7th
- 1968/69: 42 appearances, 27 League goals; Spurs finished 6th
- 1969/70: 29 appearances, 8 League goals; Spurs finished 11th
- Total: 322 appearances, 220 League goals.

INTERNATIONAL SPURS

ENGLAND HEROES

1 Ray Clemence
2 Alf Ramsey
3 Gary Mabbutt
4 Glenn Hoddle
5 Ledley King
6 Alan Mullery
7 Paul Gascoigne
8 Jimmy Greaves
9 Chris Waddle
10 Gary Lineker
11 Vivian Woodward

REST OF BRITISH ISLES

1 Pat Jennings (Northern Ireland)
2 Chris Hughton (Republic of Ireland)
3 Mel Hopkins (Wales)
4 Ron Burgess (Wales)
5 Mike England (Wales)
6 Dave Mackay (Scotland)

7 Danny Blanchflower (Northern Ireland)

8 John White (Scotland)

9 Alan Gilzean (Scotland)

10 Robbie Keane (Republic of Ireland)

11 Gareth Bale (Wales)

THE GOALKEEPERS

THE TOP FIFTEEN SPURS KEEPERS BY NUMBER OF APPEARANCES

1 Pat Jennings (1964–77): 590

2 Ted Ditchburn (1946–58): 452

3 Ray Clemence (1981–87): 330

4 Ian Walker (1991–2001): 310 (3)

5 Bill Brown (1959–66): 262

6 Erik Thorstvedt (1989–94): 216 (2)

7 Paul Robinson (2004–08): 175, and 1 goal

8 Barry Daines (1971–81): 173

9 Cyril Spiers (1927–32): 169

10 Bill Jaques (1914–22): 138

11 Heurelho Gomes (2008–): 136

12 Jim Nicholls (1927–36): 129

13 Percy Hooper (1935–39):108

14 Kasey Keller (2001–04): 99

15 Neil Sullivan (2000–03): 81

Statistics from appearances in major competitions

EIGHT INSTANCES OF
GOALKEEPING HEROICS

1. Pat Jennings, 1973, Liverpool 1-1 Spurs

Not many Spurs keepers had much joy at Anfield over the years, but Big Pat had a day to remember in 1973. League champions Liverpool were formidable at home that season but two penalty saves, first against Kevin Keegan and then Tommy Smith, and a whole host of other world-class saves, meant than Spurs were one of only four teams to emerge from Anfield with anything other than a defeat that season. Jennings' successor Barry Daines also saved a penalty at Anfield; unfortunately that was in a 7-0 defeat in 1978.

2. Neil Sullivan, 2000, Spurs 1-1 Arsenal

For a season or so, Sullivan was almost world-class, with a stack of notable displays that kept George Graham's Spurs career afloat. On a night of driving rain at White Hart Lane, he provided a faultless display of outstanding saves from most of the Goons, and even a back-header from Perry. It looked like being the match-winning effort, only for Vieira to push his marker Ferdinand out of the way at a corner and head home to break Spurs' hearts in the last minute.

3. Graham Roberts, 1984, Fulham 0-0 Spurs

Spurs were expected to progress against lowly Fulham but in the age before goalkeeper substitutes, things looked grim for Spurs after 20 minutes, when Clemence was unable to continue in goal. Roberts' 'never say die' attitude saw him claim the gloves ahead of usual stand-in Glenn Hoddle and it was soon clear that he also possessed a good deal of aptitude for his new role. Spurs restricted Fulham as best they could and where they got through, Robbo dealt with the rest, with his best moment coming from a full-stretch save from a low free kick. Roberts' clean sheet earned Spurs a replay, and to round things off, he scored one of the Lilywhites' goals in the 2-0 win.

4. Tony Parks, 1984, Spurs 1-1 Anderlecht

The injury to Clemence at Fulham meant that 21-year-old understudy Parks got an extended run in the first team, and after doing so well, he was retained even after Clemence regained fitness. After two drawn games and 30 minutes of extra time had failed to separate Spurs and Anderlecht in the UEFA Cup final, Parks was thrust into the limelight in front of the Paxton goal. The 'ice-cool Olsen', as Brian Moore described him, took a pretty decent penalty, but Parks dived to his left and saved it, giving Spurs an early advantage after Roberts had scored the opener. He did not get near the next three Anderlecht penalties but looked to have done his job as Danny Thomas came up to take the fifth, and what would have been decisive, penalty. Thomas' shot was saved and it was up to Parks to win the Cup for Spurs. Eidur Gudjohnsen's father, Arnor, stepped up to take the penalty, and in a virtual repeat of Danny Thomas' shot, Parks went to his right and made a comfortable save. Tearing off in a victory celebration, he was mobbed by the rest of the players in one of the great moments in Spurs' history.

5. Bill Brown, 1963, Slovan Bratislava 2-0 Spurs

Double-winning team keeper Bill Brown's great strength was his consistency in goal, but it is widely acknowledged that his best game came under difficult circumstances in a Cup Winners' Cup quarter-final behind the Iron Curtain in Czechoslovakia. Spurs struggled to cope with the heavy conditions and were facing an insurmountable task in the second leg, being overrun and already 2-0 down with most of the second half to play. Brown rose spectacularly to the challenge, pulling off all manner of world-class saves to prevent any further damage. He came off the pitch battered by forwards' feet but a hero, as he had done enough to allow Spurs to overturn the deficit at White Hart Lane and go on to win the final against Atlético Madrid in Rotterdam.

6. Heurelho Gomes, 2010, Spurs 2-1 Arsenal

While Brown was a consistent keeper, that could not be said of Gomes, who mixed periods of top-class keeping with dire errors. Once again, it took the challenge of Arsenal to bring out the best in a Spurs keeper, and on a magnificent night, Gomes produced a string of fantastic saves to keep Spurs ahead and maintain the Champions League push, with the team's first Premier League win over Arsenal for over a decade.

7. Barry Daines, 1978, West Bromwich Albion 0-1 Spurs

A struggling Spurs side were expected to get very little from the Hawthorns against a high-class Albion containing 'the Three Degrees', Cyrille Regis, Laurie Cunningham and Brendan Batson. An early Peter Taylor goal put Spurs in front, and despite wave after wave of WBA attacks, Spurs held firm with the much-maligned keeper on top form, making a series of outstanding saves to help Spurs hold on to an important win.

8. Espen Baardsen, 1998, Everton 0-1 Spurs

Baardsen usually made one or two mistakes during a game, but when it all came together he was superb in his brief spell at Spurs. In a last desperate attempt to save his job, manager Gross dropped Walker for this game and Baardsen responded with an almost perfect display, enabling Spurs to hold on to the lead but not Gross his job, as he was sacked after the game.

EIGHT DODGY KEEPERS

1. Barry Daines

In Spurs parlance, when people discuss changing an established player for a promising young one, 'Remember Daines' is enough to send a shudder down the spine of those advocating change, even after all these years. The Witham wonder had done well in his games as Jennings' understudy, but more often than not he came up short when he had to take centre stage, sometimes comically so.

2. Kasey Keller

Keepers who need glasses are always a worry, but somehow Keller managed two consecutive seasons in the early noughties in which Spurs shipped an incredible 119 League goals. Some moments of comedy, notably with Chris Perry, but mostly it was just bad. His one redeeming feature was providing the assist for Nielsen's winner in the 1999 League Cup final . . . as the Leicester City keeper.

3. Bobby Mimms

Mimms had impressed as understudy to Neville Southall at Everton, but the 'Remember Daines' adage should have been observed, as he proved a regular disaster merchant in the early days of Venables at the end of the 1980s.

4. Ben Alnwick

Alnwick first came to the attention of Spurs fans when, at Sunderland, he became one of the few keepers to save a Robbie Keane penalty. However, his few chances for Spurs have been very poor, almost costing the team a place in the League Cup final after a shocker at Burnley in the second leg of the semi-final.

5. Mark Kendall

After a decent start to his Spurs career, he never really shook off being the keeper on the end of the Brady shot in the 0-5 loss to Arsenal. Mistakes crept in and new signing Aleksic and even Hoddle's emergency goalkeeping cameos put pressure on Kendall, who was not helped by an expanding midriff that accentuated his clumsy demeanour. He drifted away from the first team and eventually to a job as a bobby in the South Wales police.

6. Heurelho Gomes

Gomes' time at Spurs had three distinct phases. First, there were the disasters, which took a long time to shake in the eyes of the media. Next came a spell of superb keeping which helped Spurs up to fourth and into the Champions League. And then came the slide back to calamity, coming to a head in the Champions League quarter-final against Real Madrid, which effectively ended Spurs' great run in the competition.

7. Pat Jennings

A Spurs legend seems an odd choice for the 'dodgy keepers' section, but his early days in the Spurs goal were littered with mistakes, often made to look worse by his unconventional style. Fortunately, Billy Nick believed in him and he was given time to come good, which he did in spectacular fashion over his long and distinguished career.

8. Ian Walker

Dodgy haircuts, dodgy jerseys and a dodgy rueful smile as a soft McManaman shot bobbled in one evening at the Lane. Not quite as bad as often remembered, but then again never quite as good as he promised.

Eleven unlikely middle names

1 John Okay Chiedozie
2 Jermain Colin Defoe
3 Christopher Roland Waddle
4 Aaron Justin Lennon
5 Mark Rosslyn Bowen
6 David Desire Marc Ginola
7 Gary Winston Lineker
8 Johannes Antionius Bernardus Metgod
9 William Dallas Fyfe Brown
10 Clive Euclid Aklana Wilson
11 Edwin Redvers Baden Herod

ONE-GAME WONDERS: THIRTEEN FLEETING APPEARANCES FOR SPURS

1 **Max Seeburg (1908):** A regular in the Southern League years, Seeburg only made the one appearance for Spurs in the Football League, but in doing so became the first German to play in the competition.

2 **Alex Steel (1910):** Played only one League game, a goalless draw up at Bradford City, but it was alongside his

brothers Robert and Danny, and it remains the only time three brothers have played in the same Spurs side.

3 **Aled Owen (1954):** A 2-6 home defeat to Preston North End is the nadir of one-and-only appearances.

4 **Graeme Souness (1971):** Came on as substitute for Mullery in Spurs' first ever UEFA Cup tie against Keflavik in Iceland, but a rocky relationship with Bill Nicholson saw him move on to Middlesbrough and eventually fulfil his midfield hatchetman potential with Liverpool and Scotland.

5 **Terry Lee (1974):** Despite keeping a clean sheet in a 2-0 win up at Newcastle, the combined talent of Pat Jennings and Barry Daines meant Lee had to move to Torquay for regular first team action.

6 **Noel Brotherston (1976):** The competition first from Jimmy Neighbour and then Peter Taylor meant that the Northern Ireland international only featured in a 5-2 win over Villa.

7 **Peter Southey (1979):** Would surely have made many more Spurs appearances after his impressive debut against Brighton had his life not been cut short by leukaemia at the tragically young age of 21.

8 **Diego Maradona (1987):** Pulled on the Spurs shirt for Ossie's testimonial against Inter Milan, so he'd be able to tell his grandchildren he was on the same side as the world's greatest player Glenn Hoddle at the world's greatest club.

9 **Jamie Clapham (1997):** With the likes of Justin Edinburgh and Paolo Tramezzani as direct competition, it was surprising Clapham never got much of a look in at Spurs considering his later success at Ipswich.

10 **Jamie Slabber (2003):** Had an impressive record for the stiffs, but never got more than 15 minutes' first team action in a losing battle against Liverpool, even at a time when Spurs were struggling for goals.

Three Spurs players scored on what would be their one and only appearance:

11 **Joe Allen (1933):** Scored the Spurs goal in a 1-1 draw with Bradford, but never got the number 10 shirt back from George Hall.

12 **George Jeffery (1937):** Scored in a 3-2 win over Plymouth in Division Two, but never got another chance before returning to Scotland.

13 **Dicky Dowsett (1954):** Despite having a name more likely to be associated with a Terry-Thomas character than a footballer, Dowsett scored in a 4-2 win up at Villa on the opening day but failed to get back in the team, and ended up scoring over 100 goals in the lower divisions.

The promotion team: 1977/78

1 *Barry Daines: ever present*
2 *Terry Naylor: 37 appearances (Armstrong 3, Stead 2)*
3 *Jimmy Holmes: 38 appearances (McAllister 4)*
4 *Glenn Hoddle: 41 appearances (Coates 1)*
5 *Don McAllister: 21 appearances (Osgood 18, Armstrong 3)*
6 *Steve Perryman: ever present*
7 *John Pratt: ever present*
8 *Neil McNab: ever present*
9 *John Duncan: 21 appearances (Jones 12, Moores 7, Armstrong 2)*
10 *Colin Lee: 23 appearances (Jones 8, Duncan 6, Robinson 4, Armstrong 1)*
11 *Peter Taylor: 41 appearances (Armstrong 1)*

Goals

• *John Duncan*	*16*
• *Glenn Hoddle*	*12*
• *Colin Lee*	*11*
• *Peter Taylor*	*11*

- *Chris Jones*   8
- *John Pratt*   7
- *Others*   18

EIGHTEEN MEMORABLE
TESTIMONIALS

Professional footballers have always been relatively well paid, but until the modern era it was rarely enough to set them up for life, so clubs rewarded long service with benefit matches. Well, most clubs did: Spurs belatedly agreed to testimonials in the 1970s, and for the next couple of decades there were some memorable encounters and some special guests. Here's how Spurs honoured some of the greats.

1 **Jimmy Greaves testimonial,** 17 Oct 1972. **Spurs 2-1 Feyenoord** *(Evans, Greaves):* Greaves returned to White Hart Lane for a proper send-off against the European Champions, initiating the Tottenham testimonials.

2 **Phil Beal testimonial,** 3 Dec 1973. **Spurs 2-2 Bayern Munich** *(Pratt, Gilzean):*

3 **Alan Gilzean testimonial,** 27 Nov 1974. **Spurs 2-0 Red Star Belgrade** *(Knowles, Gilzean):*

4 **Cyril Knowles testimonial,** 22 Oct 1975. **Spurs 2-2 Arsenal** *(McAllister, Knowles):*

5 **Pat Jennings testimonial,** 23 Nov 1976. **Spurs 3-2 Arsenal** *(Taylor, Greaves (2)):*
   Classic opponents in memorable mid-season encounters for four players with 1,955 first team appearances between them. Peter Knowles pulled on his boots again for his brother's testimonial after giving up the professional game to become a Jehovah's Witness, while Greaves returned once more to score his final Spurs goals in Big Pat's game.

6 **John Pratt testimonial,** 12 May 1978. **Spurs 3-5 Arsenal** *(Perryman, Moores (2)):* Pratt was lucky that Arsenal

drew a big crowd in the season there was no North London derby, and there was a treat for the old-timers as Greaves and Cliff Jones turned out.

7   **Steve Perryman testimonial,** 30 Apr 1979. **Spurs 2-2 West Ham United** *(Villa, Ardiles):* The only time both Ossie and Ricky scored in the same match at White Hart Lane, but this was probably scant consolation for appearance record-holder Perryman only getting West Ham.

8   **Terry Naylor testimonial,** 29 Apr 1980. **Spurs 0-2 Crystal Palace:** If Perryman might think himself unlucky to get West Ham, 'Meathook' must have been inconsolable at getting 'the team of the 80s'.

9   **Barry Daines testimonial,** 11 May 1981. **Spurs 2-3 West Ham United** *(Hazard, Gibson):* With only 173, mostly undistinguished, games, Daines got lucky both to land a testimonial in the first place and then have it sandwiched between the Cup final and replay against Manchester City.

10 **Bill Nicholson testimonial,** 21 Aug 1983. **Spurs 1-1 West Ham United** *(Brazil):* The first of a couple of games for Sir Bill, which also included an emotional win against Fiorentina in 2001.

11 **Keith Burkinshaw testimonial,** 29 May 1984. **Spurs 2-2 England XI** *(Hughton, Brady):* Burkinshaw may not have been enamoured of the directors of the recently formed Spurs PLC, but they gave him a match fours days after their UEFA Cup glory against Anderlecht. Arsenal favourite and 'poor man's Hoddle' Liam Brady popped up with a goal for Spurs.

12 **Glenn Hoddle testimonial,** 4 Aug 1985. **Spurs 1-1 Arsenal** *(Leworthy):* The gulf between the legend honoured and the player who scored the goal will probably never be greater than in Hoddle's game.

13 **Osvaldo Ardiles benefit match,** 1 May 1986. **Spurs 2-1 Inter Milan** *(Falco, Allen C):* Hoddle and Maradona, the two greatest footballers of that or just

about any generation, together on the same side at White Hart Lane.

14 **Paul Miller testimonial,** 2 Aug 1986. **Spurs 1-1 Rangers** *(Allen):* The off-the-field violence that marred this game was somehow fitting for Maxi's hard man image.

15 **Chris Hughton testimonial,** 10 Aug 1987. **Spurs 3-1 Arsenal** *(Thomas, Allen C, Claesen):*

16 **Tony Galvin testimonial,** 20 Oct 1987. **Spurs 2-2 West Ham United** *(Allen P, Archibald):*
Inseparable on the pitch, there were only three months between Hughton's and Galvin's testimonials, with Archie coming back from Barcelona to score in the latter.

17 **Danny Thomas benefit match,** 28 Mar 1988. **Spurs 2-3 Manchester United** *(Archibald, Hodge):* This one was for you Danny! A Spurs team containing Kenny Dalglish and John Barnes turned out to honour the Spurs fullback who'd been forced to retire after a horrific injury against QPR the previous season.

18 **Danny Blanchflower benefit match,** 1 May 1990. **Spurs 2-1 N Ireland XI** *(Howells, Gascoigne (pen)):* Fewer than 7,000 turned up to honour Spurs great Danny Blanchflower, who had recently been found to have fallen on hard times. A memorable occasion, with a meeting between Blanchflower and Gazza linking Spurs greats from different eras.

Testimonials continued into the 1990s, including an unforgettable 2-2 between the 1981 and 1991 Spurs FA Cup teams for the recently deceased Cyril Knowles and the visit of Newcastle for Gary Mabbutt, but the golden days were over.

CLUB LEGEND STEVE PERRYMAN

Perryman (noun): a model of consistency and quality over a long period of time and in a variety of roles; a record number of appearances that will never be broken.

Steve's record

Year	League		FA Cup		League Cup		Europe		Total	
	Apps	Goals	Apps	Goals	Apps	Goals	Apps	Goals	Apps	Goals
1969/70	24	1	4						28	1
1970/71	42	3	5		6	1	12	3	65	7
1971/72	39	1	5		6	1	10		60	2
1972/73	41	2	3		10	1	12		66	3
1973/74	39	1	1		1				41	1
1974/75	42	6	2		1				45	6
1975/76	40	6	2	1	6				48	7
1976/77	42	1	1		2				45	1
1977/78	42	1	2		2				46	1
1978/79	42	1	7	1	2				51	2
1979/80	40	1	6		2				48	1
1980/81	42	2	9		6				57	2
1981/82	42	1	7		8		8		65	1
1982/83	32 (1)	1	3		2		2 (1)		39 (2)	1
1983/84	41	1	4		3		11		59	1
1984/85	42	1	3		5		8		58	1
1985/86	22 (1)	1	5		4				31 (1)	1
Total	654 (2)	31	69	2	66	3	63 (1)	3	852 (3)	39

Perryman played an astonishing 173 consecutive League games from December 1975 to October 1980, all the more remarkable as given his various roles he was always in the thick of the battle. He appeared in an incredible 340 of the 344 League games from August 1974 to October 1982.

The skipper also managed to notch up at least one goal in each of his seasons with Spurs. His most famous are the pair that defeated AC Milan in the UEFA Cup semi-final in 1972, but perhaps his most important were the four in five games that sparked a revival and saved Spurs from the drop after a run of eight defeats in nine games with only three goals scored in spring 1975. And we shouldn't forget his winner against Hull to keep the promotion dream alive in 1978 either. When Spurs needed him, Stevie P was always there.

ELEVEN OF THE BEST SPURS NICKNAMES

1. HODDLE'S BALKANS

When Glenn Hoddle signed Goran Bunjevčević and 2002 World Cup star Milenko Ačimović, he described them as the Serbian Franz Beckenbauer and the Slovenian Trevor Brooking respectively. Sadly, the rough and tumble of the Premier League did not particularly suit either player and they became known as 'The Cheeky Girls', although Ačimović also acquired the moniker of 'asillymiss' after spectacularly failing to convert an open goal against Fulham.

2. OLD-TIMERS

It was probably more for reasons of convenient rhyme than polished social skills that Tommy Harmer was known as 'Harmer the Charmer' in the 1950s, while John White's nickname of 'The Ghost' had prophetic overtones given his untimely death. Frederick 'Fanny' Walden always raises a smile, George Hunt's 'Chesterfield Tough' made him sound like a boxer while Sandy 'Terrible' Tait kept the nickname warm for Ramon Vega, albeit with a different interpretation of the adjective. Bob 'Topsy' Clements and Harry 'Tiger' Erentz are other noteworthy monikers from the era.

3. DARREN ANDERTON

Anderton never really had a song, but each of the two distinct phases of his Spurs career had its own nickname. After signing as a gangly young winger in 1992 he was affectionately known as Shaggy after the character from *Scooby-Doo*. However, after the injury-ravaged latter half of his Spurs career, he became widely known as Sicknote. He was also amusingly known as 'Sharon' in some quarters, a verbal play on his first name and perceived lack of toughness.

4. THE 1980S

With Stevie, Chrissy, Robbo, Ossie, Ricky, Crooksie, Archie and Glennda, most of the 1980s heroes had fairly predictable nicknames. But Mark 'Bilko' Falco, Paul 'Ollie' Allen and Paul 'Maxi' Miller were a tad more original. Paul 'Sparrow' Moran was perfect for the light-framed player, Bobby 'Booby' Mimms was probably the most accurate nickname given his hapless stay at Spurs and Peter 'Omar' Shreeve the cleverest play on words.

5. FOREIGN NAMES

1981 FA Cup final keeper Milija Aleksic was probably called 'Elastic' everywhere he went, but Spurs fans trumped this by changing another foreign surname into the memorable 'Treacle' for Mauricco Taricco.

6. THE 1990S

Former favourite Sulzeer Campbell used the nickname 'Sol' throughout his career. He also had plenty of nicknames from the Spurs fans, most of which are unprintable after his defection to Arsenal, but putting an 'r' sound in front of the Sol usually did the trick. It was almost inevitable that Norwegian favourite would be Erik 'The Viking' Thorstvedt. 'Ricky' for Justin Edinburgh came from a period of looking like *EastEnders*' Ricky Butcher, played by Spurs fan Sid Owen. Given that it relied upon its alliterative qualities, Ronnie Rosenthal was lucky to get 'Rocket' rather than 'Rubbish', 'Ropey' or even 'Rotten' Ron.

7. TERRY NAYLOR

The 1970s fullback went by either 'Meathook' from his days as former Smithfield porter or 'Nutty', and is the one player with two great nicknames.

8. PETERBOROUGH

Simon Davies and Matthew Etherington arrived from Peterborough with the names 'Digger' and 'Mushy' respectively, for long-forgotten reasons.

9. THE NOUGHTIES

Gustavo Poyet was known as 'Radio' from his Chelsea days thanks to his non-stop talking, but there was more imagination shown in giving Young-Pyo Lee the moniker of 'Wipey' from his first two initials YP. The best nickname of the era was 'the Ginger Pelé' for Gary Doherty, deploying irony to a degree not seen since 16-stone keeper John Joyce was dubbed 'Tiny' 100 years earlier. Another chunky keeper, Paul Robinson, was known as 'ENO', as England's Number One. Other less-than-charitable nicknames were Tom Hundredstone, Steffen 'The Log' Iversen, Kasey 'Helen' Keller and 'Paolo Wanleg' for the hopelessly right-footed Chris Armstrong.

10. THE PIANOMAN

It was a cruel brilliance which paired the hastily signed Gregorz Rasiak, who was looking more and more lost and out of his depth in the Premier League, with a news story of the day of the similarly lost 'Pianoman' who turned up wandering around Kent without any knowledge of who he was or what he was doing, communicating only via the piano.

11. MUSICAL NICKNAMES

On a musical theme, there was Gordon 'Jukebox' Durie and our very own 'Disco Benny' Assou-Ekotto.

THE 100 CLUB: SIXTEEN PLAYERS WHO HAVE SCORED MORE THAN 100 GOALS FOR SPURS

Player	Appearances	Goals	Goals/game (rate)
Jimmy Greaves (1961–70)	379 (0)	266	70%
Bobby Smith (1955–64)	317 (0)	208	66%
Martin Chivers (1968–76)	355 (12)	174	47%
Cliff Jones (1958–68)	370 (8)	159	42%
George Hunt (1930–37)	198 (0)	138	70%
Len Duquemin (1947–57)	307 (0)	134	44%
Alan Gilzean (1964–74)	429 (10)	133	30%
Teddy Sheringham (1992–2003)	270 (7)	124	45%
Robbie Keane (2002–08, 2009–11)	236 (69)	122	40%
Jermain Defoe (2004–08, 2009–)	198 (97)	118	40%
Les Bennett (1946–54)	294 (0)	117	40%
Jimmy Dimmock (1919–31)	438 (0)	112	26%
Glenn Hoddle (1975–87)	478 (12)	110	22%
Bert Bliss (1912–22)	215 (0)	104	48%
Billy Minter (1908–19)	263 (0)	101	38%
Johnny Morrison (1933–39)	154 (0)	101	66%

Correct up to the end of the 2011/12 season.

ELEVEN TOTTENHAM HOTSHOTS

Players who scored over 30 goals for Spurs at a rate of more than a goal every other game:

1 **Ted Harper (1929–31); appearances 67 (0), goals 63, rate (goals/game) 94.0%.** Ted Harper's time at Spurs coincided with the team's two lowest League finishes, in Division Two, but you wonder how bad it would have been without his contribution of close to a goal a game. He became the first Spurs player to score five in a match on the opening day of the season in 1930, and ended with a then-record 36 goals in 30 games to secure Spurs' promotion. Harper's goals were not restricted to Division Two as he was record top-flight scorer in 1926 for Blackburn Rovers, with 43 League goals, and he also holds a goal-scoring record with Preston North End.

2 **Jimmy Greaves (1961–70); appearances 379 (0), goals 266, rate 70.2%.** There is little to say apart from that Greaves was quite simply the greatest, with a consistently high return each season, and that his volume will surely never be bettered.

3 **George Hunt (1930–37); appearances 198 (0), goals 138, rate 69.7%.** George Hunt was a skilful centre forward who quickly became Spurs' record scorer at the time. His haul of 65 goals in two seasons from 1932–34 helped Spurs to promotion in second place, and then a third place in the top flight the following season.

4 **Bobby Smith (1955–64); appearances 317 (0), goals 208, rate 65.6%.** A classic centre forward in the old English style, Smith broke all Spurs goal-scoring records and was leading scorer in the double season, as well as scoring in consecutive FA Cup finals in a dream career.

5 **Johnny Morrison (1933–39); appearances 154 (0), goals 101, rate 65.6%.** Morrison was a prolific marksman for Spurs in the late 1930s and would have scored even more but for the suspension of the Football League at the outbreak of World War II.

6 **Clive Allen (1984–88); appearances 124 (11), goals 84, rate 62.2%.** 'Cousin' Clive hit two on his debut in 1984, but it was not until the 49 goals of the 1986/87 season that he moved into the realms of legend. During that season, he overtook his father Les Allen's goal tally for Spurs, but the bragging rights remained with his father as he had medals from the Double season to go with his impressive 61 goals in 137 appearances.

7 **Alfie Stokes (1953–59); appearances 69 (0), goals 42, rate 60.9%.** Stokes was never a regular in the Spurs side, but he made the most of his opportunities, before being sold to Fulham.

8 **Gary Lineker (1989–92), appearances 138 (0), goals 80, rate 58.0%.** Lineker was a brilliant signing for Spurs, netting a consistently high volume of goals each season, but he was not really held in the affection he deserved as it was considered that Spurs were only borrowing him from England duty.

9 **Jürgen Klinsmann (1994–98); appearances 68 (0), goals 38, rate 55.9%.** Klinsmann formed a fantastic partnership with Teddy Sheringham during the 1994/95 season and both players scored a stack of goals. He also charmed Spurs fans and the British public off the field, remaining one of the popular overseas players of all time. He wasn't so good the second time round in 1998, but his four goals against Wimbledon secured safety for the team.

10 **Charles Wilson (1919–22); appearances 62 (0), goals 33, rate 53.2%.** Joined Spurs at the end of World War I and although never a regular, he chipped in with goals as Spurs got promoted as Division Two champions, won the FA Cup and finished runners-up in the top flight for the first time.

11 **John Duncan (1974–78); appearances 118 (2), goals 62, rate 51.7%.** Duncan arrived into a struggling side and initially helped Spurs stay up. He was leading scorer in two of the next three seasons, but not always popular with teammates, and he left for Derby soon after Spurs were promoted.

OTHER NOTABLE PLAYERS

Bert Bliss scored his 104 Spurs goals at a very respectable rate of 48.4% goals per game, just ahead of Chivers who netted his 174 at 47.4%. Dimitar Berbatov sulked his way to 46 goals at 45.1% per game, just ahead of centurions Teddy Sheringham (124 goals at 44.8%) and Len Duquemin (134 goals at 43.6%). Cliff Jones' 159 goals from the wing are an astonishing total, and they also came at an impressive rate of 42.1% per game.

Forever mentioned together, Crooks (75; 41.2%) and Archibald (77; 40.7%) had similar goals at similar rates, just ahead of modern centurions Keane and Defoe, who are around the 40% mark. Perhaps the biggest surprise is Alan Gilzean's 133 Spurs goals coming at a rate of only 30.3% per game

CROOKS AND ARCHIE

When they both scored, Spurs always won.

- Div 1, 19 Aug 1980; **Crystal Palace 3-4 Spurs** *(Archibald, Hoddle, Crooks (2))*

- League Cup second round (second leg), 3 Sept 1980; **Spurs 3-1 Orient** *(Archibald (2), Crooks)*

- Div 1, 11 Oct 1980; **Spurs 3-2 Middlesbrough** *(Archibald, Villa, Crooks)*

- Div 1, 12 Nov 1980; **Spurs 4-2 Crystal Palace** *(Archibald, Crooks (3))*

- Div 1, 17 Dec 1980; **Spurs 5-3 Ipswich Town** *(Perryman, Ardiles, Archibald, Hoddle, Crooks)*

- Div 1, 26 Dec 1980; **Spurs 4-4 Southampton** *(Brooke (2), Archibald, Crooks)*

- Div 1, 21 Mar 1981; **Spurs 2-0 Aston Villa** *(Archibald, Crooks)*

- Div 1, 9 Mar 1982; **Brighton and Hove Albion 1-3 Spurs** *(Ardiles, Archibald, Crooks)*

- Div 1, 31 Aug 1982; **Ipswich Town 1-2 Spurs** *(Archibald, Crooks)*

- European Cup Winners' Cup first round (first leg), 15 Sept 1982; **Coleraine 0-3 Spurs** *(Archibald, Crooks (2))*

- League Cup third round, 9 Nov 1982; **Gillingham 2-4 Spurs** *(Archibald (2), Crooks (2))*.

Well, almost: a couple of late goals from Southampton rescued a point one Boxing Day to spoil the otherwise perfect record.

TWENTY-FIVE NOTABLE MOMENTS FROM TEDDY SHERINGHAM

1 Premier League, 2 Sept 1992. **Spurs 2-0 Sheffield Utd** *(Sheringham, Durie)*. Sheringham scores his first Spurs goal in Spurs' first ever Premier League win.

2 Premier League, 7 Nov 1992. **Blackburn Rovers 0-2 Spurs** *(Howells, Sheringham (pen))*. After a sticky start to his Spurs career, a clear-the-air chat and a penalty at Blackburn set Sheringham back on the path to Spurs glory.

3 Premier League, 7 Feb 1993. **Spurs 4-2 Southampton** *(Sheringham (2), Anderton, Barmby)*. Scores two of the four in 4 minutes 42 seconds against the Saints as the new young team of spring 1993 go very close to perfection on a Sunday afternoon.

4 Premier League, 20 Feb 1993. **Spurs 4-0 Leeds United** *(Ruddock, Sheringham (3, 1 pen))*. Spurs had lost 5-0 to the reigning champions Leeds at the start of the season, but gained revenge thanks to Sheringham's first hat-trick, with his cushioned header looping over Lukic and into the Paxton net the pick of the bunch.

5 Premier League, 27 Feb 1993. **Spurs 3-2 Queens Park Rangers** *(Sheringham (2), Anderton)*. Backers of Sheringham for the first goal had a scare with an early penalty miss, but they were not long in working out their returns as this fine young Spurs team were more comfortable winners than the scoreline suggests.

6 Premier League, 11 May 1993. **Arsenal 1-3 Spurs**
   (Sheringham, Hendry (2)). A bit of a nothing North London
   derby, with both teams playing weakened sides, but nonetheless a great moment to score in a win at Highbury against a
   side Sheringham seemed to dislike as much as the fans.

7 **Leading Premier League goal scorer 1992/93.**
   Sheringham had a slow start to his Spurs career, but
   with 16 goals in the last 17 games he managed to clinch the
   Golden Boot in the first year of the Premier League. His
   total of 22 goals consisted of 21 for Spurs and 1 for Forest
   before his early-season move; he was two goals clear of Les
   Ferdinand at QPR.

8 Premier League, 14 Aug 1993. **Newcastle United 0-1
   Spurs** *(Sheringham)*. Newcastle came up with a fanfare but
   were shot down by a second-half Sheringham goal and a
   memorable celebration going down on one knee.

9 Premier League, 25 Aug 1993. **Liverpool 1-2 Spurs**
   (Sheringham (2, 1 pen)). Sheringham was in the form of his
   Spurs career, and bagged a couple in an all-too-rare Spurs
   League win at Anfield.

10 Premier League, 16 Oct 1993. **Manchester
   United 2-1 Spurs** *(Caskey)*. With Spurs going well and
   Sheringham in top form, it was cruel luck that a snide
   Bryan Robson challenge would all but end Sheringham's
   season in October. His value to Spurs was shown in the
   subsequent slump, which saw the Lilywhites win only two
   of the next 22 games.

11 Premier League, 2 Apr 1994. **Norwich City 1-2 Spurs**
   (Sheringham, Woodthorpe og). Sheringham's return to the
   Spurs side coincided with an upturn in form with the win
   at Norwich the second in two games, as Spurs did just
   enough to survive.

12 Premier League, 20 Aug 1994. **Sheffield Wednesday
   3-4 Spurs** *(Sheringham, Anderton, Barmby, Klinsmann)*. The
   start of something special, with Jürgen Klinsmann and
   Ossie's famous five together for the first time. Sheringham
   got the ball from out of his feet to toe-poke the opener, and

then in traditional skilful Sheringham style played a return pass for Anderton's goal and a flick header for Barmby's third.

13 Premier League, 3 Dec 1994. **Spurs 4-2 Newcastle United** *(Sheringham (3), Popescu)*. After a period out of the team, Sheringham reminded everyone of his class with a hat-trick, including one from a 'Sheringham corner' routine.

14 FA Cup sixth round, 11 Mar 1995. **Liverpool 1-2 Spurs** *(Sheringham, Klinsmann)*. Sheringham scored a brilliant curling shot to pull Spurs level, and then set up Klinsmann for one of Spurs' greatest ever cup wins.

15 Premier League, 18 Nov 1995. **Spurs 2-1 Arsenal** *(Sheringham, Armstrong)*. New Arsenal signing Dennis Bergkamp put the Goons ahead, but for a short while it looked as if Spurs had the better of the summer transfer window as Sheringham along with new strike-partner Chris Armstrong hit back to win the game.

16 Premier League, 23 Dec 1995. **Spurs 2-2 Bolton Wanderers** *(Sheringham, Armstrong)*. The Sheringham and Armstrong double act put Spurs 2-0 up midway into the second half, and it would have been good enough to move the team up to second, but chaotic defending allowed relegation-threatened Bolton back in to nick a draw.

17 Premier League, 1 Jan 1996. **Spurs 4-1 Manchester United** *(Sheringham, Campbell, Armstrong (2))*. Scores the opener in a fine win over United after Schmeichel was injured in the warm-up, but this result was the exception rather than the rule in a season of regression. Sheringham loses interest soon after and only scores two more League goals for the rest of the season.

18 Premier League, 19 Mar 1997. **Leicester City 1-1 Spurs** *(Sheringham)*. Another moderate season for Spurs, and another where Sheringham played his best football before

the team became also-rans. His last Spurs goal at Leicester was a low-key end to his first spell with the club, his body leaving at the end of the season to join his mind, which had left some time beforehand.

19 Premier League, 10 Aug 1997. **Spurs 0-2 Manchester United.** After an acrimonious summer departure, Sheringham was back on the opening day of the season as a United player. A penalty presented the opportunity to score on his debut, but as with many of his penalties it was missed. United went on to win the game but came up short in all competitions, leaving fans singing 'Oh Teddy, Teddy, went to Man United and he won f**k all'. However, a year later he had scored in the FA Cup and Champions League final to collect the Treble, which vindicated his decision to move.

20 Premier League, 16 Sept 2001. **Spurs 2-3 Chelsea** *(Sheringham (2))*. Returning to Spurs as captain under Glenn Hoddle, Sheringham was quickly into goal-scoring form to pull Spurs level from 0-2 down with a couple of classy strikes at the Park Lane end. He looked like rescuing a point for Spurs before typical Chelsea nicked a last-minute winner through Desailly.

21 League Cup semi-final, 23 Jan 2002. **Spurs 5-1 Chelsea** *(Iversen, Sherwood, Sheringham, Davies, Rebrov)*. A great all-round display from Sheringham, showing all his usual class, including a fine goal with a deliberately sliced volley. In ironing out Zenden in the first half, he also announced Spurs' intent, which Chelsea were never able to match.

22 League Cup final (Cardiff), 24 Feb 2002. **Spurs 1-2 Blackburn Rovers** *(Ziege)*. Spurs did not play well in the Cardiff rain yet had the chances to win the game easily. The last salvation fell to Sheringham, who did likewise when challenged in the box in the final minute but his chances of lifting a trophy as captain were waved away by Graham Poll.

23 Premier League, 8 Feb 2003. **Spurs 4-1 Sunderland** *(Poyet, Doherty, Davies, Sheringham)*. Sheringham scores at the Paxton end and then reveals a T-shirt below his kit with '300' on it to celebrate his 300th League goal in a great career.

24 Premier League, 21 Apr 2003. **West Bromwich Albion 2-3 Spurs** *(Keane (2), Sheringham)*. More than 11 years after his original Spurs debut, a footballing world away, Sheringham scored his 124th and last Spurs goal in a win up at the Hawthorns.

25 Premier League, 7 May 2006. **West Ham United 2-1 Spurs** *(Defoe)*. Sheringham had been gone a long time but cropped up doing charity work for the needy in the East End. Spurs needed a win at the Boleyn Ground to qualify for the Champions League, but had suffered a bout of food poisoning in the run-up to the game and were not at full strength. Into the second half with the score at 1-1, West Ham were awarded a penalty and Sheringham took the ball. Spurs fans had seen Sheringham score plenty of penalties but they'd also seen him miss a few and dared to dream. Sheringham duly scuffed his penalty, but there was to be no happy ending as Benayoun scored a late winner to sink Spurs' dreams.

A Spurs Youth Team XI

1 *Ian Walker*
2 *Stephen Carr*
3 *Chris Hughton*
4 *Phil Beal*
5 *Ledley King*
6 *Steve Perryman*
7 *Micky Hazard*
8 *Nicky Barmby*
9 *Mark Falco*
10 *Glenn Hoddle*
11 *Jimmy Neighbour*

CLIVE'S FORTY-NINE: ALL THE GOALS FROM CLIVE ALLEN'S RECORD-BREAKING 1986/87 SEASON

- Div 1, 23 Aug 1986; **Aston Villa 0-3 Spurs** *(Allen C (3))*; running total: 3.

- Div 1, 25 Aug 1986; **Spurs 1-1 Newcastle United** *(Allen C)*; 4.

- Div 1, 13 Sept 1986; **Spurs 1-3 Chelsea** *(Allen C (pen))*; 5.

- Div 1, 20 Sept 1986; **Leicester City 1-2 Spurs** *(Allen C (2))*; 7.

- League Cup second round (first leg), 23 Sept 1986; **Barnsley 2-3 Spurs** *(Roberts, Allen C, Waddle)*; 8.

- Div 1, 27 Sept 1986; **Spurs 2-0 Everton** *(Allen C (2))*; 10.

- League Cup second round (second leg), 8 Oct 1986; **Spurs 5-3 Barnsley** *(Close, Hoddle (2), Galvin, Allen C)*; 11.

- Div 1, 11 Oct 1986; **Liverpool 0-1 Spurs** *(Allen C)*; 12.

- Div 1, 18 Oct 1986; **Spurs 1-1 Sheffield Wednesday** *(Allen C)*; 13.

- League Cup third round, 29 Oct 1986; **Spurs 5-0 Birmingham City** *(Roberts, Allen C (2), Hoddle, Waddle)*; 15.

- Div 1, 15 Nov 1986; **Spurs 1-0 Coventry City** *(Allen C)*; 16.

- Div 1, 22 Nov 1986; **Oxford United 2-4 Spurs** *(Allen C (2), Waddle (2))*; 18.

- League Cup fourth round, 26 Nov 1986; **Cambridge United 1-3 Spurs** *(Allen C, Close, Waddle)*; 19.

- Div 1, 29 Nov 1986; **Spurs 2-3 Nottingham Forest** *(Allen C (2))*; 21.

- Div 1, 7 Dec 1986; **Manchester United 3-3 Spurs** *(Mabbutt, Allen C, Moran og)*; 22.

- Div 1, 20 Dec 1986; **Chelsea 0-2** *(Allen C (2))*; 24.

- Div 1, 26 Dec 1986; **Spurs 4-0 West Ham United** *(Hodge, Allen C (2), Waddle)*; 26.

- Div 1, 27 Dec 1986; **Coventry City 4-3 Spurs** *(Allen C (2), Claesen)*; 28.

- League Cup fifth round, 27 Jan 1987; **West Ham United 1-1 Spurs** *(Allen C)*; 29.

- FA Cup fourth round, 31 Jan 1987; **Spurs 4-0 Crystal Palace** *(Mabbutt, Allen C (pen), Claesen, O'Reilly og)*; 30.

- League Cup fifth round replay, 2 Feb 1987; **Spurs 5-0 West Ham United** *(Allen C (3, 1 pen), Hoddle, Claesen)*; 33.

- League Cup semi-final (first leg), 8 Feb 1987; **Arsenal 0-1 Spurs** *(Allen C)*; 34.

- FA Cup fifth round, 21 Feb 1987; **Spurs 1-0 Newcastle United** *(Allen C (pen))*; 35.

- Div 1, 25 Feb 1987; **Spurs 5-0 Leicester City** *(Allen C (2, 1 pen), Allen P, Claesen)*; 37.

- League Cup semi-final (second leg), 1 Mar 1987; **Spurs 1-2 Arsenal** *(Allen C)*; 38.

- League Cup semi-final replay, 4 Mar 1987; **Spurs 1-2 Arsenal** *(Allen C)*; 39.

- Div 1, 7 Mar 1987; **Spurs 1-0 Queens Park Rangers** *(Allen C (pen))*; 40.

- Div 1, 4 Apr 1987; **Spurs 3-0 Norwich City** *(Allen C (3))*; 43.

- Div 1, 7 Apr 1987; **Sheffield Wednesday 0-1 Spurs** *(Allen C)*; 44.

- FA Cup semi-final (Villa Park), 11 Apr 1987; **Spurs 4-1 Watford** *(Hodge (2), Allen C, Allen P)*; 45.

- Div 1, 18 Apr 1987; **Spurs 1-0 Charlton Athletic** *(Allen C)*; 46.

- Div 1, 20 Apr 1987; **Spurs 1-2 West Ham United** *(Allen C)*; 47.

- Div 1, 4 May 1987; **Spurs 4-0 Manchester United** *(Thomas M (2), Allen C (pen), Allen P)*; 48.

- FA Cup final (Wembley), 16 May 1987; **Coventry City 3-2 Spurs** *(Allen C, Mabbutt)*; 49.

Allen's total can be rounded up to 50 if the goal scored against Rangers in Maxi Miller's testimonial at the start of the season is included.

Thirteen great club men

1 **Rev. John Ripsher (1882–94):** *founder of Tottenham Hotspur, president, patron.*
2 **Bobby Buckle (1882–1900):** *founding member, player, captain, secretary, treasurer and director.*
3 **Jack Jull (1882–1920):** *founding member, player, committee member and president.*
4 **Charles D Roberts (1898–1943):** *chairman.*
5 **Arthur Turner (1906–46):** *club secretary and unofficial manager when required.*
6 **Jimmy Anderson (1908–58):** *various roles, including manager 1955–58.*
7 **Fred Bearman (1909–64):** *director, chairman and president.*
8 **Cecil Poynton (1922–34 and 1946–75):** *player, trainer and physiotherapist.*
9 **Johnny Wallis (1936–94):** *player, trainer, coach, reserve team manager and kit man.*
10 **Bill Nicholson (1936–2004):** *player, manager, chief scout and president.*
11 **Steve Perryman (1969–94):** *The skipper.*
12 **Chris Hughton (1977–90 and 1993–2007):** *player, coach, assistant manager and caretaker manager.*
13 **Gary Mabbutt (1982–):** *player and club ambassador.*

ELEVEN SPURS HAT-TRICK FACTS

1 A Spurs player has scored three goals in a match on 176 occasions. This consists of 145 hat-tricks, 27 four goal hauls and four instances of five in a match.

2 Spurs first recorded hat-trick was scored by Jack Jull in a 3-0 win over Albion in 1884.

3 Frank Osborne is the only Spurs player to score three consecutive hat-tricks, a feat he achieved in autumn 1925. Spurs' managed to lose one of those games 3-5, but Osborne's frustrations with his teammates must have been nothing compared to Jimmy Cantrell, who scored four up at Middlesbrough only to lose 5-7 in 1915.

4 Not only did Bob Clements score Spurs' first FA Cup hat-trick in a 4-0 win over Old St Stephen's in 1896, he also scored Spurs' first ever Southern League goal.

5 Three of Billy Minter's 101 Spurs goals came in a 4-0 win over Blackburn Rovers in 1910, which represented Spurs' first hat-trick in the Football League. Another member of the 100 club got Spurs' first Premier League hat-trick when Teddy Sheringham scored three in a 4-0 win against defending champions Leeds United in 1993.

6 On only four occasions has a player scored five goals in a game for Spurs:

   i   Division Two, 30 Aug 1930; Spurs 7-1 Reading (Harper (5), Cook, Dimmock)

   ii Division One, 18 Sept 1957; Spurs 7-1 Birmingham City (Harmer (pen), Stokes (5), Dyson)

   iii FA Cup fifth round, 3 Feb 1960; Spurs 13-2 Crewe Alexandra (Harmer, Smith R (4), Allen (5), Jones (3, 1 pen))

   iv Premier League, 22 Nov 2009; Spurs 9-1 Wigan Athletic (Crouch, Defoe (5), Lennon, Kirkland og, Kranjcar).

7   Bobby Smith scored four goals in a game on five occasions, including during the 13-2 record win against Crewe and the 10-4 win over Everton in Bill Nicholson's first match as manager. In total, he scored three or more on 16 occasions, one less than his former striking partner Jimmy Greaves who has a Spurs record for number of hat-tricks scored, including one on his debut against Blackpool.

8   Spurs' first hat-trick in the League Cup was scored by Martin Chivers in a low key 4-1 win against Division Two strugglers Aston Villa in September 1968. The other goal for Spurs that evening was one of the last of a distinguished Spurs career for Cliff Jones, who seven years earlier had scored Spurs' first European hat-trick in the 8-1 hammering of Górnik Zabrze in the European Cup.

9   The greatest goal-scoring debut for Spurs came from Colin Lee, who bagged four in the 9-0 win over Bristol Rovers. Alfie Conn also scored a hat-trick on his first full appearance in a shock 5-2 win at Newcastle.

10 The 13-2 win against Crewe was the only time three Spurs players – Les Allen (5), Bobby Smith (4) and Cliff Jones (3) – scored a hat-trick in the same match.

11 While it may not get in many record books, Sid McCellan scored nine in a friendly against Saskatchewan FA, which rates as the most by any Spurs player in a representative game. In all, Spurs scored 85 goals in 10 tour matches, with 12 of those coming in two matches against fellow tourists Manchester United.

TWENTY-ONE MEMORABLE SPURS HAT-TRICKS

1   FA Cup semi-final (Villa Park), 8 Apr 1901. **Spurs 4-0 West Bromwich Albion** *(Brown (4))*. In total, Sandy Brown scored 15 in the famous cup run for non-League Spurs against all the odds, including a hat-trick in a 4-2 win away at top division Preston and all four in the semi-final win over the Baggies.

2 Div 1, 18 Nov 1950. **Spurs 7-0 Newcastle United** *(Bennett, Baily, Medley (3), Walters, Ramsey (pen)).* Les Medley stars in the most stunning performance of the 'push and run' League title.

3 Div 1, 11 Oct 1958. **Spurs 10-4 Everton** *(Smith R (4), Stokes (2), Robb, Ryden, Medwin, Harmer).* Bobby Smith starts the Bill Nicholson era with a memorable win.

4 FA Cup fifth round replay, 3 Feb 1960. **Spurs 13-2 Crewe Alexandra** *(Harmer, Smith R (4), Allen (5), Jones (3, 1 pen)).* Crewe held Spurs 2-2 in the first match, but there was no stopping them in the replay with Les Allen, Bobby Smith and Cliff Jones fighting for the match ball at the end.

5 European Cup, 20 Sept 1961. **Spurs 8-1 Górnik Zabrze** *(Blanchflower (pen), Dyson, Jones (3), Smith R (2), White).* The original and probably the greatest of the 'Glory, Glory' European nights, with Cliff Jones leading the way.

6 Div 1, 16 Dec 1961. **Spurs 5-2 Blackpool** *(Allen (2), Greaves (3)).* Start as you mean to go on: Jimmy Greaves scores the first of his 17 Spurs hat-tricks.

7 Div 1, 29 Sept 1962. **Spurs 9-2 Notts Forest** *(Medwin, White, Allen (pen), Greaves (4), Jones (2)).* Jimmy Greaves always liked playing against Forest and four of his 16 goals against them came in this record-margin Division One win.

8 Div 1, 28 Oct 1972. **Manchester United 1-4 Spurs** *(Peters (4)).* In fifteen matches at Old Trafford between 1995 and 2007, Spurs managed three goals against Manchester United. Martin Peters topped that with four in an afternoon of a very different era.

9 Div 1, 11 Jan 1975. **Newcastle United 2-5 Spurs** *(Knowles, Conn (3), Duncan).* Cult hero Alfie Conn only ever scored six League goals for Spurs, but three of them came in his first full appearance, up at Newcastle, marking Spurs' only win in 14 miserable League games.

10 Div 2, 26 Oct 1977. **Spurs 9-0 Bristol Rovers** *(Lee (4), Taylor, Moores (3), Hoddle).* Signed from the obscurity of Torquay during the week before, Colin Lee announced himself in style and even Ian Moores chipped in with a second-half hat-trick.

11 Div 1, 6 Feb 1982. **Spurs 6-1 Wolves** *(Villa (3), Falco, Hoddle (pen), Crooks).* Spurs opened the 'new' West Stand in style with Ricky Villa on one of his going days.

12 Div 1, 20 Mar 1982. **Spurs 3-2 Southampton** *(Roberts (3)).* Three goals from midfield for 80s talisman Robbo against his home-town club in a top-of-the-table clash, with the last looping up and into the net after being mis-hit into the ground.

13 League Cup fifth round replay, 2 Feb 1987. **Spurs 5-0 West Ham United** *(Hoddle, Claesen, Allen C (3, 1 pen)).* A Spurs masterclass, with Clive Allen supplying three late goals.

14 Div 1, 8 Sept 1990. **Spurs 3-0 Derby County** *(Gascoigne (3)).* Some stunning long-range goals from Gazza against Peter Shilton decided this clash of that year's World Cup heroes.

15 Div 1, 21 Sept 1991. **Wimbledon 3-5 Spurs** *(Lineker (4, 1 pen), Samways).* Goal-scoring legend Gary Lineker scored two in a game 14 times, including in a certain FA Cup semi-final, to add to his four hat-tricks. Arguably the best of these occurred at Selhurst when Spurs recovered from being a goal down to take the Wombles apart with a flurry of goals either side of half time.

16 Premier League, 20 Feb 1993. **Spurs 4-0 Leeds United** *(Ruddock, Sheringham (3, 1 pen)).* Spurs had lost the reverse fixture 0-5 to the then champions, but destroyed Leeds at White Hart Lane with a superb display of class from an emerging young team, with Teddy providing the goals.

17 FA Cup sixth round, 7 Mar 1993. **Manchester City 2-4 Spurs** *(Nayim (3), Sedgley)*. A memorable game, both on and off the pitch, with the mercurial Moroccan on his best form.

18 FA Cup fifth round replay, 1 Mar 1995. **Southampton 2-6 Spurs (aet)** *(Rosenthal (3), Sheringham, Barmby, Anderton)*. Inspired Ronnie Rosenthal turns around a 0-2 half-time deficit in style.

19 Premier League, 4 Mar 1997. **Sunderland 0-4 Spurs** *(Iversen (3), Nielsen)*. If Iversen had stayed with Rosenburg, he would have been in the San Siro in the Champions League rather than running round a cold Roker Park in a meaningless mid-table game in the lost years.

20 Premier League, 2 May 1998. **Wimbledon 2-6 Spurs** *(Ferdinand, Klinsmann (4), Saib)*. With relegation looming, Spurs badly needed a win and an inspired Klinsmann saved Spurs after trailing 2-1.

21 Premier League, 22 Nov 2009. **Spurs 9-1 Wigan Athletic** *(Crouch, Defoe (5), Lennon, Kirkland og, Kranjcar)*. Spurs' record score in the Premier League, with Defoe staying onside long enough to grab a nap hand for Spurs.

ROBBIE KEANE'S TOP TWENTY MOMENTS

A skilful footballer in Spurs' best traditions, Robbie Keane is a modern Spurs legend with 122 goals helping the team out of their slumber to be contenders again . . . albeit a slightly unloved legend after his move and less successful return from Liverpool.

1 Premier League, 15 Sept 2002. **Spurs 3-2 West Ham** *(Davies, Sheringham (pen), Gardner)*. A high-quality debut, turning Ian Pearce inside out to win Spurs a penalty.

2 Premier League, 6 Oct 2002. **Blackburn Rovers 1-2 Spurs** *(Keane, Redknapp)*. First Spurs goal with a fantastic run and shot into the top corner.

3 Premier League, 24 Nov 2002. **Spurs 2-0 Leeds United** *(Sheringham, Keane)*. Another fantastic shot from the edge of the box, starting what would be a familiar pattern of scoring against former teams.

4 Premier League, 12 Jan 2003. **Spurs 4-3 Everton** *(Poyet, Keane (3))*. Keane's first hat-trick for Spurs, with the third goal coming from the only time his infuriating habit of ducking out of headers paid off. The Everton defender jumped under the ball and Keane latched on to the loose ball and dinked it over former Spurs keeper Baardsen for the winner.

5 Premier League, 5 Apr 2003. **Spurs 2-1 Birmingham City** *(Keane, Poyet)*. Birmingham keeper Andy Marriott thought the danger was over as he threw the ball down to launch another long punt upfield and the players retreated back to their positions after a Spurs attack. However, he'd failed to count them all, and Keane, who'd been quietly lurking behind him, suddenly appeared to nick the ball and roll it into an empty net for a classic moment.

6 Premier League, 6 Dec 2003. **Spurs 5-2 Wolves** *(Keane (3), Kanoute, Dalmat)*. A second hat-trick with another former club made to suffer.

7 Premier League, 24 Apr 2004. **Spurs 2-2 Arsenal** *(Redknapp, Keane (pen))*. A last-minute penalty from Keane mitigates a terrible day for Spurs as the Goons claim the title for a second time at White Hart Lane.

8 Premier League, 16 Apr 2005. **Liverpool 2-2 Spurs** *(Edman, Keane))*. A rare headed goal at Anfield, probably with his eyes shut.

9 Premier League, 1 Oct 2005. **Charlton Athletic 2-3 Spurs** *(King, Mido, Keane)*. Popped up with the winner to cap a great comeback for Spurs.

10 Premier League, 5 Mar 2006. **Spurs 3-2 Blackburn Rovers** *(Keane (2), Mido)*. Arguably his best goal at Spurs, exhibiting sensational ball control and juggling before smashing an unstoppable shot into the Park Lane net.

11 Premier League, 22 Apr 2006. **Arsenal 1-1 Spurs** *(Keane)*. A tap-in at Highbury to give Spurs the lead in a game that could have all but clinched the Lilywhites' first Champions League campaign, before a late equaliser started an end-of-season wobble.

12 Premier League, 13 May 2007. **Spurs 2-1 Manchester City** *(Keane, Berbatov)*. Spurs' best strike partnership of the decade on the mark to ensure qualification for the UEFA Cup for the second consecutive season.

13 Premier League, 7 Oct 2007. **Liverpool 2-2 Spurs** *(Keane (2))*. Perhaps some mixed feelings here, with a couple more against one of his boyhood teams.

14 League Cup semi-final, 22 Jan 2008. **Spurs 5-1 Arsenal** *(Jenas, Bendtner og, Keane, Lennon, Malbranque)*. After many years of trying, Keane finally appears in a Spurs win over Arsenal in a great night at White Hart Lane.

15 League Cup final (Wembley), 24 Feb 2008. **Spurs 2-1 Chelsea (aet)** *(Berbatov (pen), Woodgate)*. Lets Berbatov take the penalty, but lifts the Cup with Ledley to get a deserved first medal at Spurs.

16 Premier League, 15 Mar 2008. **Manchester City 2-1 Spurs** *(Keane)*. Opened the scoring at Eastlands, but was once again bizarrely substituted by bizarre manager Ramos, throwing his shirt to the ground in annoyance. Perhaps the moment when Keane thought he'd be better off somewhere else the following season.

17 Premier League, 18 Mar 2008. **Spurs 4-4 Chelsea** *(Woodgate, Berbatov, Huddlestone, Keane)*. A brilliant curling shot from the edge of the box to level things up at 4-4 against Chelsea was one of the best among his 23 Spurs goals that season.

18 Premier League, 4 Mar 2009. **Spurs 4-0 Middlesbrough** *(Keane, Pavlyuchenko, Lennon (2))*. The first goal of his mostly disappointing return to Spurs.

19 Premier League, 26 Sept 2009. **Spurs 5-0 Burnley** *(Keane (4), Jenas)*. The highlight of his second coming, as

Spurs march towards fourth place and Champions League qualification.

20 League Cup third round, 20 Sept 2010. **Spurs 1-4 Arsenal (aet)** *(Keane)*. A final Spurs goal in a low-key game as Spurs concentrated on the Champions League.

Those Robbie Keane statistics in full

Keane totals	Starts	Subs	Goals
League	189	49	91
FA Cup	16	5	12
League Cup	16	6	10
UEFA Cup	15	9	9
Total	236	69	122

- All in all, Keane scored in 101 games, of which Spurs won 67, drew 18 and lost 16, which represents a healthy 66% win percentage.

- Keane scored at least 13 goals in each of his first six seasons with Spurs.

- 57% of Keane's Spurs goals were scored at White Hart Lane.

- During his Spurs career, Keane scored 16 and missed three of his spot kicks for Spurs.

Keane's favourite teams

Team	Goals against
West Bromwich Albion	7
Birmingham City	6
Bolton Wanderers	6
Everton	6
Fulham	6
Blackburn Rovers	5
Liverpool	4
Manchester City	4
Middlesbrough	4
Wolves	4

THE TOP NINE ONE-GOAL WONDERS

1 **Justin Edinburgh:** Dean Austin (140 games, 0 goals) at right fullback and Justin Edinburgh (276 games, one goal) at the start of the 1990s were hardly the Spurs equivalent of Cafu and Roberto Carlos. Perhaps the biggest shock was that they managed a goal between them at all, with 'Ricky' popping up on a dark night with very few witnesses at Bramall Lane early on in his Spurs career.

2 **Phil Beal:** Beal was a defender's defender, but managed one goal in his 420 appearances spanning 13 seasons, against QPR in 1969 – an outfield player record for just one Spurs goal.

3 **Pat Jennings:** Beal must have endured a couple of seasons of ribbing from his goalkeeper Pat Jennings, who scored probably the most famous goal among the 'one-goal wonders' when he beat Alex Stepney with a goal kick in the 1967 Charity Shield at Old Trafford.

4 **Paul Robinson:** The only other goal from a Spurs keeper came in the Premier League in 2007 against Watford. Robbo launched a long, hopeful punt from midway inside the Spurs half towards the forwards, only to see it bounce up and over Ben Foster and into the Paxton net. Ironically, Foster was one of the keepers who would eventually take the England jersey from Robinson.

5 **Jason Cundy:** Perhaps the most stunning one-goal wonder was Jason Cundy's effort at Portman Road in 1992. There seemed no danger when Cundy slid in for an interception near the halfway line, but the ball spectacularly flew more than forty yards into the Ipswich net to earn Spurs' first away point in the newly formed Premier League.

6 **Terry Naylor:** Terry Naylor managed over 300 appearances for Spurs, but saved his one goal for the rarefied atmosphere of an away leg of a League Cup semi-final against Chelsea to earn Spurs a valuable away goal. Unfortunately for Nutty, the goal was not enough to see Spurs to the final.

7 **David Tuttle:** David Tuttle did not achieve much during his formative years at Spurs, but chose one of the special European football nights under the lights at White Hart Lane to score his only goal for the club, which helped Spurs overturn a first-leg deficit against Hadjuk Split in the early 90s.

8 **Charlie Rance:** Probably the unluckiest player to register only one true goal for the club was Charlie Rance, who netted against Notts County in 1912 only for the game to be abandoned after 80 minutes because of fog, with Spurs losing 3-1. Spurs promptly lost the rearranged game 3-0, but all was not lost for Rance, who popped up to earn a draw against Blackpool in the FA Cup, and this counted as his one and only Spurs goal.

9 **Tom Mason:** Tom Mason is probably not a well-known name for Spurs fans, but with his one goal for the team he achieved in 1912 what Spurs greats such as Greaves, Smith and Chivers failed to do, by scoring in a win at Anfield. It would be another 73 years until Garth Crooks scored a winning goal for Spurs up there.

EIGHT SUPER SUBS

1 **Jermain Defoe:** Defoe holds the record for number of substitute appearances for Spurs with in excess of 90 and counting, more than 20 clear of former strike partner Robbie Keane in second place.

2 **Jose Dominguez:** The pint-sized Portugueser made his reputation after a dazzling display on his debut against Derby in 1997. Unfortunately for Dominguez, he quickly became labelled as a 'super sub', and made 42 of his 58 appearances from the bench, the highest proportion of any player making over 30 appearances for Spurs.

3 **John Bostock:** When John Bostock came on for his debut against Dynamo Zagreb in 2008, he became Spurs' youngest ever player at 16 years, 295 days. His three subsequent appearances have also been as substitute.

4 **Ralph Coates:** Spurs were struggling to find the winning goal against lowly Norwich City in the 1973 League Cup final when Coates, an early replacement for John Pratt, rifled home a shot from the edge of the box, before embarking on an iconic goal celebration with his comb-over flapping in the wind.

5 **Adel Taarabt:** Taarabt holds the record of 15 substitute appearances without starting a game for Spurs. He's also the only person to appear for Spurs in the League, FA Cup, League Cup and in Europe without starting a game.

6 **Scott Houghton:** The only player to have scored more than one goal for Spurs without ever starting a game. He bagged a couple on one of his 14 substitute appearances to help Spurs win a freaky game over Luton in 1991.

7 **Hat-trick from the bench:** The only substitute hat-trick for Spurs came in a fifth-round Cup replay at the Dell. With Spurs already two down and the likes of Sheringham, Klinsmann and Barmby having no joy, little was expected when Francis sent on Ronnie Rosenthal. But for that evening, he was like a man possessed. The first goal was a perfectly executed half-volley, and the second an unstoppable 25-yarder after a typically shambolic run that more often than not would see Rosenthal fall over. But the best was saved until last. Into extra time, Rosenthal picked the ball up near the halfway line and, as Saints defenders backed off, he let fly a Brazilian-style 35-yarder, which swerved into the top corner.

8 **Mike England:** Mike England made all of his 397 appearances for Spurs as part of the starting XI. This remains the highest total for an outfield player never coming on as a substitute since the introduction of substitution.

Ten hirsute Hotspurs

1 *Ricky Villa: never without facial hair, either the classic droopy moustache or full beard, for that authentic pampas cowboy look.*

2 **Mike Varney:** *famous beard associated with the magic sponge of the 1970s and 1980s.*

3 **Alfie Conn:** *classic droopy 'tache, very fitting for a 1970s icon.*

4 **Sandy Tait:** *formidable moustache from the Victorian era.*

5 **Ian Moores:** *blond Abba-type beard as Spurs had their own SOS in the 1970s.*

6 **Steve Archibald:** *scraggly Scottish beard that suited his wispy brilliance in the 1980s.*

7 **Graeme Souness:** *only had one game for Spurs, but his facial hair defined a whole generation of style on Merseyside.*

8 **Ossie Ardiles:** *surprised everyone with a comical 'tache in the mid-1980s.*

9 **Vivian Woodward:** *dapper Edwardian moustache from Spurs' first England scorer.*

10 **Benoit Assou-Ekotto:** *you almost don't notice the beard with one of his mad hairstyles.*

TEN SPURS DOUBLE ACTS

1. BILL NICHOLSON AND DANNY BLANCHFLOWER

Nicholson provided the method and Blanchflower supplied the magic that made the double team work. They remain the most formidable partnership in Spurs' history.

2. TEDDY SHERINGHAM AND JÜRGEN KLINSMANN

Sheringham was reaching maturity as a top-class striker when Spurs raided the World Cup for its star player and signed Jürgen Klinsmann. The pair clicked immediately as part of Ossie's 'famous five' attacking unit, and the goals flowed for both players for the rest of the season. The partnership was over all too soon as Jurgen jumped at the end of the season and Sheringham started to lose interest in the talent downsizing which followed.

3. PAT JENNINGS AND CYRIL KNOWLES

One wonders if Jennings and Knowles would have had any career at all in the modern age of ranting fans on phone-ins and messageboards. Not because they lacked the skill, but each had error-prone starts to their careers and their unconventional styles meant that for every moment of genius they were never far away from a clanger. Perhaps the most notable of these occurred in the early 1970s against Palace when Knowles did not look up and scored a wondrous long-range own goal with Jennings off his line.

Entertaining, classy and tending to make a gaffe every now and again, they represented the perfect Spurs partnership at the back.

4. CHRIS HUGHTON AND TONY GALVIN

For most of the early and mid-1980s, a large part of Spurs' success was down to the somewhat unlikely pairing of a barrel-chested Russian-speaking Yorkshireman and his former lift engineer partner from Forest Gate, both of whom were right-footed and both of whom played for the Republic of Ireland, to be sure. The original Spurs odd couple. Best going forward, with Hughton overlapping and Galvin cutting in to deliver one of his trademark curling shots, their crowning glory was a goal apiece in a magnificent away win against Feyenoord.

5. GARTH CROOKS AND STEVE ARCHIBALD

Both signed during summer 1980, Crooks and Archie were very different characters off the pitch, but gelled instantly on it to build the platform for success in the early 1980s. In their first season, Crooks scored 22 goals, including two in the FA Cup semi-final replay and the equaliser in the Cup final replay, while Archibald, after a slower start, ended up with 25. A goal each in the 2-0 win over champions elect Aston Villa in March 1981 probably reflected their peak at Spurs, as injuries to one or both restricted the partnership over the coming seasons.

6. THE G-MEN: JIMMY GREAVES AND ALAN GILZEAN

Jimmy Greaves is undoubtedly the greatest goal-scorer in Spurs' history, and netted them with whomever he played, but he will be best remembered at Spurs alongside Alan Gilzean. Their styles complemented each other perfectly; Gilzean was skilful and good in the air, not dissimilar in style to Dimitar Berbatov, whereas Greaves had the priceless knack of making goal scoring look very simple.

Their goals helped Spurs to top-six finishes throughout the mid-to-late 1960s and were topped off by an FA Cup final win over Chelsea. Their partnership ended in a disastrous cup defeat at Crystal Palace in 1970, after which both players were among a number dropped by Bill Nicholson for the next match. Greaves sadly never played for Spurs again, but Gilzean eventually got back into the side to partner Greaves' replacement Martin Chivers, with whom he enjoyed a similarly successful partnership until his retirement in the mid-1970s.

7. GLENN HODDLE AND CHRIS WADDLE

As much as they played good football together during the overlap in their Spurs careers, the legend of 'Hoddle and Waddle' is as much 'Glenn & Chris' the pop singers. They reached number 12 in the hit parade and appeared on *Top of the Pops* with their toe-curlingly bad 'Diamond Lights'. Thoughts of a full-time pop career were shelved when the appropriately named follow-up 'It's Goodbye' peaked at 92.

8. GORAN BUNJEVČEVIĆ AND MILENKO AČIMOVIĆ

While most partnerships were based on the excellence of the pair's performance for Spurs, 'The Cheeky Girls' (as they became known) were doomed by the description from manager Glenn Hoddle when they signed. He described Bunjy as the 'Serbian Franz Beckenbauer' and Ačimović as the 'Slovenian Trevor Brooking', but both were lightweight misfits who did not hang around very long.

9. OSSIE ARDILES AND RICARDO VILLA

They were not particularly close before Spurs signed them as World Cup-winners in 1978, but the masterstroke of signing the two of them together helped both settle in England. Ossie was the impish midfield maestro who formed a great under-standing with Hoddle and was never short of a word or two for the referee, while Ricky was the enigmatic one, mixing moments of brilliance with periods of inconsistency. Their names will for-ever be associated with the 100th FA Cup final, as Chas 'n' Dave wrote about 'Ossie's Dream' beforehand, while Ricky lived the nightmare before the real dream in the replay.

10. SUGAR AND VENABLES

A partnership where the funny man wasn't particularly straight and the straight man got plenty of unintentional laughs. The acrimonious split in summer 1993 negatively echoed throughout the rest of the decade.

TWENTY GREAT MOMENTS FROM THE SPURS CAREER OF JOHN PRATT

In a career spanning 11 years, John Pratt played 415 times, scored 49 goals and won both domestic and European honours. He wore every outfield shirt number and always gave 100% in his all-action midfield role. However, he will mostly be remem-bered for the abuse he took from the Spurs faithful over that time. Here are some of his great moments:

1 **September 1969:** Pratt's first Spurs goal comes in a 3-2 away win in the North London derby.

2 **May 1972:** Becomes Spurs' first ever substitute in a major cup final when replacing Ralph Coates in the first leg of the 1971/2 UEFA Cup final against Wolves. Nearly scored a classic own goal with his first touch of the ball, but collects his first Spurs medal as an unused sub in the return leg.

3 **September 1972:** Scores his one and only European goal in a 6-3 win at Lyn Oslo in the UEFA Cup first round.

4 **October 1972:** Scores two brilliant goals against Gordon Banks as Spurs beat Stoke City 4-3 at the Lane.

5 **December 1972:** Another brilliant goal at White Hart Lane, this time an unstoppable shot that beats Ray Clemence and starts Spurs on their way to a 3-1 League Cup quarter final win against Liverpool.

6 **March 1973:** After playing a vital role in getting Spurs to Wembley for the 1973 League Cup final against Norwich City, only manages 20 minutes before getting an injury that forces him from the pitch. His replacement, Ralph Coates, scored the late winner in what was to be Pratt's only Wembley appearance.

7 **May 1974:** Plays in all 12 matches in the UEFA Cup run that saw Spurs lose out 4-2 to Feyenoord on aggregate in the final.

8 **January 1976:** JP was on target for the only goal of the match in the first leg of the League Cup semi-final against Newcastle at White Hart Lane, but it was not enough, as Spurs lost 3-1 at St James' Park a week later.

9 **April 1976:** Scores the first in a 2-0 win over Arsenal at Highbury. Only Garth Crooks has scored goals in two separate away wins against Arsenal since.

10 **May 1976:** Ends the season with 13 goals in 50 appearances across all competitions, including 10 in his 41 League appearances, marking his most successful season in terms of finding the net.

11 **September 1976:** As a second-half sub, is part of the unloved trio including Ian Moores and Ralph Coates who turn a 2-0 half-time deficit into a 3-2 win against Manchester United at Old Trafford, which ends up being Spurs' only away win of the relegation season.

12 **May 1977:** After relegation confirmed a week earlier, a Pratt goal helps Spurs beat Leicester and give a winning send-off to 27 consecutive seasons in the top flight.

13 **January 1978:** Inspires a late Spurs comeback with two goals to get a draw at Notts County, including a 30-yard stunner that was possibly his best for Spurs.

14 **May 1978:** Pratt is ever present for Spurs as they return to the top flight at the first attempt, and is rewarded with over 24,000 turning up for his testimonial against Arsenal.

15 **September 1978:** After losing his place to Ardiles and Villa at the start of the season, his reinstatement to the first team sees Spurs claim their first two wins back in the top division.

16 **October 1978:** In the era of near-post headed goals from corners, Pratt flashes one home to help beat Bolton at White Hart Lane.

17 **December 1979:** Scores Spurs' last goal of the 1970s, when his low drive at the Park Lane end is enough to get maximum points against Stoke City.

18 **March 1980:** Scores his last Spurs goal, direct from a corner, against champions Liverpool.

19 **April 1980:** Pratt plays his last ever match for Spurs, in a 1-4 defeat at Old Trafford against Manchester United – the same fixture and scoreline as the great Danny Blanchflower's last game 17 years earlier.

20 **1984–86:** Appointed assistant manager to Peter Shreeve as Spurs challenge for the title before eventually finishing third and then 10th in consecutive seasons, winning 42 of their 84 games.

The pantomime villain XI

1. Mark Bosnich

He mostly got away with his assault on Jürgen Klinsmann as it was on the same evening as Cantona's kung fu antics at Palace. This alone would probably have secured his place in our band of miscreants, but he topped things off with a Nazi salute to the Paxton end a few years later.

2. Nigel Winterburn

It was a tough choice between Dixon and Winterburn for one of the fullback slots, as both were devoid of any redeeming features, in the traditional Arsenal mould. Winterburn got the nod as he also played for anti-football Wimbledon.

3. Ben Thatcher

Dirty, limited player who once got sent off trying to ruin Ginola. How Sugar allowed Graham to spend £5 million of Spurs' money on him was as much a mystery as a tragedy.

4. Tony Adams

We loved to hate Adams as he was proper unreconstructed 'old Arsenal'. To quote the old song '. . . a pissed-up donkey, in a shit football team'. For all the eey-ore chants, Adams more often than not had the last laugh, notably when scoring the winner in the 1993 FA Cup semi-final and a spectacular volley one night at Highbury. But we needed him and players like him at Arsenal to define Tottenham. Once they stole our clothes and started playing good football, it all got a bit messed up.

5. Sol Campbell

Campbell succeeded where the likes of Descartes and the great philosophers had failed, by answering the ultimate ontological question. If there is a God in the universe, how would He have allowed the brilliant Spurs captain to leave for nothing, join our biggest rivals, and then win the double in his first season? In many ways, it was not Campbell who Spurs fans were railing at but the way the club was run down to such a state that 'rSol' (as he became known) could not stay to fulfil his ambitions. His returns to WHL were always emotional.

6. Graeme Souness

Bounced out of Spurs by Billy Nick after one substitute appearance, he spent a career as midfield hatchetman and second-rate manager but somehow fluked a League Cup final win over Spurs for Blackburn, 20 years after doing the same as a player for Liverpool in the same competition.

7. Kenny Hibbitt

It's strange to think that Hibbitt's crime, diving to win a penalty, would hardly raise more than a moment's consternation these days. But the impact of his fall, to win Wolves a last-minute equaliser, was immense at the time in 1981. Spurs won the replay in a great evening at Highbury, but Hibbitt's crime was never forgotten.

8. Robbie Savage

Has tried to reinvent himself as wooden-legged dancer and media wally, but a generation of football fans remember him as a poor player and a serial cheat. His successful attempts to get Justin Edinburgh sent off in the 1999 League Cup final ensured he was booed each and every time he touched the ball in his subsequent games against Spurs. It never mellowed, and we did not particularly laugh about it afterwards.

9. Vinnie Jones

There were a whole host of candidates for the last midfield place: Danny Maguire, Norman Whiteside, Tommy Smith, Reuben Agboola . . . But Jones gets it for being the talent void who all but ended Gary Stevens' career.

10. John Fashanu

A wrong 'un who smashed Gary Mabbutt's face at White Hart Lane in a game against Wimbledon.

11. Mark Viduka

Ian Wright probably holds stronger claims, breaking David Howell's jaw, his provocative goal celebrations and those Chicken Tonight adverts, but Viduka seemed to enjoy hearing Spurs sing 'You're just a fat Aussie wanker!' at him, and we enjoyed the banter.

Manager: George Graham, the enemy without, who became the enemy within.

Chairman: Henry Norris.

THE GAMES

A NELSON OF CLASSIC GAMES

1 Div 1, 1950. **Spurs 7-0 Newcastle United.** The 'push and run' team at their very best.

2 Div 1, 1958. **Spurs 10-4 Everton.** A goal-fest in Billy Nick's first game in charge.

3 FA Cup, 1960. **Spurs 13-2 Crewe Alexandra.** Spurs' record score, already 10-1 at half time.

4 FA Cup, 1961. **Spurs 5-0 Sunderland.** A scare in the first game, but no mistake for the double team in the replay.

5 European Cup, 1961. **Spurs 8-1 Górnik Zabrze.** Spurs overturn a 2-4 deficit in magnificent style in their first ever European Cup tie, setting up the 'Glory, Glory' nights under the White Hart Lane floodlights.

6 European Cup, 1962. **Spurs 2-1 Benfica.** Another compelling night of European football, where Spurs do everything to recover a dodgy 3-1 deficit from the first leg against the European champions, falling just short despite a win on the night.

7 Div 1, 1962. **Spurs 9-2 Notts Forest.** Arguably Billy Nick's best team, and four goals for Greaves.

8 FA Cup, 1967. **Spurs 6-0 Birmingham City.** As in '61, Spurs are taken to replay in the sixth round, but a wide margin sets them on the way to winning the cup.

9 FA Cup, 1968. **Spurs 1-0 Manchester United.** Spurs win a great cup tussle between two great clubs in extra time.

10 UEFA Cup, 1972. **Spurs 2-1 AC Milan.** Two from Stevie P put Spurs en route to the final.

11 League Cup, 1972. **Spurs 3-1 Liverpool.** A couple from John Pratt win a classic cup tie for Spurs.

12 Div 1, 1975. **Newcastle United 2-5 Spurs.** Alfie Conn nets half of his six League goals in a rare away win.

13 Div 1, 1975. **Spurs 4-2 Leeds United.** Spurs escape relegation with a fine win against the European Cup finalists on the last day of the season.

14 Div 1, 1976. **Manchester United 2-3 Spurs.** One away win in the relegation season, coming from 2-0 down at Old Trafford.

15 Div 2, 1977. **Spurs 9-0 Bristol Rovers.** Colin Lee announces himself in style as Spurs grab the extra goal difference that would prove crucial at the end of the season.

16 Div 2, 1978. **Spurs 1-0 Bolton Wanderers.** More people turned up for a Division Two match than the FA Cup semi-final at Highbury on the same day to see Don McAllister's diving header keep Spurs' promotion hopes on track.

17 Div 2, 1979. **Southampton 0-0 Spurs.** Squeaky bum time as both teams get the result they need for promotion.

18 Div 1, 1979. **Aston Villa 2-3 Spurs.** Two down with 12 minutes to go before the great Glenn turns the game on its head.

19 Div 1, 1979. **Crystal Palace 1-1 Spurs.** Spurs halt the 'team of the 80s' before the decade begins.

20 League Cup, 1979. **Spurs 2-1 Manchester United.** Hoddle scores a special goal from a worked free kick as Hughton makes his debut.

21 Div 1, 1979. **Leeds United 1-2 Spurs.** An injury to Daines sees Hoddle take the gloves after 10 minutes, and despite Miller's sending-off on the half hour, Spurs hang on for a memorable win against the odds.

22 Div 1, 1979. **Spurs 1-0 Notts Forest.** Hoddle repeats his special volley to beat Shilton and the European champions-elect.

23 FA Cup, 1980. **Manchester United 0-1 Spurs.** On a wing and a prayer with Hoddle in goal, but Ossie pops up in the 117th minute to win it for Spurs.

24 Div 1, 1981. **Spurs 2-0 Aston Villa.** The cup winners-elect beat the League champions-to-be with a goal each from Crooks and Archie.

25 FA Cup, 1981. **Spurs 3-0 Wolves.** Two first-half goals from Crooks send Spurs back to Wembley, and Ricky Villa's third is the icing on the cake.

26 European Cup Winners' Cup, 1981. **Ajax 1-3 Spurs.** Back in Europe, Spurs take apart the three-time European champions.

27 Div 1, 1982. **Spurs 6-1 Wolves.** Spurs open the 'new' West Stand in style with a Ricky Villa hat-trick.

28 FA Cup, 1982. **Chelsea 2-3 Spurs.** A second half of true Tottenham brilliance led by Hoddle and Hazard.

29 Div 1, 1982. **Spurs 3-2 Southampton.** A Graham Roberts hat-trick from midfield keeps Spurs in touch at the top.

30 Div 1, 1982. **Arsenal 1-3 Spurs.** 'Thank you very much for the North Bank, Arsenal.' A happy Easter from Highbury.

31 European Cup Winners' Cup, 1982. **Spurs 1-1 Barcelona.** A late goal from Roberts rescues a point against 'the animals' from Catalonia.

32 Div 1, 1982. **Spurs 6-0 Southampton.** A great team playing great football.

33 Div. 1, 1983. **Spurs 5-0 Arsenal.** Revenge for the Brady game with a couple from Hughton and a great volley from Falco.

34 Div 1, 1983. **Spurs 2-0 Liverpool.** Two goals from Archie are enough to beat the champions.

35 Div 1, 1983. **Spurs 2-0 Manchester United.** Another win in a strong end to the season sees Spurs up to fourth and in the UEFA Cup.

36 Div 1, 1983. **Watford 2-3 Spurs.** 'That Hoddle chip' and one from the returning Archibald see off Watford.

37 UEFA Cup, 1983. **Spurs 4-2 Feyenoord.** One of the greatest first halves ever at White Hart Lane, as Cruyff chases Hoddle's shadow at a discreet distance, and Archie and Galvin weigh in with the goals.

38 UEFA Cup, 1983. **Spurs 2-0 Bayern Munich.** A great display from Spurs, capped with a late Falco toe-poke to send Spurs through.

39 Div 1, 1984. **Everton 1-4 Spurs.** On the opening day of the season, Spurs take apart an Everton team who went on to win the League.

40 Div 1, 1984. **Spurs 5-0 QPR.** Super Spurs sparkle in the autumn sunshine, with Micky Hazard pulling the strings.

41 Div 1, 1985. **Arsenal 1-2 Spurs.** A great start to the new year as Spurs come from a goal down to win and stay top of the League.

42 Div 1, 1985. **Liverpool 0-1 Spurs.** A Garth Crooks goal ends 73 years of hurt as Spurs finally win at Anfield.

43 Div 1, 1986. **Spurs 2-0 Birmingham City.** Fewer than 10,000 watch Spurs at home as football reaches a low ebb.

44 Div 1, 1986. **Aston Villa 0-3 Spurs.** The David Pleat era gets off to a great start, with the first three of Cousin Clive's 49.

45 League Cup, 1987. **Spurs 5-0 West Ham United.** A dazzling Spurs show, and another hat-trick for Clive Allen.

46 Div 1, 1987. **Spurs 4-0 Manchester United.** Spurs thrash United to send Hoddle off to Monaco in style.

47 Div 1, 1989. **Millwall 0-5 Spurs.** Spurs mark the perilous trip to the Den with a classy win.

48 Div 1, 1989. **Manchester United 0-1 Spurs.** After a 3-0 win in the League Cup earlier that month, it seemed inconceivable that this would be the last win at Old Trafford for so long.

49 Div 1, 1990. **Spurs 3-1 Manchester City.** World Cup 1990 heroes Gazza and Lineker sparkle on their return to Spurs.

50 Div 1, 1990. **Spurs 3-0 Derby County.** A brilliant Gazza hat-trick against England keeper Shilton as Spurs are everyone's second favourite team.

51 Div 1, 1990. **Spurs 2-1 Luton Town.** Two sendings-off force a reshuffle that not only sees Spurs win but changes the course of the season, with two-goal hero Paul Stewart moving to midfield.

52 FA Cup, 1991. **Portsmouth 1-2 Spurs.** A Terry Fenwick broken leg before kick-off and a Gazza-inspired comeback on the south coast.

53 FA Cup, 1991. **Spurs 3-1 Arsenal.** Oh I Say . . . St Hotspur Day.

54 Div 1, 1991. **Manchester United 1-1 Spurs.** FA Cup winners against European Cup Winners' Cup winners in a virtual exhibition match.

55 Div 1, 1991. **Wimbledon 3-5 Spurs.** Four for Lineker as Spurs run riot either side of half time at Selhurst.

56 Premier League, 1993. **Spurs 4-2 Southampton.** Four goals in less than five minutes won this for Spurs as the Livermore/Clemence team take shape.

57 FA Cup, 1993. **Spurs 3-2 Wimbledon.** Spurs with the emerging Nicky Barmby make this Wimbledon game better than watching Ceefax for Lineker.

58 Premier League, 1993. **Spurs 4-0 Leeds United.** A fine comeback after a 5-0 drubbing at Elland Road earlier in the season.

59 FA Cup, 1993. **Manchester City 2-4 Spurs.** Madcap cup action with a Nayim hat-trick, a missed penalty, disallowed goal and a very angry pitch invasion.

60 Premier League, 1993. **Newcastle United 0-1 Spurs.** Spurs shoot down Newcastle's return to the big time with a classy Sheringham goal.

61 Premier League, 1994. **Sheffield Wednesday 3-4 Spurs.** Another opening-day classic as Ossie's famous five set the League alight and Jürgen Klinsmann scores the winner on his debut.

62 Premier League, 1995. **Spurs 3-1 Blackburn Rovers.** Champions-elect Blackburn are no match for an excellent Spurs performance.

63 FA Cup, 1995. **Sunderland 1-4 Spurs.** Spurs serve up a Sunday afternoon treat at the old Roker Park.

64 FA Cup, 1995. **Southampton 2-6 Spurs.** 2-0 down before Rocket Ronnie Rosenthal sets up a remarkable win.

65 FA Cup, 1995. **Liverpool 1-2 Spurs.** Spurs' greatest performance at Anfield was applauded by both sets of fans.

66 Premier League, 1996. **Spurs 4-1 Manchester United.** All was quiet in the away end on this new year's day.

67 Premier League, 1997. **Sunderland 0-4 Spurs.** A Steffen Iversen hat-trick encouraged the early delusion he was a superstar.

68 Premier League, 1997. **Spurs 3-2 Sheffield Wednesday.** Ginola-inspired Spurs edge this relegation scrap.

69 Premier League, 1998. **Spurs 3-3 Liverpool.** The much-needed three points in this entertaining game looked to be heading Spurs' way before a young Michael Owen secured a late draw for the visitors.

70 Premier League, 1998. **Crystal Palace 1-3 Spurs.** Chris Armstrong's diving header and Klinsmann swinging on the bar in the celebration feature in a vital away win for Spurs, as 'Can't smile without you' becomes the relegation season song.

71 Premier League, 1998. **Wimbledon 2-6 Spurs.** Survival secured with a glorious win led by Ginola and four-goal Klinsmann.

72 League Cup, 1998. **Spurs 3-1 Manchester United.** A Ginola masterclass set Spurs on the way to Wembley.

73 Premier League, 1998. **Spurs 2-2 Manchester United.** A stirring fight-back capped by a couple of Sol Campbell headers.

74 FA Cup, 1999. **Spurs 2-0 Leeds United.** Spurs' best performance under George Graham, with Ginola top-class once again.

75 FA Cup, 1999. **Barnsley 0-1 Spurs.** A superb individual goal from FWA and PFA Player of the Year Ginola.

76 Premier League, 1999. **Spurs 3-1 Manchester United.** A Stephen Carr wonder goal lit up a wet White Hart Lane with an all too rare win against United.

77 Premier League, 1999. **Spurs 4-0 Watford.** Almost an exhibition match for Ginola, to give the crowd a Christmas treat.

78 Premier League, 2000. **Spurs 1-0 Liverpool.** The first goal of the new millennium, is a quality strike from Chris Armstrong which settles another entertaining game against the Scousers.

79 Premier League, 2000. **Spurs 7-2 Southampton.** Within a year, Spurs had signed the manager and centre-back from the shambolic Saints.

80 Premier League, 2000. **Spurs 3-1 Sunderland.** Spurs end the season in style with Stephen Carr at the top of his form.

81 Premier League, 2001. **Spurs 4-2 Newcastle United.** Crazy match, with three sendings-off, two penalties and six goals.

82 FA Cup, 2001. **West Ham United 2-3 Spurs.** Rebrov finally delivers for Spurs to win a memorable game at a wet Upton Park.

83 Premier League, 2001. **Sunderland 2-3 Spurs.** The Ginger Pelé is an unlikely hero as Spurs come back to win 3-2.

84 Premier League, 2001. **Spurs 3-1 Derby County.** An almost perfect performance for Glenn Hoddle's Tottenham.

85 Premier League, 2001. **Newcastle United 0-2 Spurs.** Classy Spurs dominate a strong Newcastle side.

86 League Cup, 2002. **Spurs 5-1 Chelsea.** Spurs end the decade-long run without a win against Chelsea in style.

87 Premier League, 2002. **Spurs 2-0 Leeds United.** A Venables assist from the Leeds bench for the first, and an early example of Robbie Keane's brilliance for the second.

88 Premier League, 2004. **Spurs 5-1 Southampton.** A Defoe hat-trick in a Spurs win at the start of the Jol era.

89 Premier League, 2005. **Spurs 3-1 Portsmouth.** An exceptional debut from Mido.

90 Premier League, 2005. **Spurs 5-1 Aston Villa.** A rousing end to the season culminated in the thrashing of Villa, with Andy Reid's belter the pick of the goals.

91 Premier League, 2005. **Charlton Athletic 2-3 Spurs.**
A trademark comeback from 2-0 down to win 2-3 in the
best Spurs tradition.

92 Premier League, 2006, **Spurs 2-1 Middlesbrough.**
Berbatov and Keane score, Carrick runs the midfield and
yet Spurs only win 2-1 – the quintessential Martin Jol
game at Spurs.

93 Premier League, 2007. **West Ham United 3-4 Spurs.**
Perennial strugglers West Ham thought they'd won it enter-
ing the final minutes 3-2 ahead, but a Berbatov free kick
and a breakaway Stalteri goal help their relegation cause.

94 Premier League, 2007. **Spurs 4-4 Aston Villa.** Spurs
come back from 1-4 down in the game set aside to
commemorate a quasquicentennial anniversary, and
launch a one-game-only replica kit.

95 Premier League, 2007. **Spurs 6-4 Reading.** Four for the
'Incredible Sulk' as Spurs score 11 in two home games
over Christmas.

96 League Cup, 2008. **Spurs 5-1 Arsenal.** Another
hoodoo broken with 5-1 win in a League Cup semi-final.

97 Premier League, 2008. **Spurs 4-4 Chelsea.** A thrilling
League match played a few weeks after Spurs had beaten
Chelsea at Wembley, with Robbie Keane scoring a late
equaliser to share the points between two high-class sides
playing great open football.

98 Premier League, 2008. **Arsenal 4-4 Spurs.** A spectacular
Bentley opener and two very late goals earn Spurs a precious point at the Emirates at the start of the Redknapp era.

99 Premier League, 2009. **Spurs 2-1 Liverpool.** Disco
Benny ends Liverpool's title hopes in the opening game of
the season.

100 Premier League, 2009. **Spurs 9-1 Wigan Athletic.**
A record Premier League win, with Defoe becoming the
fourth Spurs player to score five in a match.

101 Premier League, 2010. **Spurs 2-1 Arsenal.** Danny Rose is the unlikely hero as Spurs beat Arsenal for the first time in the League for a decade.

102 Premier League, 2010. **Spurs 2-1 Chelsea.** And a few days after the Arsenal game, another bogey side are vanquished to maintain the challenge for a Champions League place as Spurs hit a modern-era high.

103 Premier League, 2010. **Manchester City 0-1 Spurs.** A Peter Crouch goal is enough to win what is effectively a play-off for the Champions League.

104 Champions League, 2010. **Spurs 4-0 Young Boys Berne.** As with the first tie in the old European Cup, Spurs avenge a 4-2 away defeat in style back at White Hart Lane.

105 Champions League, 2010. **Inter Milan 4-3 Spurs.** The finest ever individual performance in a Spurs shirt from Gareth Bale nearly rescues something against the odds at the reigning European Champions.

106 Champions League, 2010. **Spurs 3-1 Inter Milan.** A Gareth Bale-inspired Spurs tear the reigning European Champions apart.

107 Premier League, 2010. **Arsenal 2-3 Spurs.** Yet another comeback to win 2-3, with Younes Kaboul heading home a famous winner.

108 Champions League, 2011. **AC Milan 0-1 Spurs.** Spurs' greatest ever European away performance rounded off with a Peter Crouch goal.

109 Champions League, 2011. **Spurs 0-0 AC Milan.** Comfortably holding Milan to 'out-Italian' the masters and qualify 1-0 on aggregate.

110 Premier League, 2011. **Spurs 4-0 Liverpool.** Modric sets Spurs on their way to a classy win against some chippy has-beens to set up a title challenge.

111 Premier League, 2012. **Manchester United 2-3 Spurs.** AVB succeeds where the last 11 Spurs managers and caretaker Pleat have failed in winning at Old Trafford in the League, breaking a run going back to 1989.

TWENTY-TWO IGNOMINIOUS DEFEATS

1 UEFA Cup final, 29 May 1974. **Feyenoord 2-0 Spurs.** Despite the club losing its first major final, the horror of this defeat was as much off the pitch as on it. Rather than a team talk to get Spurs back in the game, Bill Nicholson spent his half time trying to calm the Spurs fans who'd been causing havoc in the stadium. The fall-out from this match was immense, with a lifetime European ban for Spurs (later overturned) and the resignation of Nicholson a few months later, after 16 glorious years at the helm.

2 Div 1, 16 Oct 1976. **Derby County 8-2 Spurs** *(Osgood (pen), Perryman).* Spurs shipped eight for the first time in the League at the Baseball Ground as things fell apart in the relegation season.

3 Div 1, 7 May 1977. **Manchester City 5-0 Spurs.** This Maine Road hammering was the final nail in the relegation coffin of 1976/77.

4 Div 1, 23 Aug 1978. **Spurs 1-4 Aston Villa** *(Hoddle (pen)).* Spurs unveiled new World Cup winning Argentinians Ardiles and Villa to a ticker-tape welcome in front of an expectant White Hart Lane. Instead, it was another Villa, the dull Brummies, who stole the show with a thumping defeat as Spurs got a very rude awakening.

5 Div 1, 2 Sept 1978. **Liverpool 7-0 Spurs.** If the home defeat to Aston Villa was a shock, the 7-0 drubbing two games later, which included Barry Daines saving a penalty, was the single worst defeat suffered by Spurs both emotionally and in the record books. A playground ribbing from glory-hunting Liverpool fans on the Monday after ensured a lifelong dislike of the red Scousers.

6   Div 1, 23 Dec 1978. **Spurs 0-5 Arsenal.** Liam Brady and
    chums removed all the Christmas spirit in 1978 with one
    of the worst home defeats in living memory.

7   Div 1, 2 Sept 1981. **Spurs 0-4 West Ham United.**
    Losing to West Ham is embarrassing at the best of times,
    but after winning away at Boro on the opening day of
    the season, the fans were looking forward to welcoming
    the 1981 cup winners in their first outing at White Hart
    Lane since the Wembley triumph. David Cross had other
    ideas, and scored all four for the visitors.

8   Div 1, 11 May 1985. **Spurs 1-5 Watford** *(Hoddle (pen))*.
    Considering Spurs led the League for most of the season,
    were still in third place and won the two games either side,
    the demoralising upset by mid-table cloggers Watford was
    as shocking as it was awful.

9   FA Cup semi-final, 9 Apr 1995 (Elland Rd). **Everton
    4-1 Spurs** *(Klinsmann (pen))*. After initially being
    denied entry into the FA Cup and then overcoming
    Sunderland, Southampton and Liverpool in memorable
    away wins once reinstated, it was desperately disappointing
    to go out to a moderate Everton side. Spurs were
    sluggish from the start and paid for errors by emergency
    fullback Stuart Nethercott, before Daniel Amokachi
    put Spurs out of their misery with a couple of late
    goals. A 'Jürgen's dream' with English football's greatest
    fixture awaited, and given how poor United were in
    the final, it's another case of being left to think what
    might have been . . . perhaps even Spurs' greatest ever
    cup triumph.

10 Premier League, 11 May 1997. **Spurs 1-2 Coventry City**
    (McVeigh). Ten years after the shock FA Cup final defeat,
    Spurs had a chance to relegate Coventry, yet
    served up a very lame display that allowed the Sky Blues
    to perform one of their miraculous end-of-season
    escapes.

11 Premier League, 6 Dec 1997. **Spurs 1-6 Chelsea** *(Vega).*
    It's fair to say Christian Gross' first home game could have
    gone better.

12 FA Cup third round replay, 23 Dec 1999. **Newcastle
    United 6-1 Spurs** *(Ginola).* As soon as it was announced
    that the FA Cup third round was to be held in December,
    there was a fear that Spurs would be gone before
    Christmas. They were drawn with Newcastle, who'd cheat-
    ed Spurs out of an FA Cup semi-final win after the referee
    missed a blatant handball the previous season. After a
    drawn first match, Spurs were quite simply abject in the
    North East with no fight, turning a defeat into a humilia-
    tion, and the Magpies became the only club to knock Spurs
    out of the FA Cup twice in a calendar year.

13 League Cup third round, 30 Oct 2000. **Spurs 1-3
    Birmingham City** *(Anderton (pen)).* Plenty of Spurs per-
    formances during the Graham era were boring, but this one
    with a full-strength team against second-tier opposition
    was dire as well. No class or spirit, and Spurs were done for
    by half time.

14 **The three 0-4s in 2002**
    Premier League, 6 Mar 2002. **Manchester United 4-0
    Spurs**
    FA Cup, 10 Mar 2002. **Spurs 0-4 Chelsea**
    Premier League, 13 Mar 2002. **Chelsea 4-0 Spurs**
    The referee ensured United had a player advantage and a
    penalty to start the ball rolling, while Diego Forlan's finish-
    ing kept the score down to four. That was just one of those
    games, but the consecutive home and away 0-4 defeats to
    Chelsea, a side Spurs had thrashed a few weeks earlier in a
    League Cup semi final, on top of the United defeat within
    the space of a week ripped a fatal hole in Glenn Hoddle's
    Tottenham project.

15 Premier League, 10 Nov 2002. **Sunderland 2-0 Spurs.**
    Away days do not come much worse than this, when Spurs

gave Sunderland one of only two home wins during a season they were relegated with a record-low points total.

16 Premier League, 16 Nov 2002. **Arsenal 3-0 Spurs.** A week after the Sunderland defeat, and Spurs were beaten as much by Thierry Henry running the length of the pitch to slide on his knees in front of the Spurs fans as in the game itself, which was just another anaemic away performance, where the only fight displayed was at half time in the traditional smashing up-of the Clock-end toilets.

17 FA Cup third round, 4 Jan 2003. **Southampton 4-0 Spurs.** A south-coast shocker as Hoddle's former employers wreaked a terrible revenge on the great man, Spurs folding in predictably tame fashion to lose in what was Hoddle's least favourite scoreline.

18 Premier League, 11 May 2004. **Spurs 0-4 Blackburn Rovers.** Coming after a 1-5 away defeat at Middlesbrough, there were no wheels on Hoddle's wagon after another 0-4 shocker saw season tickets raining down on the pitch for most of the second half.

19 UEFA Cup Group Stage, 25 Oct 2007. **Spurs 1-2 Getafe** *(Defoe)*. Spurs' proud record of only one defeat – to multiple European champions Real Madrid – in more than 70 home European ties was ruined against Spanish nobodies in a terrible night for the club. To make matters even worse, the club leaked the sacking of Martin Jol during half time.

20 Premier League, 1 Mar 2008. **Birmingham City 4-1 Spurs** *(Jenas)*. After winning the League Cup against Chelsea the week before, manager Ramos tried to embrace British culture by allowing the players to let their hair down for a few days after the win. It was to be a terrible mistake – he never got them back, and the defeat to a dreary Birmingham team who generally needed half a

season to score four marked the start of the slide that saw
him sacked six months after his Wembley triumph.

21   FA Cup semi-final, 10 Apr 2010 (Wembley). **Spurs 0-2
Portsmouth (aet).** Aside from playing a Watford side with
a wine-bar owner in goal, semi-finals do not come any easier than a game against relegation-haunted rivals who also
faced great financial uncertainty off the pitch. It's not even
as if Pompey were that good on the day either, in what must
rank as Spurs' worst performance ever at Wembley outside
the Makita trophy defeats.

22   Premier League, 28 Aug 2011. **Spurs 1-5 Manchester City**
(Kaboul). Just over 16 months after winning at Eastlands to
pinch Champions League qualification from under the noses
of the newly moneyed City, Spurs were given a harsh lesson in
what cash can buy in football these days. City were inspired all
over the pitch, and gave a breathtaking display of the speed and
skill of modern football, to which a high-class Spurs side had
no answer on the day.

THIRTY LEGENDARY AWAY DAYS

1   UEFA Cup final, 1974. **Feyenoord 2-0 Spurs.** Legendary
for all the wrong reasons, as a full-scale terrace war won
Spurs a European ban but helped lose the game, and
manager.

2   Div 1, 1975. **Newcastle United 2-5 Spurs.** A hatrick
from enigmatic legend Alfie Conn ensured it was a rocking
trip back to King's Cross on the football special.

3   Div 2, 1978. **Notts County 3-3 Spurs.** Almost every away
game in the 1977/78 season has a claim to fame, but this
one makes the list for a memorable 30-yarder from John
Pratt in the fight-back from 3-1 down, all set against the
typical hoolie background of the era.

4   Div 2, 1978. **Mansfield Town 3-3 Spurs.** Spurs played
in an all-white kit on a very muddy pitch and looked to be
heading for defeat after a famous Barry Daines

miskick, but a last-minute Hoddle special free kick won Spurs a precious point at another new ground for the fans to tear up on the Second Division odyssey.

5 Div 2, 1978. **Southampton 0-0 Spurs.** Ninety minutes of frayed nerves before the draw won Spurs promotion and allowed the fans to celebrate in traditional fashion by going on the rampage.

6 Div 1, 1979. **Aston Villa 2-3 Spurs.** With Spurs 2-0 down going into the final 10 minutes, the brilliance of Glenn Hoddle produces three goals in six minutes for a magical comeback.

7 FA Cup, 1980. **Manchester United 0-1 Spurs.** A packed Old Trafford under lights, 117 minutes gone, Hoddle in goal for Spurs after Joe Jordan becomes Aleksic's dentist, and up pops Ossie, an infrequent goal scorer, to curl home the winner from the edge of the box against all the odds. When they talk about 'The magic of the cup', this is it.

8 FA Cup semi-final replay (Highbury), 1981. **Wolves 0-3 Spurs.** After being cheated of a win in the first game by a late penalty, Spurs made no mistake against Wolves on a beautiful spring evening at Highbury. Crooks nodded home the first and then scorched through to score a second in the first half and Ricky Villa rounded things off with a brilliant shot into the Clock-end net. Spurs fans rampage through Arsenal territory after the game to celebrate Spurs' first FA Cup final in 14 years.

9 Div 1, 1981. **Arsenal 1-3 Spurs.** 'Thank you very much for the North Bank, Arsenal,' sang the hoolies from said stand as Crooks and co. shifted the balance of power in North London back to Spurs, on and off the pitch.

10 FA Cup, 1982. **Chelsea 2-3 Spurs.** The early kick-off and black cover of the programme pleaded against hooliganism to little avail; Spurs went on the rampage on the pitch with three goals in 30 breathtaking minutes of class in the best tradition of brand Tottenham, with Hoddle's second goal almost perfect in every respect.

11 Div 1, 1985. **Liverpool 0-1 Spurs.** Seventy-three years of heartache ended with a second-half Garth Crooks winner at Anfield.

12 Div 1, 1985. **Arsenal 1-2 Spurs.** Spurs come back from a goal down to win at Arsenal and go top of the League on new year's day. Could it be more perfect? Only if Graham Roberts celebrates the second and winning goal with a two-fingered salute to the Arsenal fans.

13. FA Cup, 1991. **Blackpool 0-1 Spurs.** Wild and windy on the North West coast and a 'name on the cup' fortunate win to start the ball rolling on the road to Wembley in 1991.

14. FA Cup, 1991. **Portsmouth 1-2 Spurs.** The Spurs fans jammed in the open away end at Fratton Park did not have to think back long to the lower league exits to Bradford and Port Vale as Pompey went in one up at half time, but with the wind and an inspired Gazza, Spurs' date with destiny was maintained.

15. FA Cup, 1991. **Arsenal 1-3 Spurs.** 'Threeeeeeee one, we beat the Scum three one' on the most enjoyable visit to Wembley of them all.

16 FA Cup, 1993. **Manchester City 2-4 Spurs.** Some great football from Spurs and a Nayim hat-trick looked to be enough before a full-scale pitch invasion by uppity City fans put the game at risk of being abandoned. After the restart, a possibly deliberately missed Sheringham penalty and disallowed Spurs goal were accepted, to allow the game to reach full-time without further pitch invasion.

17 Premier League, 1994. **Sheffield Wednesday 3-4 Spurs.** The eagerly awaited debut of Jürgen Klinsmann for Spurs playing in Ossie's 'famous five' ensured the away end was packed at the start of the 1994/95 season. Spurs raced into a 2-0 lead before Wednesday pulled a couple back, including a spectacular own goal from Calderwood. Barmby put Spurs ahead again before Klinsmann powered home a header on his debut and celebrated with his now-famous dive. There was still time for Klinsmann to be stretchered

off with a head injury as Wednesday pressured Spurs up to the final whistle, but Spurs held on for the win that defined Ossie's managerial ethos.

18 FA Cup, 1995. **Southampton 2-6 Spurs.** 2-0 down and Ronnie Rosenthal on as sub was not the most promising of starts for the second half, but an inspired Israeli scored a hat-trick, with Spurs running riot in extra time.

19 FA Cup, 1995. **Liverpool 1-2 Spurs.** Klinsmann set up Sheringham to equalise at the end of the first half, and Sheringham returned the compliment for Klinsmann to nab the late winner in front of the Kop, earning a standing ovation from the Scousers.

20 FA Cup, 1996. **Notts Forest 0-0 Spurs.** Heavy snow saw this game abandoned after 18 minutes, but that was only the start of the fun as the travelling fans all had epic journeys back to London in the inclement weather.

21 Premier League, 1997. **Everton 0-2 Spurs.** There was not much joy around as the dark clouds of relegation gathered around both Spurs and Everton in November 1997, but the new reign of Christian Gross got off to the best possible start with a brilliant Ginola goal and one from Vega to give the fans some hope.

22 Premier League, 1998. **Crystal Palace 1-3 Spurs.** As the relegation run intensified, Spurs produced a much-needed win at Selhurst, the best of the goals coming from a brilliant diving header from Chris Armstrong that was memorably celebrated by Klinsmann swinging on the crossbar.

23 Premier League, 1998. **Wimbledon 2-6 Spurs.** Spurs were in a tight spot at the bottom of the League as the returning Klinsmann struggled for goals in his second spell with Spurs. Things looked a bit iffy when Wimbledon went 2-1 up in the first half, but four special goals from the great man saw Spurs to a memorable victory and safety.

24 League Cup semi-final, 1999. **Wimbledon 0-1 Spurs.** Five matches in a month against Wimbledon in all three domestic competitions were rounded off with a 1-0 win

and a post-match pitch invasion to celebrate Spurs reaching the League Cup final.

25 FA Cup, 2001. **West Ham 2-3 Spurs.** Spurs' record signing Sergei Rebrov had struggled since his summer move, but on a wet Sunday at the Boleyn Ground he earned his Spurs. A magnificent volley into the goal at the away end and another just after half time set Spurs on the their way, but the usual Tottenham panic saw Spurs hanging on at the end in the classic cup tie.

26 Premier League, 2007. **West Ham 3-4 Spurs.** West Ham thought they'd won a valuable three points for their relegation struggle when they went 3-2 up with minutes remaining. Spurs had other ideas, though, and a brilliant Berbatov free kick on 90 minutes levelled things, before Stalteri of all people popped up to knock home the winner on a breakaway with the last kick of the game.

27 Premier League, 2010. **Arsenal 2-3 Spurs.** Giving away two-goal leads is de rigueur these days in North London derbies. The Goons thought they'd done enough, but a spirited Spurs would not lie down and a late Kaboul header won the points and bragging rights for Tottenham.

28 Premier League, 2010. **Manchester City 0-1 Spurs.** The fates had decreed that this game would decide the final Champions League place, and Spurs for once showed great mental strength to see it through, with Peter Crouch scoring the all-important goal.

29 Champions League, 2010. **Inter Milan 4-3 Spurs.** Although Spurs lost the match, coming from 0-4 down with 10 men against the reigning European champions and almost getting a result, thanks to an inspired Gareth Bale, felt like a win.

30 Champions League, 2011. **AC Milan 0-1 Spurs.** Spurs' greatest European away performance subdued the seven-times European champions before Spurs took the lead near the end from a Crouch header to reward the travelling faithful with the ultimate 'I was there' badge.

THIRTEEN CUP SHOCKS

1 FA Cup fifth round, 1955. **York City 3-1 Spurs** *(Robb)*. With the 'push and run' team dominating League football in the 1950s, a trip to York looked the ideal draw for Spurs to improve upon the semi-final and sixth-round near misses in the previous seasons. York had other ideas, and in a game played in a snowstorm they added Spurs to Stanley Matthews' Blackpool in their list of giants killed, in a cup run that took them to the semi finals. York also had the good grace to memorably eject Arsenal from the competition in the 1980s.

2 FA Cup fifth round, 1957. **AFC Bournemouth 3-1 Spurs** *(Medwin)*. After another semi-final defeat in 1956, Spurs looked on course for a good cup run again in 1957, when Bournemouth and Boscombe Athletic of Division Three South stood between Spurs and the last eight. Spurs eventually went on to finish runners-up in the League, but had no answer to the Cherries on the day.

3 FA Cup fifth round replay, 1959. **Norwich City 1-0 Spurs.** Bill Nicholson was in charge two years later when Spurs were drawn at home to Norwich City of Division Three South. After their defeat of the Busby Babes in the third round, no-one was taking Norwich lightly, but Spurs still needed a late Cliff Jones equaliser to force a replay at Carrow Road. This time there was no reprieve, Spurs losing to the only goal in front of a sell-out crowd.

4 FA Cup fourth round replay, 1970. **Crystal Palace 1-0 Spurs.** The scoreline was only 1-0, but the defeat to Palace in 1970 saw Bill Nicholson read the riot act, dropping several first-teamers including Jimmy Greaves, who was never to play for Spurs again. John Pratt took over Greaves' number 8 jersey.

5 League Cup fifth round, 1983. **Spurs 1-4 Burnley** *(Gibson)*. A high-class Spurs side contested this quarter-final with big hopes for another return to Wembley to avenge the defeat to Liverpool in the previous season's final. Burnley were apparent no-hopers from the third tier,

but they pulled off one of the greatest shocks of the era with a wide margin and a fully deserved win, with Northern Ireland international Billy Hamilton their hero. To further put the win into context, Spurs won eight and drew two of their remaining home League games that year to finish fourth, including a 5-0 hammering of Arsenal.

6 League Cup semi-final, 1983. **Spurs 1-2 Arsenal** *(Allen C)*. Spurs won the first leg 1-0 at Highbury, and were up by the same margin at half time in the return fixture, only for Arsenal to score two late goals and force a replay. Spurs were again leading 1-0 in the replay only for Arsenal to once again score two late goals and go through. A shocking state of affairs, made worse by the announcer giving Spurs fans details of cup final arrangements at half time.

7 FA Cup final (Wembley), 1987. **Spurs 2-3 Coventry City** *(Allen C, Mabbutt)*. Although Coventry had beaten Spurs 4-3 at Highfield Road earlier in the season and finished a respectable 10th in Division One, Spurs went into the game overwhelming favourites. They were looking to win the cup for a record eighth time, while Coventry had yet to win a trophy in their history. With only half the team wearing shirts with the sponsors' logo, Spurs got off to a great start, with a goal after two minutes, but the easy win did not materialise and Spurs were sunk by a cruel deflection off Gary Mabbutt's knee in extra time.

8 FA Cup third round, 1988. **Bradford 1-0 Spurs.** Dark satanic mills overlooked a dark cup exit with no saving grace.

9 FA Cup fourth round, 1989. **Port Vale 2-1 Spurs** *(Ruddock)*. The curse of 1987 cup final extended for another season as lowly Port Vale picked up the baton from Bradford.

10 League Cup third round, 1994. **Notts County 3-0 Spurs.** Recent defeats had put pressure on manager Ardiles and the players did little to help him out, with an embarrassing display against a struggling County, not helped by Dumitrescu's early sending off.

11 FA Cup fourth round replay, 2004. **Spurs 3-4 Manchester City** *(King, Keane, Ziege).* The two managers Pleat and Keegan looked on helplessly as Spurs first raced into a 3-0 lead, and looked to have the game in safe keeping when City were reduced to ten men at the break. But Spurs are always vulnerable with too much time to worry away an advantage, and City came storming back and won it in extra time.

12 League Cup second round, 2005. **Grimsby Town 1-0 Spurs.** Spurs had suffered the occasional upset against the likes of Orient, Lincoln and Torquay at this stage of the League Cup only to be bailed out in the return leg at White Hart Lane. This time, with no second chance, and despite fielding pretty much the same team who went on to win the next three League games and finish fifth, Spurs were sent crashing out by a last-minute goal.

13 Rescued by replays: There have been plenty of near-disasters rescued by a replay victory. The unheralded Worksop and New Brighton both held Spurs 0-0 between the wars, and Altrincham held Spurs 1-1 at White Hart Lane in 1979 before being overcome in the replays. However, one team who may in hindsight regret their cup shock was Crewe Alexandra in 1960. The Division Three North side held Spurs to a 2-2 at Gresty Road but were 10-1 down by half time in the replay, before falling 13-2 behind in Spurs' record score.

Eleven early-season hammerings

It is traditional for Spurs to make a slow start to the season then recover, to be in top form as the leaves start to fall and hand out a decent beating for the unfortunate opponents.

  1 Div 1, 18 Sept 1957. ***Spurs 7-1 Birmingham City*** *(Harmer (pen), Stokes (5), Dyson). One win in* seven before Alfie Stokes became the second of just four players to have scored five in a match for Spurs.

2 Div 1, 3 Sept 1958. **Spurs 4-0 Chelsea** *(Medwin (3), Robb). Three consecutive defeats in three League games before Terry Medwin's finest hour.*

3 Div 1, 7 Sept 1968. **Spurs 7-0 Burnley** *(Jones (2), Robertson, Greaves (3, 1 pen), Chivers). Spurs had won only one of the previous six League games before they managed to put Burnley in their place.*

4 Div 1, 8 Sept 1982. **Spurs 6-0 Southampton** *(Brooke (pen), Perryman, Galvin (2), Villa, Crooks). One win in three before Saints were dispatched to heaven in a superb evening at White Hart Lane.*

5 Div 1, 4 Sept 1985. **Spurs 4-1 Chelsea** *(Roberts, Miller, Falco, Chiedozie). Division One, 7 September 1985. 5-1 Newcastle United (Falco, Chiedozie (2), Hoddle, Hazard). Three straight defeats preceded Spurs scoring nine in four days (and for good measure, another five in the next home game against Sheffield Wednesday).*

6 Div 1, 15 Sept 1984. **Spurs 5-0 Queens Park Rangers** *(Falco (2), Allen C (2), Hazard). Spurs had had two wins in five before Micky Hazard at his peak put QPR back in their box.*

7 Premier League, 18 Sept 1993. **Spurs 5-0 Oldham Athletic** *(Sedgley (2), Sheringham, Durie, Dozzell). Sedge and co. show us the way to Oldham in the early days of the Premier League, following three games without a win.*

8 Premier League, 4 Oct 2003. **Spurs 3-0 Everton** *(Kanoute, Poyet, Keane). The margin may not technically be classed as a hammering, but after one win in seven and the spectre of another spell with*

caretaker Pleat hanging over the club, it was very welcome with dark days ahead.

9 Premier League, 11 Nov 2007. **Spurs 4-0 Wigan Athletic** *(Jenas (2), Lennon, Bent). After one win in 12 while the sword of Levy hung over Jol's head, Spurs got the season back on track with a pounding of Wigan under new man Ramos.*

10 Premier League, 26 Sept 2009. **Spurs 5-0 Burnley** *(Keane (4), Jenas). An initially bright start to the season looked in danger with consecutive defeats but a Robbie Keane-inspired Spurs regained the momentum which would eventually lead to Champions League qualification.*

11 Premier League, 18 Sept 2011. **Spurs 4-0 Liverpool** *(Modric, Defoe, Adebayor (2)). After two defeats conceding a total of eight goals, Spurs bounced back in no uncertain terms, with a spectacular goal from Modric setting them on their way.*

THE HIGHS AND LOWS OF SPURS ATTENDANCES

HIGHEST ATTENDANCE TO WATCH A SPURS GAME

The biggest crowed watching Tottenham was the 114,815 who packed out Crystal Palace to watch the 1901 FA Cup final. Two goals from Sandy Brown should have been enough to win the cup at the first attempt, but a controversial Sheffield United equaliser sent the game to a replay at Burnden Park that Spurs won 3-1 in front of only 20,470.

Spurs' highest recorded attendance to watch a game other than a final was the 90,000 that turned up to see Falco's disallowed goal in the UEFA Cup quarter-final against Real Madrid in 1985, which ended scoreless.

HIGHEST ATTENDANCE TO WATCH A LEAGUE GAME

The highest recorded total watching Spurs in the League was the 76,000 who witnessed a 4-0 away win at Stamford Bridge in October 1920. The highest non-rounded totals have been the last seven visits to Old Trafford, ranging from 75,223 to 75,696 with 75,566 choking on their prawn sandwiches during the winning visit in 2012.

LARGEST ATTENDANCE AT WHITE HART LANE

Spurs' two highest home attendances occurred in sixth-round FA Cup ties in consecutive seasons before the war. In March 1937, 71,913 filed in to watch Tottenham lose 2-1 to Preston North End. A year later, the record 75,038 showed up for the visit of Sunderland, but again Second-Division Spurs let the crowd down with a 0-1 defeat.

LARGEST ATTENDANCE TO WATCH SPURS WIN AT WHITE HART LANE

The FA Cup was again the game of the season when 71,853 braved post-war austerity in January 1948 to watch Spurs beat West Bromwich Albion 3-1 in the fourth round on the way to the semi-final. The 'push and run' side were very popular, with three attendances over 70,000 during the consecutive championships in 1950 and 1951. The highest of these was the 70,882 who saw Manchester United defeated 2-0 with goals from the two Leses: Medley and Bennett.

SMALLEST CROWD TO WATCH A SPURS MATCH

The lowest recorded crowd for a Spurs game in one of the major competitions is the 1,300 who turned up to watch them beat south London team the Vampires in an FA Cup replay in 1895. The lowest ever League gate at White Hart Lane was the unlucky 5,000 that turned up to watch Spurs suffer the joint heaviest home defeat, a 0-6 thrashing by Sunderland on 19 December 1914.

SMALLEST CROWD EVER TO WATCH A LEAGUE MATCH

The smallest crowd ever to watch a Spurs League match were the 3,000 spectators recorded for the away matches at Bolton in 1910, which Spurs won 2-0, and the 1-1 draws with Glossop in 1908 and Sheffield United in 1910.

LOWEST RECENT EBB

With football in the doldrums in the mid-1980s, only 9,359 showed up for a midweek League game against Birmingham City in 1986, which Spurs won 2-0. A month earlier, only 10,841 turned up to watch the Lilywhites beat West Brom 5-0. Things must have been bad, as the games were in the middle of eight wins over 12 games with 32 goals scored!

Another low ebb was the game after Bill Nicholson left the club, when only 12,813 turned up to see Martin Chivers earn Spurs a 1-1 draw against Carlisle United.

PREMIER LEAGUE ERA

Ground limitations mean there is little difference in most sell-out crowds at the modern White Hart Lane these days. There have been over 130 Premier League crowds between 36,000 and the record 36,310 who turned up to watch Spurs beat Liverpool 2-1 in November 2010.

At the other end of the scale, and during a time when the ground was being modernised, only 17,452 turned up to see two missed penalties in a 1-1 relegation scrap with Aston Villa in March 1994. Earlier that season, in another midweek game, only 17,744 were there to see John Fashanu's awful challenge on Gary Mabbutt in another 1-1 against Wimbledon.

WHEN SPURS ARE IN TOWN

A visit from Tottenham is usually the biggest attraction in the fixture list of most clubs, and the Spurs game is the record attendance at five clubs:

1 FA Cup fifth round (Filbert Street), 18 February 1928; Leicester City: 47,298, Spurs won 3-0.

2 Division One (Boleyn Ground), 17 October 1970; West Ham United: 42,322, Spurs drew 2-2.

3 Division One (Baseball Ground), 20 September 1969; Derby County: 41,826, Spurs lost 0-5.

4 FA Cup fifth round, (Recreation Ground), 12 February 1938; Chesterfield: 30,561, Spurs drew 2-2.

5 FA Cup fourth round (Gresty Road), 30 January 1960; Crewe Alexandra: 20,000, Spurs drew 2-2 before winning the replay 13-2.

SEVENTEEN GOALS AND A MISS THAT DEFINE THE TOTTENHAM WAY

1 **Jimmy Greaves,** Spurs 5-1 Manchester United (1965): Greaves received the ball with his back to goal midway inside the United half, before turning and just running past the whole defence and keeper then rolling it home into an empty net. Simple but brilliant: the essence of the Greaves and the great Bill Nick Spurs teams.

2 **Glenn Hoddle,** Spurs 2-1 Manchester United (1979); **Glenn Hoddle,** Spurs 1-0 Notts Forest (1979): Two carbon-copy volleys out of the top drawer: Hoddle jumps to reach the ball in the iconic pose with his left leg tucked in, and flashes spectacular volleys past England keepers Gary Bailey and Peter Shilton. Goals of total genius in their creation and execution.

3 **Ricky Villa,** Spurs 3-2 Manchester City (1981): From trudging off after being replaced in the first game to dribbling past the City defenders to score the most famous goal in FA Cup history in the replay and cement Spurs' status as the 'cup kings' with a then-record seventh win.

4 **Glenn Hoddle,** Chelsea 2-3 Spurs (1982): Hughton to Archie, flick to Hazard, lay-off to Hoddle and a raking shot to score. Great players at the top of their game, expressing themselves in the true Tottenham way.

5 **Glenn Hoddle,** Watford 2-3 Spurs (1983): The vision to see and the technique to carry out the turn and chipped shot that featured on the *Match of the Day* title sequence for years after – something that only Glenn Hoddle could have achieved. And what defined Glenn Hoddle defined Spurs.

6 **Graham Roberts,** Spurs 3-0 Bruges (1984): Two thunderbolt volleys from 30 yards showed that even the team hard man had more than his fair share of skill. His decision to chest the ball rather than head it from distance for the equaliser in the 1984 UEFA Cup final also showed another dimension to his brilliance.

7 **Glenn Hoddle,** Spurs 3-1 Oxford United (1987): The farewell-to-a-legend goal. Breaking from inside his own half, Hoddle glided up the pitch, evading challenges with body swerves and 'giving eyes', before rolling the ball into an empty net. Arsenal have never had a player who could do that, and if you chose to follow another team while this man was playing football there was something wrong with you.

8 **Chris Waddle,** Spurs 2-0 Aston Villa (1988): In his own very distinctive style, no-one embodied Tottenham flair more than Chris Waddle. His first goal against Villa had all the elements of a Waddle goal, running at their defence with his familiar hunched gait, twisting one way then the other, before unleashing a shot into the top of the net. His second of the match wasn't bad either.

9 **Gary Lineker,** Spurs 3-1 Porto (1991): In the days before the modern Barcelona, Spurs show the way with a multi-pass move culminating in Lineker stabbing home.

10 **Paul Gascoigne,** Spurs 3-1 Arsenal (1991): Plenty of brilliant goals from Gazza, but this bold and spectacular free kick came from a player who recognised no limit to his talent. Like Villa's goal in 1981 it inspired another generation of Spurs fans (to the misery of Spurs in the 90s) which saved the club financially.

11 **Jürgen Klinsmann,** Sheffield Wednesday 3-4 Spurs (1994): The iconic goal of an iconic game, with an iconic goal celebration that helped redefine post-Gazza Spurs.

12 **David Ginola,** Barnsley 0-1 Spurs (1999): In an era low on flair, Ginola lit up a cup tie at Barnsley with a trademark mazy run through the whole of the Barnsley defence before rolling home the winning goal.

13 **Allan Nielsen,** Spurs 1-0 Leicester City (1999): A last-minute diving header to win a Wembley Cup final with the team down to 10 men was real Harry Hotspur stuff.

14 **Darren Anderton and David Ginola,** Spurs 2-0 Leeds (1999): One great game and two great long-range goals, but perhaps the thing that best defines the Tottenham way was the run across the Leeds box and shot by Ginola that came back off the inside of the post.

15 **Christian Ziege,** Spurs 3-1 Derby (2001): A sweeping move across White Hart Lane is finished by Ziege slotting home with the outside of his left foot from Sheringham's threaded pass. A goal radiating 'Glenn Hoddle sunshine football'.

16 **Teddy Sheringham,** Spurs 5-1 Chelsea (2002): While the spectacular second goal by Sherwood from a Sheringham corner routine earlier in the game is one of the all-time greats, the one-touch move down the Spurs left and Sheringham's volley home from a chest trap from Poyet for the third showed that the Spurs spirit was still alive after the lost decade in the 1990s.

17 **Jermaine Jenas,** Spurs 5-1 Arsenal (2008): A flowing one-touch move with modern Spurs heroes involved, before it's rounded off by a strong run and shot from Jenas to set up a famous semi-final win.

THE TWENTY-SIX MAJOR CUP FINAL MATCHES

Where a draw in normal time is usually a good bet.

1 FA Cup final (Crystal Palace), 1901. **Spurs 2-2 Sheffield United.** 1 George Clawley, 2 Harry Erentz, 3 Sandy Tait, 4 Tom Morris, 5 Ted Hughes, 6 Jack L Jones, 7 Tom Smith,

8 John Cameron, 9 Sandy Brown, 10 David Copeland, 11 John Kirwan. *Scorer:* Sandy Brown (23, 51). *Player-manager:* John Cameron.

2 FA Cup final replay (Burnden Park, Bolton), 1901. **Spurs 3-1 Sheffield United.** 1 George Clawley, 2 Harry Erentz, 3 Sandy Tait, 4 Tom Morris, 5 Ted Hughes, 6 Jack L Jones, 7 Tom Smith, 8 John Cameron, 9 Sandy Brown, 10 David Copeland, 11 John Kirwan. *Scorers:* John Cameron (52), Tom Smith (76), Sandy Brown (87). *Player-manager:* John Cameron.

3 FA Cup final (Stamford Bridge), 1921. **Spurs 1-0 Wolverhampton Wanderers.** 1 Alex Hunter, 2 Tommy Clay, 3 Bob McDonald, 4 Bert Smith, 5 Charlie Walters, 6 Arthur Grimsdell, 7 Jimmy Banks, 8 Jimmy Seed, 9 Jimmy Cantrell, 10 Bert Bliss, 11 Jimmy Dimmock. *Scorer:* Jimmy Dimmock (53). *Manager:* Peter McWilliam.

4 FA Cup final (Empire Stadium, Wembley), 1961. **Spurs 2-0 Leicester City.** 1 Bill Brown, 2 Peter Baker, 3 Ron Henry, 4 Danny Blanchflower, 5 Maurice Norman, 6 Dave Mackay, 7 Cliff Jones, 8 John White, 9 Bobby Smith, 10 Les Allen, 11 Terry Dyson. *Scorers:* Bobby Smith (66), Terry Dyson (75). *Manager:* Bill Nicholson.

5 FA Cup final (Empire Stadium, Wembley), 1962. **Spurs 3-1 Burnley.** 1 Bill Brown, 2 Peter Baker, 3 Ron Henry, 4 Danny Blanchflower, 5 Maurice Norman, 6 Dave Mackay, 7 Terry Medwin, 8 John White, 9 Bobby Smith, 10 Jimmy Greaves, 11 Cliff Jones. *Scorers:* Jimmy Greaves (3), Bobby Smith (51), Danny Blanchflower (pen, 80). *Manager:* Bill Nicholson.

6 European Cup Winners' Cup final (Rotterdam), 1963. **Spurs 5-1 Atlético Madrid.** 1 Bill Brown, 2 Peter Baker, 3 Ron Henry, 4 Danny Blanchflower, 5 Maurice Norman, 6 Tony Marchi, 7 Cliff Jones, 8 John White, 9 Bobby Smith, 10 Jimmy Greaves, 11 Terry Dyson. *Scorers:* Jimmy Greaves (16, 80), John White (35), Terry Dyson (67, 85). *Manager:* Bill Nicholson.

7 FA Cup final (Empire Stadium, Wembley), 1967. **Spurs 2-1 Chelsea.** 1 Pat Jennings, 2 Joe Kinnear, 3 Cyril Knowles, 4 Alan Mullery, 5 Mike England, 6 Dave Mackay, 7 Jimmy Robertson, 8 Jimmy Greaves, 9 Alan Gilzean, 10 Terry Venables, 11 Frank Saul. *Sub (not used):* 12 Cliff Jones. *Scorers:* Jimmy Robertson (40), Frank Saul (67). *Manager:* Bill Nicholson.

8 League Cup final (Empire Stadium, Wembley), 1971. **Spurs 2-0 Aston Villa.** 1 Pat Jennings, 2 Joe Kinnear, 3 Cyril Knowles, 4 Alan Mullery, 5 Peter Collins, 6 Phil Beal, 7 Alan Gilzean, 8 Steve Perryman, 9 Martin Chivers, 10 Martin Peters, 11 Jimmy Neighbour. *Sub (not used):* 12 Jimmy Pearce. *Scorer:* Martin Chivers (57, 87). *Manager:* Bill Nicholson.

9 UEFA Cup final first leg (Molineux), 1972. **Wolverhampton Wanderers 1-2 Spurs.** 1 Pat Jennings, 2 Joe Kinnear, 3 Cyril Knowles, 4 Alan Mullery, 5 Mike England, 6 Phil Beal, 7 Alan Gilzean, 8 Steve Perryman, 9 Martin Chivers, 10 Martin Peters, 11 Ralph Coates (sub: 15 John Pratt, 68). *Scorer:* Martin Chivers (78, 81). *Manager:* Bill Nicholson.

10 UEFA Cup final second leg (White Hart Lane), 1972. **Spurs 1-1 Wolverhampton Wanderers.** 1 Pat Jennings, 2 Joe Kinnear, 3 Cyril Knowles, 4 Alan Mullery, 5 Mike England, 6 Phil Beal, 7 Alan Gilzean, 8 Steve Perryman, 9 Martin Chivers, 10 Martin Peters, 11 Ralph Coates. *Scorer:* Alan Mullery (29). *Manager:* Bill Nicholson.

11 League Cup final (Empire Stadium, Wembley), 1973. **Spurs 1-0 Norwich City.** 1 Pat Jennings, 2 Joe Kinnear, 3 Cyril Knowles, 4 John Pratt (sub: 12 Ralph Coates, 25), 5 Mike England, 6 Phil Beal, 7 Alan Gilzean, 8 Steve Perryman, 9 Martin Chivers, 10 Martin Peters, 11 Jimmy Pearce. *Scorer:* Ralph Coates (72). *Manager:* Bill Nicholson.

12 UEFA Cup final first leg (White Hart Lane), 1974. **Spurs 2-2 Feyenoord.** 1 Pat Jennings, 2 Ray Evans, 3 Terry

Naylor, 4 John Pratt, 5 Mike England, 6 Phil Beal (sub: Mike Dillon, 80), 7 Chris McGrath, 8 Steve Perryman, 9 Martin Chivers, 10 Martin Peters, 11 Ralph Coates. *Scorers:* Mike England (39), van Daele (og, 64). *Manager:* Bill Nicholson.

13 UEFA Cup final second leg (Rotterdam), 1974. **Feyenoord 2-0 Spurs.** 1 Pat Jennings, 2 Ray Evans, 3 Terry Naylor, 4 John Pratt (sub: Phil Holder, 76), 5 Mike England, 6 Phil Beal, 7 Chris McGrath, 8 Steve Perryman, 9 Martin Chivers, 10 Martin Peters, 11 Ralph Coates. *Manager:* Bill Nicholson.

14 FA Cup final (Empire Stadium, Wembley), 1981. **Spurs 1-1 Manchester City (aet).** 1 Milija Aleksic, 2 Chris Hughton, 3 Paul Miller, 4 Graham Roberts, 5 Steve Perryman, 6 Ricky Villa (sub: 12 Gary Brooke, 66), 7 Ossie Ardiles, 8 Steve Archibald, 9 Tony Galvin, 10 Glenn Hoddle, 11 Garth Crooks. *Scorer:* Hutchinson (og, 81). *Manager:* Keith Burkinshaw.

15 FA Cup final replay (Empire Stadium, Wembley), 1981. **Spurs 3-2 Manchester City.** 1 Milija Aleksic, 2 Chris Hughton, 3 Paul Miller, 4 Graham Roberts, 5 Ricky Villa, 6 Steve Perryman, 7 Ossie Ardiles, 8 Steve Archibald, 9 Tony Galvin, 10 Glenn Hoddle, 11 Garth Crooks. *Sub (not used):* 12 Gary Brooke. *Scorers:* Ricky Villa (6, 76), Garth Crooks (80). *Manager:* Keith Burkinshaw.

16 League Cup Final (Empire Stadium, Wembley), 1982. **Spurs 1-3 Liverpool (aet).** 1 Ray Clemence, 2 Chris Hughton, 3 Paul Miller, 4 Paul Price, 5 Micky Hazard (sub: 12 Ricky Villa, 65), 6 Steve Perryman, 7 Ossie Ardiles, 8 Steve Archibald, 9 Tony Galvin, 10 Glenn Hoddle, 11 Garth Crooks. *Scorer:* Archibald (11). *Manager:* Keith Burkinshaw.

17 FA Cup final (Empire Stadium, Wembley), 1982. **Spurs 1-1 Queens Park Rangers (aet).** 1 Ray Clemence, 2 Chris Hughton, 3 Paul Miller, 4 Paul Price, 5 Micky Hazard (sub: 12 Gary Brooke, 104), 6 Steve Perryman,

7 Graham Roberts, 8 Steve Archibald, 9 Tony Galvin, 10 Glenn Hoddle, 11 Garth Crooks. *Scorer:* Glenn Hoddle (110). *Manager:* Keith Burkinshaw.

18 FA Cup final replay (Empire Stadium, Wembley), 1982. **Spurs 1-0 Queens Park Rangers.** 1 Ray Clemence, 2 Chris Hughton, 3 Paul Miller, 4 Paul Price, 5 Micky Hazard (sub: 12 Gary Brooke, 66), 6 Steve Perryman, 7 Graham Roberts, 8 Steve Archibald, 9 Tony Galvin, 10 Glenn Hoddle, 11 Garth Crooks. *Scorer:* Glenn Hoddle (pen, 6). *Manager:* Keith Burkinshaw.

19 UEFA Cup final first leg (Brussels), 1984. **Anderlecht 1-1 Spurs.** 1 Tony Parks, 2 Danny Thomas, 3 Chris Hughton, 4 Graham Roberts, 5 Paul Miller, 6 Steve Perryman, 7 Micky Hazard, 8 Steve Archibald, 9 Mark Falco, 10 Gary Stevens (sub: 12 Gary Mabbutt, 81), 11 Tony Galvin. *Scorer:* Paul Miller (57). *Manager:* Keith Burkinshaw.

20 UEFA Cup final second leg (White Hart Lane), 1984. **Spurs 1-1 Anderlecht (aet). Spurs won 4-3 on penalties.** 1 Tony Parks, 2 Danny Thomas, 3 Chris Hughton, 4 Graham Roberts, 5 Paul Miller (sub: 12 Ossie Ardiles, 77), 6 Gary Mabbutt (sub: 16 Ally Dick, 73), 7 Micky Hazard, 8 Steve Archibald, 9 Mark Falco, 10 Gary Stevens, 11 Tony Galvin. *Scorer:* Graham Roberts (84). *Penalty scorers:* Graham Roberts, Mark Falco, Gary Stevens, Steve Archibald; Danny Thomas – saved. *Manager:* Keith Burkinshaw.

21 FA Cup final (Empire Stadium, Wembley), 1987. **Spurs 2-3 Coventry City (aet).** 1 Ray Clemence, 2 Chris Hughton (sub: 12 Nico Claesen, 97), 3 Mitchell Thomas, 4 Steve Hodge, 5 Richard Gough, 6 Gary Mabbutt, 7 Clive Allen, 8 Paul Allen, 9 Chris Waddle, 10 Glenn Hoddle, 11 Ossie Ardiles (sub: 14 Gary Stevens, 90). *Scorers:* Clive Allen (2), Gary Mabbutt (40). *Manager:* David Pleat.

22 FA Cup final (Empire Stadium, Wembley), 1991. **Spurs 2-1 Notts Forest (aet).** 1 Erik Thorstvedt, 2 Justin Edinburgh, 3 Pat Van den Hauwe, 4 Steve Sedgley, 5 David

Howells, 6 Gary Mabbutt, 7 Paul Stewart, 8 Paul Gascoigne (sub: 12 Nayim, 17), 9 Vinny Samways (sub: 14 Paul Walsh, 81), 10 Gary Lineker, 11 Paul Allen. *Scorers:* Paul Stewart (55), Des Walker (og, 94). *Manager:* Terry Venables.

23 League Cup final (Empire Stadium, Wembley), 1999. **Spurs 1-0 Leicester City.** 1 Ian Walker, 2 Steve Carr, 12 Justin Edinburgh, 15 Ramon Vega, 23 Sol Campbell, 4 Steffen Freund, 6 Allan Nielsen, 9 Darren Anderton, 14 David Ginola (sub: 22 Andy Sinton, 90), 18 Steffen Iversen, 10 Les Ferdinand. *Subs (not used):* 13 Espen Baardsen, 32 Luke Young, 20 Jose Dominguez, 11 Chris Armstrong. *Scorer:* Allan Nielsen (90). *Manager:* George Graham.

24 League Cup final (Millennium Stadium, Cardiff), 2002. **Spurs 1-2 Blackburn Rovers.** 1 Neil Sullivan, 3 Mauricio Taricco (sub: 29 Simon Davies, 79), 26 Ledley King, 6 Chris Perry, 18 Ben Thatcher, 23 Christian Ziege, 8 Tim Sherwood, 7 Darren Anderton, 14 Gus Poyet (sub: 16 Steffen Iversen, 83), 10 Teddy Sheringham, 9 Les Ferdinand. *Subs (not used):* 13 Kasey Keller, 30 Antony Gardner, 11 Sergei Rebrov. *Scorer:* Christian Ziege (31). *Manager:* Glenn Hoddle.

25 League Cup final (New Wembley Stadium), 2008. **Spurs 2-1 Chelsea (aet).** 1 Paul Robinson, 28 Alan Hutton, 39 Jonathan Woodgate, 26 Ledley King, 2 Pascal Chimbonda (sub: 22 Tom Huddlestone, 60), 25 Aaron Lennon, 8 Jermaine Jenas, 4 Didier Zokora, 15 Steed Malbranque (sub: 6 Teemu Tainio, 74), 9 Dimitar Berbatov, 10 Robbie Keane (sub: 5 Younes Kaboul, 101). *Subs (not used):* 12 Radek Cerny, 23 Darren Bent. *Scorers:* Berbatov (pen, 70), Woodgate (94). *Manager:* Juande Ramos.

26 League Cup final (New Wembley Stadium), 2009. **Spurs 0-0 Manchester United (aet). Spurs lost 1-4 on penalties.** 1 Heurelho Gomes, 22 Vedran Corluka, 32

Benoit Assou-Ekotto, 20 Michael Dawson, 26 Ledley King, 7 Aaron Lennon (sub: 5 David Bentley, 102), 8 Jermaine Jenas (sub: 3 Gareth Bale, 98), 4 Didier Zokora, 14 Luka Modric, 10 Darren Bent, 9 Roman Pavlyuchenko (sub: 24 Jamie O'Hara, 65). *Subs (not used):* 27 Ben Alnwick, 6 Tom Huddlestone, 16 Chris Gunter, 19 Adel Taarabt. Penalty scorer: Corluka; O'Hara – saved, Bentley – missed, wide. *Manager:* Harry Redknapp.

Oh what fun it is to see Spurs score six away!

1 Div 1, 25 Aug 1962. **West Ham Utd 1-6 Spurs** *(Medwin, White, Greaves (2), Jones, Lyall og). The clanging irons were no match for a great Spurs side, who recorded their largest ever away League win.*

2 UEFA Cup first round first leg, 14 Sept 1971. **Keflavik 1-6 Spurs** *(Mullery (2), Coates, Gilzean (3)). Iceland was far enough away to give Graeme Souness a run-out in a Spurs shirt, and while losing 6-1 on your home turf might have seemed bad, worse was to follow for the Icelanders with a 9-0 defeat at White Hart Lane, making Spurs' record aggregate score in Europe.*

3 UEFA Cup first round first leg, 13 Sept 1972. **Lyn Oslo 3-6 Spurs** *(Peters, Pratt, Gilzean (2), Chivers (2)). Norwegian part-timers did at least have the distinction of getting three consolation goals from a generous Spurs before shipping another six without reply in the return leg.*

4 FA Cup third round, 13 Jan 1973. **Margate 0-6 Spurs** *(Knowles, Pratt, Pearce, Chivers (2), Peters). You can keep the Costa Brava and all that palaver as Spurs were very happy to have an FA Cup knees-up beside the sea in 1973.*

5   UEFA Cup first round, first leg, 14 Sept 1983.
     Drogheda Utd 0-6 Spurs *(Falco (2), Crooks,
     Galvin, Mabbutt (2)). As with Keflavik, a bad first leg
     got even worse at White Hart Lane where Spurs scored
     another eight to equal the greatest ever winning margin
     in Europe.*

6   League Cup second round first leg, 21 Sept
     1994. **Watford 3-6 Spurs** *(Anderton, Klinsmann
     (3), Sheringham, Dumitrescu). It was a good job Spurs
     racked up six at Vicarage Road as the chaotic magic of
     Ossie's famous five team saw Spurs lose the second leg
     3-2 at home and only limp through to the next round.
     The subsequent defeat at Notts County saw Ossie sacked
     soon after.*

7   FA Cup fifth round replay, 1 Mar 1995.
     Southampton 2-6 Spurs *(Rosenthal (3),
     Sheringham, Barmby, Anderton). Spurs needed extra
     time to complete the astonishing comeback led by
     Rocket Ronnie Rosenthal.*

8   Premier League, 2 May 1998. **Wimbledon 2-6
     Spurs** *(Ferdinand, Klinsmann (4), Saib). Twice
     behind, but the second coming of Klinsmann blossomed
     on a sunny spring afternoon to secure Spurs' safety.*

9   League Cup second round, 23 Sept 2004. **Oldham
     Athletic 0-6 Spurs** *(Kanoute (2), Keane, Defoe,
     Bunjevcevic, Gardner). Spurs accumulated as many goals
     in this game as they did in the 11 League matches
     manager Jacques Santini survived in his brief reign.*

BEING THERE: ELEVEN UNMISSABLE TERRACE MOMENTS

The history books record the score, but there are some times
when the shared experience of 'being there' is more memorable than the result.

1. DANNY THOMAS

The UEFA Cup final had gone to penalties, and with their four previous takers all successful, Spurs were a Danny Thomas penalty away from lifting the trophy. A crescendo of expectation built around White Hart Lane, but Thomas' kick was saved. As the crestfallen Thomas made his way back to the halfway line and captain Roberts ran out to console him, the chant of 'Only one Danny Thomas!' began to grow in a very moving moment of solidarity between players and supporters. Seconds later, Tony Parks saved the next penalty to win the Cup for Spurs and immortalise the moment.

2. BOLTON FANS

The death of club legend Bill Nicholson was announced on the morning of a fixture against Bolton Wanderers in 2004. Before the game, Spurs presented a special tribute film dedicated to the life and works of the great man. As the Spurs fans watched on in contemplative silence while the rain drummed on the roof, the Bolton fans gave a spontaneous, respectful round of applause, which quickly caught on around the whole stadium. It's hard to say how many of the Bolton fans knew about the death or indeed the Spurs legend from another sporting era, but their simple action was the most wonderful gesture that added a perfect touch to a very special moment.

It was fitting therefore that Spurs fans should be able to repay the compliment in the aftermath of Fabrice Muamba's collapse at White Hart Lane in 2012, where their immediate and sensitive reaction won many plaudits, most importantly from Bolton.

3. SOL CAMPBELL'S RETURN TO SPURS

Hate is such a negative emotion, but White Hart Lane was full of it in November 2001 as Sol Campbell returned to the ground as an Arsenal player after his controversial Bosman move the previous summer. Everywhere, supporters had balloons and placards with 'Judas' inscribed on them, and the atmosphere crackled with anticipation. Campbell chants dominated the fans' songsheet, and he was booed every time he went near the ball with an intensity not seen before or since. As ever, he had a strong match, but looked visibly shaken by the reception and nearly gave the crowd something special to cheer by going close to scoring own goals in both halves.

4. GÓRNIK ZABRZE

Much like their first game in the Champions League, the first leg of Spurs' first ever European tie was little short of a disaster, and they needed to recover a 4-2 deficit in the return leg. In an all-white kit and with over 56,000 creating a special atmosphere, Spurs tore into Gornik from the first whistle, quickly erasing the deficit before eventually running out spectacular 8-1 winners, in what was the first and definitive 'Glory, Glory' night atmosphere under the floodlights at White Hart Lane.

5. CHARLIE IN THE STAND

Spurs visited Arsenal on consecutive new year's day fixtures in 1985 and 1986. In the first game, Roberts entered into the spirit of things by celebrating Spurs' second and winning goal by running back to his position and giving a two-fingered salute to the Arsenal faithful. A year later during a 0-0 draw on a freezing cold day, he topped this by clattering Arsenal's so-called star player Charlie Nicholas and sending him and the ball into the stand, to the rapturous applause of the travelling Spurs fans.

6. THE ATMOSPHERE AT THE 'ARFA ARFA' GAME

There have been plenty of big games with great atmosphere over the years, but having gone more than 10 years without a win against Chelsea, Spurs' League Cup semi-final second leg against the Blues in 2001 was very special. Led by the Spurs drummer, the fans did their bit before the game and once Iversen had levelled the scores on aggregate in the opening minutes, the intensity went even higher as the crowd began to dare to dream. In a brilliant display of skill and desire, Spurs never looked back and scored at regular intervals to not only win the tie but to end the bad run in spectacular style. Coming out of the ground Spurs sang 'Who put the ball in the Chelsea net? Arfa, arfa! Who put the ball in the Chelsea net? Half of Tottenham!' to give the game its name and seal one of the greatest nights at White Hart Lane.

7. WORLD CUP 1990 HEROES

The 1990 World Cup in Italy returned the feelgood to football, and the opening-day fixture of the following season against Manchester City allowed fans to view two of England's best players in Gazza and Lineker. It was a beautiful sunny day and a goal for Gazza, plus a couple for Lineker in a 3-1 Spurs win, was the perfect outcome.

8. THE TOTTENHAM ANGELS, 1962

Before Spurs' European Cup semi-final against Benfica, a couple of fans dressed as angels and carried a placard 'Lisbon Greaves Tonight' around the boundary of the pitch to help create the fantastic atmosphere of that famous but ultimately unsuccessful night.

9. ALFIE CONN SITTING ON THE BALL

Spurs went into the final match of the 1974/75 season with only Carlisle United below them and needing a last-game win to climb out of the relegation zone. Spurs' opponents Leeds were comfortably in mid-table and had half an eye on a forthcoming European Cup final against Bayern Munich. In front of nearly 50,000, Cyril Knowles put Spurs ahead early in the game with a trademark free kick, but despite continual pressure Spurs had to wait until the second half for further goals, which eventually arrived from Chivers, a Knowles penalty and a brilliant individual effort from Alfie Conn. With the score at 4-1 and Spurs virtually safe, Conn contemptuously sat on the ball, mocking a perceived lack of intent. While Leeds were probably not bothered about the scoreline and wanted an easy game without injuries before their big final, they did not take kindly to the gesture and promptly went up the other end and scored. The Leeds goal served as a reminder not to get too cocky, as they could still go through the gears if sufficiently riled, but Spurs held on for a famous victory to everyone's delight.

10. FEYENOORD, 1974

The second leg of the 1974 UEFA Cup final was played among widespread crowd trouble from the Spurs supporters, who smashed up the stadium and had a tear-up with the Feyenoord fans and Dutch police before rampaging through the streets of Rotterdam for the rest of the night. With Spurs losing 1-0 on the night but still in the tie, Bill Nicholson was diverted from his half-time team talk to try to plead with the crowd, but to little avail. The night had a big impact on Sir Bill, who resigned a few months later, and Spurs were served with a lifetime European ban which was later overturned.

11. HIGHBURY, 1981

It seemed a little unfair that a midweek semi-final replay between Spurs and Wolves should be held only a few miles from Tottenham at Highbury, but that was the least Spurs deserved considering the controversial nature of Wolves' equaliser in the first game. Spurs had at least three of the four stands and quickly dominated on the pitch, with a couple from Crooks in the first half almost guaranteeing victory, which was sealed by a brilliant long-range shot from Ricky Villa in the second half. The win got Spurs to the FA Cup final for the first time in 14 years at the home of their nearest rivals, and the fans celebrated accordingly, running riot all over N5.

THIRTEEN GAMES WITH THE CLASSIC SPURS SCORE 3-2

If you had to explain Spurs to someone who knew about football but nothing about the club, simply saying 3-2 should be sufficient to provide a path into the swashbuckling magic with a hint of vulnerability that is Tottenham Hotspur. Here are some of the best.

1 FA Cup quarter-final, 13 Oct 1894. **Spurs 3-2 West Herts** *(Hunter, Goodall (2))*. Spurs' greatest moments are often associated with the FA Cup, and it's fitting that the club's first tie in the competition ended as a 3-2 win against West Herts, a forerunner of the modern Watford.

2 Div 1, 4 Sept 1976. **Manchester United 2-3 Spurs** *(Coates, Pratt, Moores)*. That Spurs won only one away game in the relegation season of 1976/77 makes this victory at Old Trafford all the more remarkable. They were 2-0 down at half time and things did not look good, but the mostly unloved trio of Coates, Pratt and Moores were heroes for the day.

3 Div 1, 24 Mar 1979. **Aston Villa 2-3 Spurs** *(Hoddle (2), Jones)*. With 12 minutes at Villa to go, Spurs were losing 2-0 and seemingly heading for defeat until Glenn Hoddle cracked home a low shot from the edge of the area. With the atmosphere changed, Chris Jones pulled Spurs level before the great Glenn put a seal on an amazing six minutes by chipping the advancing Jimmy Rimmer to win the game.

4 FA Cup final replay (Wembley), 14 May 1981. **Manchester City 2-3 Spurs** *(Villa (2), Crooks)*. The 1981 cup final replay is probably the most famous game in Spurs' history. After escaping from the first game with a draw, the euphoria of an early Spurs goal had subsided by the time City went ahead with a penalty midway through the second half. Staring into the abyss, a chipped pass from Hoddle broke to Crooks who stabbed Spurs level. With the game in the balance, Ricky Villa picked the ball up on the left wing midway inside the City half, and the magic of Spurs and of the FA Cup combined to produce one of football's enduring moments. Subbed in the first game after an indifferent performance, the revitalised Argentinian

threaded his way through City defenders before slotting
home for the Empire Stadium's most famous goal, securing
the win for Spurs.

5   FA Cup sixth round, 6 Mar 1982. **Chelsea 2-3 Spurs**
    (Archibald, Hoddle, Hazard). Despite being in the second tier,
    Chelsea had knocked out Liverpool in the round before and
    went in at half time with a one-goal lead. However, the tide
    turned with three goals from Archibald, Hoddle and
    Hazard and 30 minutes of some of the best football ever
    played by a Spurs side. A late Chelsea goal ensured it was
    more frantic at the final whistle than Spurs' dominance
    entitled it to be.

6   FA Cup fifth round, 14 Feb 1993. **Spurs 3-2 Wimbledon**
    (Anderton, Sheringham, Barmby). In his fledgling broadcasting
    career, Gary Lineker remarked he'd rather watch
    Wimbledon on Ceefax; soon after, Wimbledon and his for-
    mer side were drawn together in the Cup and the pressure
    was on Spurs. An emerging young team displayed great
    attacking instincts and Nicky Barmby capped a fine display
    with a long-range header that put Spurs 3-0 up at the
    break. Although the Dons pulled a couple back in the
    second half, it was a win for the beautiful game over
    the ugly one.

7   Premier League, 3 Oct 1993. **Spurs 3-2 Everton**
    (Sheringham, Anderton, Caskey). Spurs had started the season
    brightly under new manager Ardiles, but in front of a
    live Sunday afternoon audience on Sky, Everton came in
    determined mood. The visitors took the lead twice
    before Spurs launched a rousing comeback attacking the
    Paxton end. First Sheringham equalised with seconds
    of normal time remaining. There was a feeling of momen-
    tum in the ground and sure enough, former England
    youth captain Darren Caskey fired home the winner in
    injury time. This was the third home win of the season,
    which put Spurs on the heels of the leaders. However, dis-
    aster struck in the next game with an injury to Teddy
    Sheringham and Spurs managed to win only one more

home game for the rest of the season, and narrowly avoided relegation.

8 Premier League, 19 Oct 1997. **Spurs 3-2 Sheffield Wednesday** *(Dominguez, Armstrong, Ginola).* Things were so bad at Spurs towards the end of Francis' reign that this game was already a relegation six-pointer in October. The good feeling from his sparkling debut carried over for Dominguez, who settled a few nerves with an early goal, and when Ginola risked his precious hair by scoring a rare header to put Spurs three up it looked as if the rot had stopped. However a 3-0 scoreline is never a comfortable one for Spurs players to worry themselves with for 15 minutes over half time, and Wednesday came back strongly in the second period, though Spurs managed to hang on in a desperate finish.

9 FA Cup sixth round, 11 Mar 2001. **West Ham United 2-3 Spurs** *(Rebrov (2), Doherty).* For most of his first season, Sergei Rebrov had struggled to make an impact commensurate with his £11 million fee. In the goalless League game a few months before, he had been substituted for former non-League player Dave McEwan, while Andy Booth stayed on the pitch. All this changed midway through the first half when Rebrov flashed home a brilliant volley in front of the travelling Spurs fans. Another Rebrov goal and a header from Gary Doherty gave Spurs what should have been a comfortable 3-1 lead, but Todorov pulled another one back to ensure a nervy finish.

10 Premier League, 14 Apr 2001. **Sunderland 2-3 Spurs** *(Clemence, Doherty (2)).* Visiting the then high-flying Sunderland and being 2-0 down at half time with a forward line of Korsten and Doherty, things did not look good. But a classy goal from Stephen Clemence and a couple from the Ginger Pelé served to fuel the short-lived optimism at the start of the Hoddle era.

11 Premier League, 1 Oct 2005. **Charlton Athletic 2-3 Spurs** *(King, Mido, Keane).* Going 2-0 down to nuisance

team Charlton was made worse by scorer Darren Bent taunting the scoreline to the Spurs fans. But his joy was short-lived, as King and Mido brought Spurs level before Robbie Keane smashed home the winner to leave Bent looking rather silly.

12 Premier League, 20 Nov 2010. **Arsenal 2-3 Spurs** *(Bale, van der Vaart (pen), Kaboul)*. Spurs travelled to the Emirates stadium having not beaten Arsenal in 19 visits and had only once scored more than one goal in that dismal run. They were 2-0 down after 27 minutes, the game had all the hall-marks of its recent predecessors; but Harry Redknapp's Spurs side were different gravy. Gareth Bale gave the travelling faithful some hope with a goal at the start of the second half and even before van der Vaart slotted home a pressure penalty you could feel momentum growing for Spurs. Arsenal had a goal disallowed before Kaboul thumped home a header to not just win the game, but to formally announce that Spurs were back.

13 Premier League, 29 Sept 2012. **Manchester United 2-3 Spurs** *(Vertonghen, Bale, Dempsey)*. An early goal for Vertonghen and the obligatory big game goal for Bale took Spurs into a 2-0 lead. Memories shifted back to recent away games at Arsenal and United, which had ended in 2-5 defeats, and the omens did not look when United pulled a goal back soon after half time but Spurs went up the other end to restore the two goal advantage and hung on for a famous win to exorcise the second half collapse demons which had blighted so many recent Spurs sides.

. . . and 3-2 was of course the score of Spurs' most famous defeat in the 1987 Cup final to Coventry.

NINETEEN SPURS ABANDONMENTS

1 11 Nov 1883. **Spurs 1-0 Brownlow Rovers.** The first abandoned Spurs match was against Brownlow Rovers, when the game was called off as the ball had burst, with Spurs leading 1-0.

2 Friendly, 19 Nov 1887. **Spurs 2-1 Royal Arsenal (unknown scorers). Abandoned 75 mins: bad light.** Arsenal would try anything to nick a result, and with Spurs leading 2-1 in the first ever match between the clubs, the game was abandoned due to 'bad light'.

3 FA Cup qualifier, 2 Nov 1895. **Spurs 2-4 Vampires (Pryor, Clements). Abandoned 90 mins: pitch markings.** Not strictly an abandonment, but a post-match complaint about the pitch markings worked to Spurs' advantage as they won the replayed game 2-1.

4 **Broken legs.** Two Spurs games were abandoned within a month of each other in spring 1897 as a result of an opposition player with a broken leg, and both ended at the 1-1 mark.

   i   United League, 15 March 1897; Kettering Town 1-1 Spurs (Milliken). Abandoned 25 mins: broken leg.

   ii Friendly, 26 April 1897; London Caledonians 1-1 Spurs (Newbigging). Abandoned 45 mins: broken leg.

5 S&D League, 24 Apr 1900. **Spurs 1-2 Woolwich Arsenal (Pratt). Abandoned 75 mins: bad language.** Perhaps the word 'arse' offended Victorian sensibilities – and no doubt there were more harsh words when the result was allowed to stand.

6 FA Cup second round, 20 Feb 1904. **Spurs 0-1 Aston Villa. Abandoned 38 mins: crowd trouble.** Maybe the Villa fans heard there were no Cup-a-Soups at half time, as this game was abandoned for off-the-field reasons. But Spurs profited from the abandonment by winning the rearranged game at Villa Park 1-0.

7 FA Cup first round replay, 17 Jan 1907. **Hull City 0-0 Spurs. Abandoned 100 mins: bad light.** After the first game at White Hart Lane ended 0-0 and another 100 minutes of goalless football into extra time in the replay, the clubs decided to accept the result and hold a second replay, which Spurs edged 1-0 with a Herbert Chapman goal.

8 Div 1, 23 Oct 1909. **Preston North End 0-0 Spurs. Abandoned 50 mins: rain.** Spurs' visit to the North West was ended by rain, and they lost the rearranged game 4-1.

9 Div 1, 28 Jan 1911. **Spurs 1-1 Oldham Athletic (Crompton). Abandoned 45 mins: fog.** This would have been Ellis Crompton's only goal in his few appearances, but Spurs won the rearranged game comfortably 2-0.

10 Div 1, 6 Jan 1912. **West Bromwich Albion 0-0 Spurs. Abandoned 57 mins: fog.** Baggies turned Smoggies – but Spurs lost the rearranged game 2-0.

11 Div 1, 12 Oct 1912. **Spurs 1-3 Notts County (Rance). Abandoned 80 mins: fog.** As much as it seemed like a reprieve, Spurs being 3-1 down with ten minutes to go, Tottenham lost the rearranged game 3-0.

12 London Professional Charity Cup, 3 Nov 1924. **Clapton Orient 2-1 Spurs (Hargreaves (pen)). Abandoned 110 mins: bad light.** The Charity Cup was probably not top of everyone's priorities, as the teams agreed to accept the result rather than go through a replay.

13 Football League South A, 23 Dec 1939. **Spurs 3-4 Southend United (Bennett, Hall AE (2)). Abandoned 60 mins: fog.** The highest-scoring abandoned match, ended by the gloom surrounding the first wartime Christmas.

14 **Blitz Abandonments.** The Luftwaffe forced a premature end to three Regional League South matches at the start of World War II:

    i Regional League South, 7 September 1940; West Ham United 1-4 Spurs (Burgess (3), Duncan). Abandoned 80 mins: air raid.

    ii Regional League South, 12 October 1940; Spurs 2-3 Arsenal (Skinner, Medley). Abandoned 47 mins: air raid.

iii   Regional League South, 23 November 1940; Spurs 2-1 Luton Town (Duncan, Ludford). Abandoned 60 mins: air raid.

15   Div 2, 27 Nov 1948. **Spurs 0-0 Nottingham Forest. Abandoned 17 mins: fog.** This proved to be the last game abandoned as a result of fog before the Clean Air Act was introduced in London. Spurs won the rearranged fixture 2-1.

16   Friendly, 29 Nov 1954. **Accrington Stanley 0-0 Spurs. Abandoned 52 mins: rain.** An abandonment as a result of the ever-present rain was probably seen as a blessing by the players, who were on a long weekend in the North West having beaten Burnley in the League a couple of days before.

17   Div 1, 17 Dec 1969. **Spurs 0-0 Everton. Abandoned 29 mins: floodlight failure.** In an age before Far Eastern betting syndicates, the lights went out at White Hart Lane and did not return. Spurs lost the rearranged game 0-1 later in the season.

18   FA Cup fifth round, 15 Feb 1996. **Nottingham Forest 0-0 Spurs. Abandoned 18 mins: snow.** It was quickly apparent that this game was not going to go the distance as the snow kept falling and spawned a number of heroic tales of how Spurs fans managed to get back to London in adverse conditions. Spurs drew the rearranged game and the replay at White Hart Lane before succumbing on penalties.

19   FA Cup sixth round, 17 Mar 2012. **Spurs 1-1 Bolton Wanderers (Walker). Abandoned 41 mins: injury.** A well-contested cup tie nearly took a tragic turn when Fabrice Muamba collapsed shortly before half time. It was evident to everyone in the ground that it was something serious as the medics battled to save his life on the pitch. After a long period in intensive care, Muamba was on the way to recovery by the time Spurs won 3-1 in the rescheduled match 10 days later.

SIX OF THE BEST OVER MANCHESTER CITY

When Man City are not needing late injury-time goals and penalties to win a third tier promotion play-off against Gillingham, they are usually very welcome opponents for Spurs.

1 **FA Cup final replay (Wembley), 1981.** *Spurs 3-2 Man City*. City were very helpful to Spurs in the greatest cup final of all time. They disposed of the altogether more dangerous Ipswich in the semi, provided an equaliser in the first game, scored the best but forgotten goal of the replay, before furnishing the shop-room dummies for Ricky Villa to dribble around for the winning goal.

2 **World Cup 1990 heroes: Division One, 1990.** *Spurs 3-1 Man City*. Basking in the sunshine summer of 1990, returning World Cup heroes Lineker and Gazza maintained the feelgood vibe to put City away.

3 **The classic cup tie: FA Cup sixth round, 1993.** *Man City 2-4 Spurs*. A commanding performance featuring a Nayim hat-trick before the shenanigans of pitch invasions, 'missed' penalties and disallowed goals gave a scoreline that flattered City in a classic cup tie.

4 **Breaking the spell: Premier League, 2001.** *Man City 0-1 Spurs*. Gooner George looked on with Gooner glee as Spurs seemed to be heading for their fifth straight 0-0, but little Rebrov popped up in the last minute to rescue Spurs from his evil plan to give Tottenham a rare away win in that dark era.

5 **The UEFA game: Premier League, 2007.** *Spurs 2-1 Man City*. Only a few years ago qualification for the UEFA cup was a big deal for Spurs. City arrived at White Hart Lane as the final obstacle in a season that had seen Martin Jol's team overcome a 1-1-4 start to be on the precipice. It wasn't a classic but Spurs just did enough and the relief was palpable on an emotional Martin Jol in the end of season lap of honour.

6   **The big money match: Premier League, 2010.** *Man City 0-1 Spurs.* Effectively a play-off for the Champions League qualification, Spurs went up to a moneyed but nervous City and did enough to comfortably win the richest single prize in their history with a goal from Peter Crouch. Good job they sorted it at City as they had a shocker and lost to relegated Burnley in the next game.

EIGHT VERY SPURS COLLAPSES

1   Div 1, 19 Mar 1966. **Spurs 5-5 Aston Villa** *(Brown L, Robertson, Greaves, Saul, Gilzean).* Spurs sauntered into a 5-1 lead just after the break and looked to be heading for another wide-margin win over Villa like the 4-0 scoreline from the previous season. Tony Hateley started the Villa comeback giving ex-Arsenal defender Laurie Brown a torrid time at the heart of the Spurs defence. Villa had the game level with 10 minutes to go and could have even won it but for a last-gasp clearance from Mullery.

2   FA Cup fourth round replay, 7 Feb 1973. **Spurs 3-5 Derby County (aet)** *(England (pen), Gilzean, Chivers).* All sorts of Spurs teams from different eras manage to snatch defeat from the jaws of victory. A high-class Tottenham had managed to get a draw against high-flying Derby at the Baseball Ground, and looked to be coasting in the replay with a three-goal advantage before it all went badly wrong in extra time.

3   League Cup fourth round, 27 Nov 1996. **Bolton Wanderers 6-1 Spurs** *(Sheringham).*

Premier League, 28 Dec 1996. **Newcastle United 7-1 Spurs** *(Nielsen).* The Bolton defeat was made worse as the Trotters were in the second tier at the time. But when Spurs played against Newcastle a month later, they were in the top half of the table, and would have gone level with the high-flying Geordies had they won. However, for the second time in a month, a last quarter without any fight saw Spurs not just beaten but hammered as the cracks started to appear in Francis' team.

4   Premier League, 6 Dec 1997. **Spurs 1-6 Chelsea** *(Vega)*. Things did not look too bad in Christian Gross' first home game come half time, with Ramon Vega levelling the scores just before the break. Gross must have given a half-time team talk akin to his opening 'train ticket' press conference, though, as a fragile Spurs team offered little resistance to complete humiliation in the second half. The one saving grace was that this proved to be the last home defeat in a season-long struggle with relegation.

5   Premier League, 15 Apr 2000. **Spurs 2-4 Aston Villa** *(Iversen, Armstrong)*. Goals either side of half time looked to have made the game safe for Spurs, but once again Villa were about to stage another remarkable comeback at White Hart Lane. A dodgy penalty got Villa back into things, then three unstoppable shots from Dion Dublin, Benny Carbone and even balding fullback Alan Wright in a devastating 10-minute spell turned the game on its head and left Spurs reeling.

6   Premier League, 29 Sept 2001. **Spurs 3-5 Manchester United** *(Richards, Ferdinand, Ziege)*. When Ziege scored a spectacular diving header to put Spurs 3-0 up just before half time, it looked like Glenn Hoddle's new Spurs team had announced themselves as serious challengers in the Premier League. With 15 minutes to think about it at half time, Spurs worried themselves out of the game, and an early United goal started a tidal wave that washed over Spurs, who were a laughing stock by the final whistle.

7   Premier League, 11 Sept 2002. **Fulham 3-2 Spurs** *(Richards, Sheringham)*. Spurs travelled to Loftus Road knowing that a win against Fulham would take Spurs to the top of the Premier League. The first half went well, with goals from Richards and Sheringham giving Spurs a comfortable 2-0 lead and allowing the fans to taunt Fulham 'Shit ground, not yours'. It was all Spurs in the early part of the second half, and there was even time for Perry to execute one of his infamous 'Cruyff turns'. The turning point came when

Ačimović headed home a Davis cross, but what would have been his one and only goal for Spurs was controversially disallowed for offside. Fulham gained some urgency, and all of a sudden Spurs were on full-scale retreat looking for the final whistle. A soft shot from former Goon Inamoto managed to beat Keller, and worse was to follow as the linesman awarded a penalty that the referee had missed, which allowed Malbranque to equalise. The game seemed to be heading for a draw before the big Legwinski beat Thatcher to score with virtually the last kick of the game.

8   Premier League, 25 Feb 2012. **Arsenal 5-2 Spurs** *(Saha, Adebayor (pen))*. Spurs went into this match on the crest of a wave, having just beaten Newcastle 5-0 to remain 10 points clear of Arsenal, and #mindthegap was regularly trending on Twitter. With Arsenal having a bad run and fans calling for Wenger's resignation, things looked very good for Spurs when former Arsenal player Adebayor scored from the spot to give Tottenham their first two-goal advantage away at Arsenal for 19 years. However, that point may as well have marked not only the end of the game but the end of the season for Spurs. Arsenal grabbed one back before half time and Spurs found nothing, and were rolled over with a further four goals. This result sparked a catastrophic loss of form that saw Spurs fall out of the title race and then out of the guaranteed Champions League places as the season imploded.

YOU WIN SOME, YOU LOSE SOME, YOU WIN SOME, YOU LOSE SOME: SPURS' FA CUP SEMI-FINALS

Win the first two, lose the next four, win the next seven and then lose the next six . . .

- FA Cup SF (Villa Park), 1901. **Spurs 4-0 West Bromwich Albion** *(Brown (4))*. As for much of the cup run, Spurs were massive underdogs, but four of Sandy Brown's 15 FA Cup goals that season proved more than enough to win a virtual away game in the Midlands.

- FA Cup SF (Hillsborough), 1921. **Spurs 2-1 Preston North End** *(Bliss (2))*. Despite home and away defeats to Preston in the League, a couple from Bert Bliss ignited the magic of the cup for Spurs.

- FA Cup SF (Hillsborough), 1922. **Spurs 1-2 Preston North End** *(Seed)*. A year later and the complete opposite: two League wins against North End help Spurs finish runners-up, but there is a semi-final upset after a controversially disallowed goal sees Spurs miss out on the last final before the Empire Stadium was opened at Wembley.

- FA Cup SF (Villa Park), 1948. **Spurs 1-3 Blackpool (aet)** *(Duquemin)*. As a plucky Division Two side, Spurs came within four minutes of a massive shock against a Blackpool side including the legendary Stanley Matthews. However, it was Mortensen, who did the damage with the equaliser, the first of his hat-trick in only Spurs' second experience of extra time.

- FA Cup SF (Villa Park), 1953. **Spurs 1-2 Blackpool** *(Duquemin)*. Just as in the 1920s, Spurs repeated semi-final opponents from the North West in quick succession. A much stronger Spurs side, consisting of Arthur Rowe's 'push and run' heroes, were up against the still strong Blackpool side. An equaliser from 'the Duke' looked likely to take the game into extra time before a last-minute error allowed Blackpool to nick the winner and enter football folklore with the 'Matthews Final' against Bolton.

- FA Cup SF (Villa Park), 1956. **Spurs 0-1 Manchester City.** Another semi-final at Villa Park, and another defeat by a team from the North West. A controversial decision not to award Spurs a late penalty cost Jimmy Anderson's team a chance of extra time. Danny Blanchflower's instigation of tactical changes against the manager's wishes towards the end of the game to try to get Spurs level cost him the captaincy for a few seasons.

- FA Cup SF (Villa Park), 1961. **Spurs 3-0 Burnley** *(Smith R (2), Jones)*. With four semi-final defeats stretching back nearly 40 years, three of which were at Villa Park against opposition from the North West, the double team could have been forgiven for thinking the omens were against them as they took on fellow title rivals. However, Burnley had a rare off-day and Spurs ran out comfortable winners, with a brace from Bobby Smith setting up the win.

- FA Cup SF (Hillsborough), 1962. **Spurs 3-1 Manchester United** *(Greaves, Jones, Medwin)*. March 1962 had not been a good month for Spurs' defence of the League title, with a crucial home defeat to Ipswich, but the retention of the FA Cup proved more straightforward. A couple from Jimmy Greaves and Cliff Jones before half time put Spurs in a strong position, and although United pulled one back, Terry Medwin ensured there would be no way out for Busby's men.

- FA Cup SF (Hillsborough), 1967. **Spurs 2-1 Nottingham Forest** *(Greaves, Saul)*. Spurs went into this semi in one of the greatest runs of form in the club's history, and duly came out on top with the customary Jimmy Greaves goal against Forest. A second-half strike from Frank Saul meant a Forest consolation goal was not enough to prevent the first all-London FA Cup final between Spurs and Chelsea.

- FA Cup SF (Hillsborough), 1981. **Spurs 2-2 Wolves (aet)** *(Archibald, Hoddle)*. Tragedy at Hillsborough nearly occurred eight years before the 1989 disaster, as the larger Spurs contingent were wedged into the Leppings Lane end. Fortunately, the absence of fences meant that the fans could escape the crush. Hoddle scored a brilliant free kick just before half time to restore Spurs' lead after Wolves had responded quickly to Archie's early goal. This looked to be enough for Spurs, before Clive Thomas decided that a legitimate tackle from Hoddle outside the box and a dive from Kenny Hibbitt were enough for a penalty.

- FA Cup SF replay (Highbury), 1981. **Spurs 3-0 Wolves** *(Crooks (2), Villa)*. The injustice of the first game was more than made up for in the replay. Spurs filled out

Highbury on a sunny evening so the replay felt almost like a home game. Crooks nodded home from close range to put Tottenham ahead and then scored arguably his best goal, scorching on to another perfect Hoddle through-ball and firing home to all but secure a trip to Wembley. A Ricky Villa special in the second half was the perfect end to a memorable evening that made the controversy of the first game a blessing.

- FA Cup SF (Villa Park), 1982. **Spurs 2-0 Leicester City** *(Crooks, Wilson og)*. Spurs struggled to play their best football, but Garth Crooks once again came to the rescue with the opening goal. On its own it looked to be enough, before a bizarre own goal finished Leicester off.

- FA Cup SF (Villa Park), 1987. **Spurs 4-1 Watford** *(Hodge (2), Allen P, Allen C)*. Injuries before the game meant that Watford had to call up wine bar-owner Gary Plumley to play in goal. It was cocktails all round for Spurs as they coasted to the easiest of semi-final wins, with goals from Steve Hodge book-ending goals from the Allen cousins.

- FA Cup SF (Wembley), 1991. **Spurs 3-1 Arsenal** *(Gascoigne, Lineker (2))*. Not just Spurs' greatest semi-final, but one of the greatest Spurs matches of all time. Financial troubles had overshadowed the cup run, while star player Paul Gascoigne had needed emergency surgery after the sixth round win and was in a race against time to line up at Wembley. Fortunately, Gazza made the team and the recall of Samways for Nayim allowed Venables to out-think his Arsenal counterpart George Graham, who was looking to win the double with the League title almost assured. Just as Spurs often mess things up when too much is in our favour, in the face of adversity we rise magnificently to the challenge, and never looked likely to give away the early advantage from the Empire stadium's greatest free kick.

- FA Cup SF (Wembley), 1993. **Spurs 0-1 Arsenal.** Two years on, a stronger all-round Spurs side including Mabbutt, Anderton, Sheringham, Ruddock and Barmby from the bench went into the game ahead of Arsenal in the League. Unfortunately, what should have been an early penalty for Spurs and a red card for Arsenal defender Linighan was only a free kick outside the box and a yellow card. Spurs did well without scoring, but were undone by a late Tony Adams header.

- FA Cup SF (Elland Road), 1995. **Spurs 1-4 Everton** *(Klinsmann (pen))*. Spurs had originally been banned from the FA Cup as part of the punishment meted out for the Sugar–Venables fall-out, but earned a late reprieve. An emerging side, with all the flair of Ossie's famous five allied to some defensive nous, had scored 10 away goals to see off Sunderland and Southampton and recorded a famous win at Anfield in the sixth round. All the omens pointed to it being Spurs' year – but no-one told Everton, who exposed an inexperienced Stuart Nethercott and won it with late Daniel Amokachi goals in what was a heart breaking defeat.

- FA Cup SF (Old Trafford), 1999. **Spurs 0-2 Newcastle United (aet).** Another cup run that included one of the best Spurs displays of the era to see off Leeds and an iconic Ginola goal to do for Barnsley. In a tight match of few chances, Spurs should have had a blatant penalty from Nikos Dabizas' handball on the hour. It was not given, and by a cruel irony it was from the penalty spot that Alan Shearer scored the first of his two extra-time goals to end Spurs' dreams of returning to Wembley after winning the League Cup.

- FA Cup SF (Old Trafford), 2001. **Spurs 1-2 Arsenal** *(Doherty)*. The decade since the 1991 semi-final had been kinder to Arsenal than Spurs. The Spurs boardroom takeover had seen George Graham sacked in the run-up to the game, which turned out to be new manager Glenn Hoddle's first in charge. Spurs took an early lead through the Ginger Pelé, but by the end had Neil Sullivan in goal to thank for keeping the scoreline respectable.

- FA Cup SF (Wembley), 2010. **Spurs 0-2 Portsmouth.** On paper a formality, against a soon-to-be relegated team in financial crisis, but in practice a lacklustre shambles. One of the few low points of the Redknapp era.

• FA Cup SF (Wembley), 2012. **Spurs 1-5 Chelsea** *(Bale)*. Spurs started well and hit the woodwork, as well as having a van der Vaart header cleared off the line before a brilliant goal from Drogba put Chelsea ahead before half time. Referee Martin Atkinson awarded Chelsea a contro-versial 'goal' during a goalmouth scramble that never looked remotely justified. Gareth Bale pulled one back, but as Spurs pressed for an equaliser (which should really have been a winner), they were undone at the back and fell apart, to lose a sixth semi-final by the widest margin.

SIXTEEN PENALTY SHOOT-OUTS

It's fair to say that the glory of Spurs' first ever proper penalty shoot-out in the 1984 UEFA Cup final has not been replicated in subsequent showdowns, with only one successful round of spot kicks against Peterborough since the night of European glory.

1 Tour, 2 June 1979. **San Lorenzo 3-3 Spurs** *(Lee, Pratt, Galvin)*. **Spurs won 5-3 on penalties.** A full set of spot kicks, including one from Gordon Smith, allowed Spurs to progress to the final of the Japan Cup to eventually beat Dundee United.

2 Tour, 15 Aug 1982. **FC Cologne 0-0 Spurs. Spurs lost 1-3 on penalties.** Only Archie is on target as Spurs become one of the first English teams to suffer at the hands of Germans on penalties, this time in the Amsterdam 707 tournament third-place play-off.

3 Tour, 11 June 1983. **Manchester Utd 2-0 Spurs** *(Perryman, Mabbutt)*. **Spurs won 3-2 on penalties.** Spurs won the Royal Swazi Hotel Tournament in the shoot-out with Alan Brazil, Steve Perryman and unlikely hero Paul Price on target.

4 UEFA Cup final second leg, 25 May 1984. **Spurs 1-1 Anderlecht** *(Roberts)*. **Spurs won 4-3 on penalties.** The epic end to an epic competition. Roberts, Falco, Stevens and Archibald all scored before Danny Thomas' penalty was saved, only for Parks to become the hero by saving the next penalty to win the cup.

5 Friendly, 19 Aug 1986. **PSV Eindhoven 1-1 Spurs** *(Falco)*. **Spurs lost 3-4 on penalties.** Waddle on target, but it's not enough for Spurs in this pre-season warm-up.

6 Fiorucci Cup, 27 Apr 1993. **Spurs 0-0 Inter Milan. Spurs lost 5-6 on penalties.** Short matches in the Fiorucci Cup, but a long and ultimately unsuccessful penalty competition.

7 FA Cup third round replay, 19 Jan 1994. **Spurs 1-1 Peterborough United** *(Barmby)*. **Spurs won 5-4 on penalties.** Spurs' last successful penalty competition was against lowly Peterborough in the Ossie era, but they may as well have lost it given their terrible display at Ipswich in the next round.

8 Youth Cup, 1994/95. **Manchester United 2-2 Spurs. Spurs lost 4-3 on penalties.** Even in youth football Spurs have struggled on penalties, with a young Stephen Carr missing and blubbing as Spurs lost the Youith cup final.

9 Friendly, 26 May 1995. **Singapore Lions 1-1 Spurs** *(Anderton)*. **Spurs lost 2-4 on penalties.** No joy for Spurs in the Far East, as they clearly miss the recently departed Klinsmann.

10 FA Cup fifth round replay, 9 Mar 1996. **Spurs 1-1 Notts Forest** *(Sheringham)*. **Spurs lost 1-3 on penalties.** A disappointing end to the marathon cup tie, with Forest keeper Crossley saving from Wilson, Rosenthal and Sheringham, to add to the Lineker penalty he saved in the 1991 cup final.

11 League Cup fifth round, 17 Dec 2003. **Spurs 1-1 Middlesbrough** *(Anderton)*. **Spurs lost 5-4 on**

penalties. Spurs' South Americans Poyet and Tarrico miss as Spurs exit to the Smoggies.

12 Kappa Cup, 5 Aug 2004. **Spurs 1-1 Partizan Belgrade** *(Defoe)*. **Spurs lost 1-0 on penalties.** Another penalty competition defeat, this time without a single successful spot kick.

13 League Cup fifth round, 1 Dec 2004. **Spurs 1-1 Liverpool** *(Defoe)*. **Spurs lost 4-3 on penalties.** Kanoute is the villain as Spurs go out at the same stage of the competition, to the same score as they did the season before against Boro, and to another team in red.

14 UEFA Cup third round second leg, 12 Mar 2008. **PSV Eindhoven 0-1 Spurs** *(Berbatov)*. **Spurs lost 5-6 on penalties.** A better show from Spurs, taking things to sudden death where Pascal Chimbonda's miss sends Spurs out.

15 League Cup final, 1 Mar 2009. **Spurs 0-0 Manchester United (aet). Spurs lost 1-4 on penalties.** A miss from Bentley after O'Hara's kick had been saved was enough to sink Spurs, after a goalless 120 minutes at the new Wembley stadium.

16 League Cup third round, 21 Sept 2011. **Stoke City 0-0 Spurs (aet). Spurs lost 6-7 on penalties.** A young Spurs side had held out for a draw, before someone called Massimo Luongo missed the decisive penalty on his debut and only appearance in the first team thus far.

Cold discomfort: fourteen New Year shockers

George Graham managed Spurs for three seasons, and in each of these, Spurs went into spiritual hibernation after the third round of the FA Cup until the middle of February. Fourteen games, no wins and only three goals, and none in the six games at White Hart Lane.

1 *Premier League, 9 Jan 1999; Sheffield Wednesday 0-0 Spurs*
2 *Premier League, 16 Jan 1999; Spurs 0-0 Wimbledon*
3 *Premier League, 30 Jan 1999, Blackburn Rovers 1-1 Spurs (Iversen)*
4 *Premier League, 6 Feb 1999; Spurs 0-0 Coventry City*
5 *Premier League, 20 Feb 1999; Middlesbrough 0-0 Spurs*
6 *Premier League, 12 Jan 2000; Chelsea 1-0 Spurs*
7 *Premier League, 15 Jan 2000; Everton 2-2 Spurs (Armstrong, Ginola)*
8 *Premier League, 22 Jan 2000; Spurs 0-1 Sheffield Wednesday*
9 *Premier League, 5 Feb 2000; Spurs 0-1 Chelsea*
10 *Premier League, 12 Feb 2000; Leeds United 1-0 Spurs*
11 *Premier League, 13 Jan 2001; Everton 0-0 Spurs*
12 *Premier League, 20 Jan 2001; Spurs 0-0 Southampton*
13 *Premier League, 31 Jan 2001; West Ham United 0-0 Spurs*
14 *Premier League, 3 Feb 2001; Spurs 0-0 Charlton Athletic.*

THE TEN EVENTS WHICH KILLED THE OLD SPURS

Spurs have emerged from a decade or more of slump to be a high-class Premier League side, but it all feels very different to what went before. Here are the 10 moments that killed the old Spurs.

1. CUP WINNERS' QUARTER-FINAL V FEYENOORD (1992)

Spurs had already put out a much better Porto side and looked to have a great chance of progressing to the semi-finals against regular European foes Feyenoord. However, a host of missed chances against the dour cloggies led by former Spur Johnny Metgod saw Tottenham lose 1-0 on aggregate. This was to be Spurs' only shot at European glory in the 1990s, and ended their chance of becoming one of the European giants to win trophies in the 1960s, 1970s, 1980s and 1990s alongside AC Milan and Barcelona.

2. FA CUP SEMI-FINAL V ARSENAL (1993)

While Spurs had been the clear underdogs against champions-elect Arsenal in 1991, this time a bright Lilywhite side looked to have a better chance than a regressive Arsenal outfit. The pivotal moment came in the first half when Darren Anderton was felled by Andy Linighan. Instead of awarding a penalty and reducing the Goons to ten men, the referee only gave Spurs a free kick that was squandered. Near the end of the game, Donkey Adams nodded home a late winner for Arsenal who went on to lift the cup, and Linighan scoring the winner in the final replay added insult to injury. This game started Spurs on the road to losing six FA Cup finals over the next 20 years.

3. SUGAR–VENABLES FALL-OUT (1993)

While it may have been necessary for the long-term viability of the club, the messy way in which Sugar expelled Venables from Spurs damaged both internal morale and external respect for the club. Spurs lost a de facto manager at the height of his considerable powers and descended into a laughing stock, with the likes of Dozzell, Kerslake and Scott recruited to ward off relegation. The separation set Spurs on a downward trajectory for the rest of the decade where flair was feared and being ordinary was seen as a relative success compared to being rubbish, in a most un-Spurs and unsuccessful way.

4. THE PREMIER LEAGUE TAKES OFF IN THE MID 90s (WITHOUT SPURS)

Spurs were one of the old 'big four' who'd helped instigate the Premier League, but a changes in the interim saw other teams embracing the new realities more effectively. Presumably piqued by Klinsmann's short stay, the esteemed chairman offered Arsenal a few words of advice when they signed their very own 'Carlos Kickaball' Dennis Bergkamp, while Spurs paraded Chris Armstrong from lowly Palace.

Spurs had messed about with a couple of stand redevelopments at the start of the 1990s but had not increased capacity, Manchester United were on their way to building the largest ground in the country and collecting more than a million a match.

Meanwhile, Arsenal could see that Rioch was yesterday's man as a manager and found a genius in Wenger on the other side of the world. In terms of yesterday's men, Spurs could not have done much better than a pigeon-fancier with a proud mullet. And when a foreign manager was positively de rigueur a few years later, Spurs copied Arsenal by plucking a virtual unknown from a footballing backwater. Unfortunately, Spurs hired Christian Gross and the game was almost up.

5. THE DEPARTURE OF SHERINGHAM (1997)

The Spurs slide made 31-year-old Sheringham realise he needed to leave to collect the medals his distinguished career deserved. In an acrimonious departure, Sheringham was virtually given away to United for £3.5 million, while Spurs spent nearly double that on Sir Les, who struggled to fill the void. It could be argued that Sheringham left too early, as silverware arrived for Spurs the season after in the form of the League Cup, but by then Sheringham had scored in the FA Cup and Champions League finals to add to his League Championship. It was the first time that someone had to leave Spurs to win trophies, and set a precedent that subsequently took Campbell, Carrick and Berbatov away.

6. APPOINTMENT OF GEORGE GRAHAM AND DAVID PLEAT (1998)

With Spurs in a mess and supporter patience with the chairman wearing thin, Sugar thought the unthinkable and appointed the epitome of Arsenality in its most unreconstructed form, George Graham, to manage Spurs. The official line was that it would bring success to Tottenham, but the Goonersaurus was already beyond his footballing sell-by date and there was a feeling that it was as much done to hurt the fans who'd failed to fully appreciate what Sugar had done for the club. A Spurs team that was not built on flair was a Spurs team in name only, and it was compounded by the successful sides of the era, including Arsenal, stealing our old clothes and embracing progressive football ideologies usually associated with Spurs. A second disaster was to bring in David Pleat as director of football. It is often said that the Director of Football system works outside the UK but its English translation is frustrated manager-in-waiting. This malign influence over subsequent managers lasted for more than 10 years in various guises, and was arguably the most damaging aspect of the whole affair.

7. KAISERSLAUTERN (1999)

A League Cup win in 1999 provided Spurs with the opportunity to take part in UEFA Cup football the following season. After disposing of Zimbru, Spurs travelled to Kaiserslautern with a 1-0 advantage from the first leg. News that George Graham was to leave his best player, David Ginola, out of his team filtered through to the home dressing room, and his man-marker was replaced by an attacking player. Spurs seemed to have got away with it as the game went into the 90th minute goalless, but a disastrous injury time saw Spurs first concede the goal to level the tie on aggregate, and then Stephen Carr put through his own net to send Spurs out.

To lose to an ordinary Kaiserslautern team was bad enough, but to do it in such dramatic circumstances after preventing your best player from participating was a very dark day for a club with 'Audere est Facere' as its motto.

8. LEAGUE CUP FINAL AND 0-4 RESULTS (2002)

After a decade of despair, Spurs' last hope was Glenn Hoddle. The hope was that the footballing genius would follow in the footsteps of the two greatest Spurs managers, Rowe and Nicholson, by playing for both Spurs and England before leading the club to glory. Progress was not always smooth but the football was a marked improvement on the previous era, and when Spurs lined up to face a weakened Blackburn Rovers at the Millennium Stadium in Cardiff, it looked as if the Hoddle era was to produce a trophy in the first season. However, a combination of bad luck and bad finishing saw Spurs lose the game and with it confidence, and they lost 4-0 three times in a week soon after. An uneasy relationship with the director of football did not help behind the scenes, and the vision of Glenn Hoddle's 'sunshine football' was all but over. And so passed the last of the old Spurs.

9. THIERRY HENRY'S SLIDE (2002)

With Hoddle unable to revive the old Spurs, the final breath came at Highbury during the North London derby in November 2002. After scoring a jammy goal at the North Bank, Thierry Henry turned and ran the length of the pitch before doing a knee slide full of his poncy attitude in front of the Spurs fans. A memorable photograph taken from the other end of the pitch captures the Spurs faces looking on, a few angry but most resigned and beaten.

Although the celebration broke all sorts of protocols, Arsenal chose it as their image for Henry's statue outside the new ground as they realised the power of the image that broke Spurs.

10. THE RESURRECTION (2005 ONWARDS)

During 2003/04, after the best part of a decade struggling and no links to the past in either style or personnel, Spurs were a club who'd lost their raison d'être in the modern footballing world. But from the ashes, a new Spurs began to form. First through Martin Jol, Harry Redknapp and now AVB, Spurs are back at the top table of English football if not quite among the elite just yet, all achieved with sustainable funding that is a remarkable achievement in itself.

Spurs are different these days: no longer do the club have the best player in the League but no team ethic, they are not the cup kings, and the cocky arrogance has been replaced by a more understated consistency, with a range of high-class players. The financial glass ceiling prevents Spurs from going much higher, which is frustrating, but in 2012, they finished three consecutive seasons in the top five for the first time since 1965, and this is a welcome world away from some of the shambles of the previous 20 years.

4

THE SPURS SPIRIT

THIRTY-TWO RANDOM FACTS ABOUT SPURS

1 Spurs have been level at 90 minutes in seven of the last nine cup finals they have contested: FA Cup finals in 1981, 1982, 1987 and 1991; League Cup finals in 1982, 2008 and 2009. Of the other two domestic finals, Spurs got a late winner from Allan Nielsen in the 1999 League Cup final against Leicester and were denied a last-minute penalty to level things against Blackburn in the 2002 final in the same competition. For good measure, three of the four UEFA Cup final matches they played in were drawn in this period.

2 Gary Lineker scored in six of the seven games he played against Norwich. His nine goals in these games represented 11% of his 80 for Spurs.

3 Steve Perryman has appeared on children's TV favourite *Crackerjack* and even more remarkably, Tony Galvin was a guest on the lesser-known *Crosswits*, hosted by Tom O'Connor.

4 Spurs have only played one competitive match in June, when a penalty from Ronnie Dix was enough to share the points with Barnsley in 1947.

5 Olympic cyclist Chris Hoy was surprised to get abuse on Twitter from Spurs fans after the controversial defeat by Stoke in November 2011. Hoy's 'crime' was to have a name a bit like match referee Chris Foy, who contrived a whole host of funny decisions to let Stoke win.

6　John Piercy was the 500th player used by Spurs.

7　Gazza took the ball away from the keeper and scored with his sock against Arsenal in 1988, after having his boot ripped off getting to the through ball from Waddle.

8　The opposing goalkeepers Joe Corrigan and Peter Hucker were named respective man of the match in all four games of the 1981 and 1982 cup finals and replays.

9　From 31 December 1966, Spurs won 19, drew seven and lost only once in the remaining 27 games of the season in 1967, earning them a third-place finish and FA Cup glory against Chelsea at Wembley.

10　The original protest on Sol Campbell's return to White Hart Lane was to be the 'minute of contempt', an internet campaign urging fans to turn their back on the former captain when he came on to the pitch. As it turned out, passions were so raw, vitriol and 'Judas' balloons were the order of the day.

11　The only change between the cup final and replay in 1981 was that Ricky Villa changed his 'unlucky' number 6 shirt for a much luckier number 5 and scored two goals in the final, with Steve Perryman returning to his more familiar number 6 to lift the cup.

12　Eddie Baily, Spurs' 'push and run' forward and later Bill Nicholson's number two, was reported missing in action during the World War II and Spurs did not register him as a player at the end of the conflict . . . Until he turned up for training at the start of the following season.

13　Jermaine Jenas' goal in the 1-1 draw in 2005 is the only one of eight goals scored in Spurs' first 20 Premier League visits to Old Trafford to have earned the team a point. Spurs collected only three points in all these matches, a total they could have collected in one had Pedro Mendes' famous long-range goal been allowed to stand earlier that year.

14 Norfolk-born Ruel Fox has international caps for Montserrat.

15 Between 1946 and 1977, the Spurs goalkeeper's jersey was consecutively worn by three players – Ditchburn, Brown and Jennings – for 1,112 of the 1,302 League games in that period. Spurs' custodian was less certain on the return to the top flight, when three keepers – Barry Daines, Mark Kendall and Milija Aleksic – were all used in the first season back in 1978/79.

16 From the 1919/20 season to 1923/24, Spurs played each team home and away in the League in consecutive weeks.

17 Cliff Jones was Spurs' first substitute in a major final, but did not leave the bench in the 1967 FA Cup win over Chelsea.

18 Former manager George Graham once played for the glamorous-sounding California Surf – surely the greatest mismatch of imagery in footballing history.

19 At 5' 2", Fanny Walden is the shortest recorded player to play for Spurs.

20 Both Mike England and John Pratt scored at each end in a game against Burnley at White Hart Lane in 1974 that Spurs eventually lost 2-3.

21 The self-proclaimed 'biggest club in the world' and sometime Premier League opponents when not in the second flight, Newcastle United have not won a major trophy since before the moon landings in 1969, while Winston Churchill was the Prime Minister the last time they won a trophy that is still in existence, back in 1955.

22 Walter Tull was the first black player to represent Tottenham, scoring two goals in 10 League appearances between 1909–11. Chris Hughton was the next black player for Tottenham, seven decades later in 1979.

23 Spurs have played the Blues of Chelsea and Leicester in Wembley finals in both the 1960s and the modern era. Spurs won all four matches, and even gave Leicester a player advantage and Chelsea a goal start to make things more interesting in the most recent victories.

24 Given that the 'Z' is silent in most Scottish names such as Menzies, Dalziel etc, why was Gilzean not pronounced Gil-ean?

25 The tie against Stevenage in 2012 means that there are now only 16 League sides who Spurs have never met in the FA Cup, namely: Accrington Stanley, Aldershot, Barnet, Burton Albion, Colchester, Crawley Town, Dagenham & Redbridge, Gillingham, Hartlepool, Macclesfield, Morecambe, Rochdale, Shrewsbury, Swansea City, Wycombe and Yeovil.

26 Of the 43 goals Spurs have scored in major cup finals, three have been provided by opposition players: van Daele for Feyenoord in 1974; Tommy Hutchinson for Manchester City in 1981; and Des Walker of Forest, who provided the winner in 1991.

27 In the 1935/36 season, Spurs had three players called Hall, two Hunts and two Evanses. Fortunately for the early commentators, they never all played in the same game.

28 Steve Archibald holds the unique distinction of appearing twice in the same episode of *Top of the Pops* in 1982. He sang 'We Have a Dream' with the Scotland World Cup squad, and then joined his Spurs teammates and Chas 'n' Dave for the FA Cup final song 'Tottenham, Tottenham'.

29 Between his debut in August 2007 and Spurs' 5-0 win over Burnley in September 2009, Gareth Bale appeared in a record 24 Premier League games without being on the winning side.

30 When Ricky Villa was about to pull the trigger for his cup-winning goal in 1981, Garth Crooks was so engrossed in the moment as he looked on from the edge of the box that he kicked an imaginary ball at the same time.

31 Carlisle United, Glossop, Mansfield Town and Swindon Town are the only teams Spurs have met in the League but failed to beat having met each of them for one season only.

32 There have been eight Browns, seven Smiths and five Joneses who have played first-team football for Spurs.

EIGHT ITEMS OF SPURS SYMMETRY

1 Spurs thumped Manchester United 5-1 in front of over 58,000 at White Hart Lane in October 1965. Two months later, United had their exact 1-5 revenge. Presumably they could not have been as confident, because only 39,511 turned up at Old Trafford.

2 Gerry Francis' and Martin Jol's managerial careers had distinct similarities exactly 10 years apart in the 1990s and 2000s, as the table below shows.

Francis	Jol
Francis appointed Spurs manager in the November of the fourth year of the decade.	Jol appointed Spurs manager in the November of the fourth year of the decade.
First official game was a high-scoring home defeat, 3-4 against Aston Villa.	First official game was a high-scoring home defeat, 4-5 against Arsenal.
Beat Norwich 2-0 away on Boxing Day with goals from Barmby and Sheringham before a disappointing home draw against Palace in his seventh and eighth matches in charge.	Beat Norwich 2-0 away on Boxing Day with goals from Keane and Brown before a disappointing home draw against Palace in his seventh and eighth matches in charge.
Secured a top-half finish in his first season and had a good run in the FA Cup.	Secured a top-half finish in his first season and had a good run in the FA Cup.
After 50 matches, a 1.6-point-per-game record.	After 50 matches, a 1.6-point per-game record.
Restores Spurs' credibility with 60-plus League points in total, but not always appealing to fans' sense of style in his first full season.	Restores Spurs credibility with 60-plus League points in total, but not always appealing to fans' sense of style in his first full season.

Loses his 87th game in charge to Newcastle with an embarrassing 1-7 defeat.	Loses his 87th game in charge to Newcastle, with a poor 2-3 defeat.
After 90 matches, has a 1.52-point-per-game record.	After 90 matches, has a 1.52-point-per-game record.
A seven-goal thriller at Upton Park in his 93rd game in charge, where a late goal from a fullback proves decisive, Dicks scoring the winner for West Ham.	A seven-goal thriller at Upton Park in his 93rd game in charge, where a late goal from a fullback proves decisive, Stalteri scoring the winner for Spurs.
A home win against Derby in August of the seventh year of the decade is not enough to stop the dark clouds gathering.	A home win against Derby in August of the seventh year of the decade is not enough to stop the dark clouds gathering.
Is sacked in early November of the seventh year of the decade after a short run of bad form.	Is sacked in late October of the seventh year of the decade after a short run of bad form.

3 John Gorman played 15 League matches and one FA Cup match in his first season in 1976/77. He missed the whole of the next season through injury, before playing 15 League matches and one FA Cup match, which proved to be his last, in the 1978/79 season.

4 When Spurs first met Watford in Division One in the 1980s, all results were away wins and all were the same score in reverse for the first two seasons. Watford's 1-0 win at Spurs was reversed with a Falco winner later in the season, and the Hornets had the best of the five goals at the Lane after Spurs' 2-3 win with Hoddle's famous chip at Vicarage Road. The games in the subsequent season were also away wins, but Spurs' 1-2 victory at Vicarage Road was comprehensively trumped by a 5-1 home defeat later in the season as the sequence was broken.

5 In the 2000s, Spurs won two League Cup semi-finals 5-1 against London opposition that had some remarkable similarities, as can be seen in the following table.

2002	2008
Spurs open the scoring against Chelsea in 2002 with Iversen stabbing home into the Park Lane goal after a couple of minutes.	Spurs open the scoring against Arsenal in 2008 with a great run and shot by Jenas into the Park Lane goal after a couple of minutes.
Spurs' second goal comes from a player with Arsenal connections, putting Spurs 2-0 up at the break, as Sherwood hits home a 'Sheringham corner'.	Spurs' second goal comes from a player with Arsenal connections, putting Spurs 2-0 up at the break, as Bendtner heads an own goal under pressure from Dawson.
Teddy Sheringham, a Spurs legend with 100-plus goals in two spells with the club, uses the outside of his foot to hit home the third goal at the Paxton end.	Robbie Keane, a Spurs legend with 100-plus goals in two spells with the club, uses the outside of his foot to hit home the third goal at the Paxton end.
Spurs' nippy right-winger Simon Davies runs through to shoot home Tottenham's fourth.	Spurs' nippy right-winger Aaron Lennon runs through to shoot home Tottenham's fourth.
The fifth goal is a tap in from a low cross, which arcs its way into the net from Rebrov.	The fifth goal is a tap in from a low cross, which arcs its way into the net from Malbranque.
Spurs go a goal down to a crap team in the final and eventually lose 2-1.	Spurs go a goal down to a good team in the final but come back to win 2-1.

6   Spurs clinched both Division One League titles with home wins over Sheffield Wednesday. On 28 April 1951, a Len Duquemin goal was enough for Spurs, while 10 years later on 17 April 1961, Bobby Smith and Les Allen combined to clinch the first part of the double for Tottenham in a 2-1 win in front of 61,205 at White Hart Lane.

7   Two Spurs managers left on 16 March in different years, both of them Scotsmen. The first was popular FA Cup-winning manager John Cameron who resigned on the date in 1907, while a wave of euphoria washed over Spurs when the less popular George Graham was escorted to the door on the fateful day in 2001.

8 Bill Nicholson's and Harry Redknapp's managerial careers had similarities in results if not trophies in the first four years in charge, as shown below.

Sir Bill	Harry
Nicholson appointed to take over a struggling Spurs side in the October of the eighth year of the decade.	Redknapp appointed to take over a struggling Spurs side in the October of the eighth year of the decade.
After a transitional season and some important summer signings, Spurs win 5-1 away in the first week of the next season on the North East coast.	After a transitional season and some important summer signings, Spurs win 5-1 away in the first week of the next season on the North East coast.
In his 43rd game in charge, he has a high-scoring home win (5-1) against a team beginning with W (Wolves), and main forward Bobby Smith scores four.	In his 43rd game in charge, he has a high-scoring home win (9-1) against a team beginning with W (Wigan), and main forward Jermain Defoe scores five.
Beats Arsenal away 3-2 in his 80th game in charge.	Beats Arsenal away 3-2 in his 82nd game in charge.
Wins his 87th League game in charge against Newcastle United and has a point-per-game record of 1.74 (retrospectively, with the present system of three points for a win).	Wins his 87th League game in charge against Newcastle United, and has a point-per-game record of 1.75.
After 115 games, Spurs win the League and FA Cup double.	After 115 games, Spurs beat QPR and are riding high in the League again, a season after a great run to the last eight of the Champions League.
Nicholson's record was: played 115; won 62; drawn 22; lost 31; he is a Tottenham legend forever.	Redknapp's record was: played 115; won 57; drawn 29; lost 29. He is seven draws more and five wins away from Billy Nick, but never a defeat or two away from 'Harry out' in this complicated modern era.

In the midwinter of the 1/2 season of the decade, Spurs break the British record transfer fee for Jimmy Greaves.

In the midwinter of the 1/2 season of the decade, Spurs get Everton reserve Louis Saha on loan.

After 144 League games, Nicholson's record was: played 144; won 77; drawn 28; lost 39.

After 144 League games, the length of Redknapp's tenure at Spurs, his record was: played 144; won 71; drawn 36; lost 37.

Spurs spirits: thirteen Spurs drinks

1 'Chivers Regal' (Martin Chivers)
2 'Cream Toda' (Kazuyuki Toda)
3 'Ginola and tonic' (David Ginola)
4 'Pienaar Colada' (Stephen Pienaar)
5 'Whyte & Mackay Whisky' (John White/Dave Mackay)
6 'Bailys Liqueur' (Eddie Baily)
7 'Brooke Bond Tea' (Gary Brooke/Dennis Bond)
8 'Noilly Pratt' (John Pratt)
9 'Lennonade' (Aaron Lennon)
10 'Grand Marneyier' (Dean Marney)
11 'Rosé Dominguez' (Jose Dominguez)
12 'JD & Coke' (Jermain Defoe)
13 'Paul Robinson's Barley Water' (self-explanatory)

And for our friends at West Ham . . . bitter lemons all round.

SPURS DATES

Everyone knows it's lucky for Spurs when the year ends in 'one', but certain days are also luckier than others for Spurs.

NINE GREAT DATES TO WATCH SPURS

1 **19 September: played 21; won 14; drawn 6; lost 1; goals for 54; goals against 24.** Statistically, this is Spurs'

best day, with the only defeat coming back in 1914. However, many of the wins are fairly unremarkable, although Ziege did score a spectacular long-range effort to set up a 2-1 win at Sunderland in the most recent of them in 2001.

2 **3 December: P19; W14; D3; L2; F53; A21.** Starting out with a 3-1 win over Woolwich Arsenal back in 1910, Spurs have won the first and most recent six fixtures on this date, perhaps the best of which was a spirited second-half comeback inspired by Sir Les to beat Bolton 3-2 in 2001.

3 **7 January: P17; W13; D3; L1; F47; A14.** A great day for Spurs, consisting mostly of FA Cup wins, including the third-round victories on the way to FA Cup glory in 1961 and 1981 against Charlton and QPR respectively. The only defeat was the shock reverse at Bradford in 1988, but perhaps the most memorable 7 January saw Graham Roberts' heroics in goal to keep a clean sheet and earn Spurs a replay at Fulham after he took over from the injured Ray Clemence.

4 **27 October: P17; W13; D2; L2; F34; A14.** Spurs have won every one of the eight matches on this date since returning to the top flight in 1978, the best of which featured Howell's brace to beat Forest 2-1 in 1990.

5 **9 October: P16; W12; D2; L2; F45; A14.** A 5-0 triumph over Chelsea in 1920, but largely League Cup wins in recent times, the most memorable of which was a tricky-looking tie at regular giant killers Tranmere a few days after the 5-3 defeat to Manchester United, but Spurs got back on track with a 4-0 win.

6 **10 January: P17; W11; D3; L3; F36; A22.** Mostly fun in the cup, although Spurs needed a Peter Taylor penalty to avoid the biggest shock of all time when non-League Altrincham left White Hart Lane with a draw in 1979.

7 **7 October: P14; W10; D3; L1; F27; A14.** One of the great days for John Pratt, with a couple against the legendary Gordon Banks helping Spurs to a 4-3 win over Stoke in 1972. The 3-0 win over Torquay in the League Cup in 1987 at least went some way to recover from the embarrassment of a 1-0 defeat in the first leg.

8 **8 March: P15; W10; D3; L2; F35; A15.** A tale of two 5-0 wins. Only 10,841 showed up for the demolition of West Brom in 1986, but around 64,800 crammed into White Hart Lane in 1961 for the FA Cup sixth round replay against Sunderland, on the way to Spurs' double glory later in the season.

9 **5 May: P17; W10; D4; L3; F30; A20.** A generally good day for Spurs, topped by retaining the FA Cup against Burnley in 1962 and the 1-0 away win at Manchester City in 2010 that clinched Champions League qualification for the first time. Not so good in 2012, when a poor draw at Villa cost Spurs the chance of securing a podium finish in the Premier League for the first time.

AND FIVE DAYS TO AVOID

Some days are unluckier . . .

1 **6 March: P18; W3; D6; L9; F16; A31.** The date that Spurs dazzled Chelsea on the way to cup glory in 1982 is more associated with some of Tottenham's darkest occasions. There cannot be many worse days than losing 0-6 at home to Arsenal, and if we add in two of the four home defeats in Europe, losing at home to Cardiff, failing to beat Plymouth and never having won a top-flight match, it becomes apparent that 6 March is not the day to watch Spurs.

2 **1 February: P18; W4; D3; L11; F21; A30.** Spurs have not won in the last eight games on this date, not since an FA Cup win against Millwall on the way to the trophy in 1967, and they've never won a top-flight fixture on the first day of February either.

3 **13 March: P17; W5; D1; L11; F24; A39.** Spurs failed to win in their first nine matches on this date, lost a League Cup final to Liverpool in 1982 and suffered a third consecutive 0-4 loss in a week in 2002.

4 **14 March: P18; W4; D3; L11; F26; A37.** Spurs won only one of their first nine games on this date, but at least had the compensation of watching Chris Waddle perform a masterclass for Sheffield Wednesday in the last defeat on this day back in 1992.

5 **7 May: P14; W2; D2; L10; F14; A30.** With players' minds no doubt on their summer holidays, Spurs have served up some shockers on this date, with seven consecutive defeats between 1966 and 2006, including the 5-0 reverse at Maine Road that confirmed relegation in 1977.

THREE OTHER NOTABLE DAYS

1. **Unbeaten on . . . 15 February: P9; W4; D5; L0; F8; A4.** The unbeaten record was given its most severe test in 2011, with a Champions League away game in the San Siro against seven times European champions AC Milan, but a late Crouch goal saw Spurs record their most impressive away win in Europe.

2. **Most draws on . . . 11 September: P18; W3; D11; L4; F31; A35.** Spurs drew eight consecutive matches on this date between 1926 and 1973, and eight of the 11 overall draws on this date were 2-2. The draw tradition was maintained in the last game on this date in 2010, when a Modric goal earned Spurs a point at the Hawthorns against West Brom.

3. **Most matches on . . . 26 December: P74; W31; D19; L-24; F132; A102.** Despite the old song, Spurs have only played Arsenal three times on Boxing Day and lost each time. At eight matches, West Ham are the most frequent opponents, and more often than not they entered into the giving spirit of Christmastime.

TWELVE ICONIC SPURS OBJECTS

1. THE SPURS COCKEREL

The Spurs cockerel on a ball is quite simply the club's most iconic object. Standing nearly 10 feet tall, it was built by former Spurs player and coppersmith William J. Scott and set atop the mock-Tudor gable of the West Stand in November 1909. It remained in place, aside from a cleaning in 1934, through two world wars and the 'push and run' League title until 1957, when the new floodlights meant it had to come down. After a year's absence, it reappeared on the East Stand and oversaw the majestic reigns of Bill Nicholson and Keith Burkinshaw until the stand was redeveloped in 1989. Now retired from the elements, the celebrated centenarian statue now greets visitors in the reception area of White Hart Lane.

2. THE FLAG OVER THE TUNNEL

Before the old West Stand was demolished in 1980, some of the greatest players in the history of the club emerged from the tunnel under a navy blue banner that had 'Up the Spurs' written on it in big white letters.

3. THE DAVE MACKAY/BILLY BREMNER PHOTO

Dave Mackay had just come back from a second broken leg and did not take kindly to fellow Scot Billy Bremner trying to damage it again. The iconic photo perfectly captures the moment, with a snarling Mackay grabbing the pleading Bremner's shirt, and symbolises the sometimes-forgotten steel that has always gone with the great skill of Spurs.

4. #WWWWDWWWWWW

After losing the opening two games of the 2011/12 season 8-1 on aggregate, Spurs embarked on a remarkable run over the next 11 games. As the run grew, fans on Twitter started to use the sequence as a hashtag to celebrate the emergence of Spurs again at the top table of English football.

5. RIBBONS FROM THE 1901 FA CUP WIN

The tradition of putting ribbons in the winning team's colours on the FA Cup stems from Spurs' win in 1901, when a wife of one of the directors thought it a good idea to adorn the cup in this fashion.

6. ORIGINAL SPURS SHARE CERTIFICATE

Spurs were ahead of the game when they became the first club to be floated as a company on the London Stock Exchange in 1983. Like most things from the era, it was a decent idea that was badly implemented, and others looked, learned and did it all a whole lot better.

7. GÓRNIK ZABRZE COAL TRUCK

The new European Cup was a magical event for both players and fans, with games under floodlights against mysterious continental opponents. They also had a tradition of exchanging gifts before the match: Spurs always present our opponents with a silver cockerel, and in return our visitors from a Polish coal-mining area offered a small black coal truck with 'Zabrze' written on the side, a wonderful memento of a special night.

8. GROSS TRAIN TICKET

Spurs were in a mess and eyebrows were raised when Alan Sugar recruited top Swiss coach – a footballing oxymoron – Christian Gross to save the season. In the press conference, Gross produced his train ticket from the airport and announced it was his ticket to glory. A tumbleweed moment that destroyed what little credibility he had, before more ridicule was unloaded on an already-suffering Spurs.

9. THE SPURS SUPPORTERS CLUB BADGE

The Spurs supporters club produce a simple oval badge featuring a cockerel on a ball on a navy blue background, for new members. A simple design classic.

10. KLINSMANN'S SHIRT

There was plenty of embarrassment for Spurs during the Sugar years, but not much could top the chairman appearing on TV saying he wouldn't use Klinsmann's shirt to wash his car after the German's departure. Crass and embarrassing at the time, it had a wonderful twist when Sugar then re-signed Klinsmann for a second stint at Spurs a few years later.

11. 'COLONEL BURGERS'

No trip to White Hart Lane is complete without a visit to the burger van at the back of the Paxton end and hearing the owner in full flow selling his wares. To be addressed with one of his catchphrases – 'Onions wiv that Colonel?', 'Haaaaaave a looooook at thaaaat, handsome!' – is a modern 'I was there' moment.

12. THE RIVALDO LETTER

With Spurs struggling to land a big name after the 2002 World Cup, someone at the PR excuses department thought it would be a good idea to tell the press that although Spurs had failed to sign the Brazillian Rivaldo, he was impressed enough to write a letter of appreciation to the club. An epic fail.

The Spurs days of Christmas

12-yard hero Tony Parks in 1984.

11 wins at the start of the 1960/61 double season.

10 players poisoned before facing West Ham in 2006.

9 against Wigan, Bristol Rovers, Keflavik, Forest, Tranmere and Port Vale.

8 games and only two points when Harry Redknapp took over in 2008. Triffic!

7 consecutive FA Cup semi-finals won between 1961 and 1991.

6 *years of Arthur Rowe and 'push and run'.*

5 *gold forwards in Ossie's 'famous five'.*

4 *League Cup final wins.*

3 *European trophies.*

2 *League titles*

And a cartilage injury to Paul Gascoigne in the final.

A FEW MEMORABLE SENDINGS-OFF OVER THE YEARS

Playing in the white shirts of the good guys, Spurs don't have too many villains. But there have been a few memorable sendings-off over the years.

1. FIRST SENDING-OFF

Spurs' first recorded sending-off was Joe Walton in a 1-1 draw with Brighton and Hove Albion in the Southern League in 1904.

2. SPURS' FIRST EUROPE SENDING-OFF

Jimmy Greaves was Spurs' first player to be sent off in Europe under murky circumstances in a Cup Winners' Cup semi-final in Belgrade. As he trudged off the pitch protesting the injustice, he was greeted by Spurs trainer Cecil Poynton, who by a strange twist of fate had been the previous Spurs player to be sent off, 12,597 days (or $34\frac{1}{2}$ years) before in 1928 against Stoke City.

3. ALWAYS LIKELY

Johnny Blair only played 30 times for Spurs in the mid-1920s, but remarkably he picked up two red cards in that time, which must have taken some doing given the more lenient rules of the era. These days, almost any player can get sent off for a whole range of real and imagined offences, but one who would have collected red cards in any age was Ramon Vega. He started as he meant to go on by getting his marching orders on his debut against Forest, and collected a couple more before his Spurs career was cut short by chronic lack of ability.

4. SPURS' FIRST FA CUP SENDING-OFF

Future Wimbledon boss Joe Kinnear became the first Spurs player to see red in an FA Cup game as Tottenham overcame European champions-elect Manchester United in a pulsating cup tie at White Hart Lane in 1968. It would be 30 years before Spurs' next red card in the competition, with Stephen Clemence walking in a rather less memorable tie with Barnsley.

5. ALAN MULLERY

In an explosive incident against Lyon in 1967, Mullers was kicked in the face and knocked unconscious by Lyon player André Guy. As the Spurs players converged to help the stricken player, a full-scale free-for-all occurred that also included Lyon supporters who'd taken part in a pitch invasion. At the end of the mêlée, a cowardly bit of refereeing saw both aggressor and blood-spattered victim sent off.

6. SPURS' FIRST RED CARD IN THE LEAGUE CUP

The sight of West Ham gloating about 'winning the World Cup for England' was probably enough to make Alan Gilzean see red in Spurs' first ever League Cup game in September 1966.

7. GOALKEEPERS

Gilzean's fellow 'Scotsman' Neil Sullivan became the first goalkeeper to be sent off against Brentford in the League Cup in 2000. For good measure, Sully was also the first Spurs keeper to be dismissed in a League game a few months later when taking out Newcastle United's Kieron Dyer, who coincidentally also saw red later in the game.

8. SPURS CONNECTIONS

Tony Galvin (on the wing) and West Brom's Spurs-manager-to-be Martin Jol were sent off for a bit of heavyweight argy-bargy in a tense League Cup semi-final at the Hawthorns in 1982.

9. CUP FINAL RED CARD

Justin Edinburgh is the only Spurs player to have been sent off in a major final, when he fell victim to Robbie Savage's snide tricks midway through the second half of the 1999 League Cup showdown. This served to spur the team on, and justice was done with Allan Nielsen's last-minute winner for Spurs.

10. GRAHAM ROBERTS

Robbo had the reputation of 1980s hardman, but also had the bizarre experience of being sent off on a stretcher after being 'done' by Wimbledon's Lawrie Sanchez in a bad-tempered League game against everyone's least favourite team in 1984.

11. SPURS' FIRST PREMIER LEAGUE SENDING-OFF

Neil Ruddock was Tottenham's first sending-off in the Premier League era, leaving the field against Palace in 1992 after some typical thoughtless bravado.

12. DOWN TO NINE MEN

When Pat Van Den Hauwe followed Nayim for an early bath in the League game against Luton in December 1990, things looked particularly bleak – both in the game and the season as a whole, which was falling away after a bright start. However, the enforced tactical reshuffle was to prove the turning point of the season and Paul Stewart's Spurs career. Brought back from a lumbering forward role without many goals, Stewart was a revelation in central midfield and he scored twice in the game for a 2-1 win.

EIGHT FA CUP SEMI-FINAL INJUSTICES

Spurs have a great cup record, but it could have been even better without some dodgy decisions in semi finals.

1 FA Cup SF (Hillsborough), 1922. **Spurs 1-2 Preston North End** *(Seed)*. With the score at 1-1, Bert Bliss scored a goal for Spurs that would have probably won the game but the referee had stopped play earlier in the build-up for treatment of an injured Preston player. What should have been a 2-1 win for Spurs went the other way when Preston scored a late winner.

2 FA Cup SF (Villa Park), 1956. **Spurs 0-1 Manchester City.** With Spurs trailing 1-0 into the closing stages, City goalkeeper Bert Trautmann – who would later enter legend by playing through the final with a broken neck – took out George Robb as he was about to score. But the officials managed to avoid giving an obvious penalty and Spurs were done for.

3 FA Cup SF (Wembley), 1993. **Spurs 0-1 Arsenal**. After about 20 minutes, Anderton was taken down just inside the box, deserving a penalty and a red card for the offending Arsenal player. The referee saw things differently and gave Spurs a free kick outside the box, also allowing Andy Linighan to stay on the pitch. Arsenal toughed it out with 11 men and nicked it near the end.

4 FA Cup SF (Elland Road), 1995. **Spurs 1-4 Everton** *(Klinsmann (pen))*. Spurs had the injustice of having to play Stuart Nethercott against Anders Limpar, and the great run of cup wins – in the season that Spurs had originally been banned from the competition – counted for nothing.

5 FA Cup SF (Old Trafford), 1999. **Spurs 0-2 Newcastle United (aet).** Spurs put up a good showing and looked set to return to the old Wembley for the second time in a few

weeks when the big hairy arm of Newcastle defender Dabizas clearly handled a cross. Referee Durkin managed to miss it and Shearer put Spurs away in an extra time that shouldn't have been required.

6 FA Cup SF (Wembley), 2010. **Spurs 0-2 Portsmouth.** A desperate performance on a desperate new Wembley pitch could have been salvaged had the referee not disallowed a Peter Crouch goal for some obscure pushing offence by Krancjar.

7 FA Cup SF (Wembley), 2012. **Spurs 1-5 Chelsea** *(Bale).* After an upturn in League form on the back of some dodgy refereeing, Chelsea were once again given a helping hand in the form of a 'goal' awarded during a scramble where the ball wasn't within a foot of the goal line, let alone over it.

And one more, although it did not deny Spurs glory as we won the replay . . .

8 FA Cup SF (Hillsborough) 1981. **Spurs 2-2 Wolves (aet)** *(Archibald, Hoddle).* A trademark Glenn Hoddle free kick looked to have won the game for Spurs until a fair but ungainly tackle by the same player saw Kenny Hibbitt con the referee, Clive Thomas, with an obvious dive, and this enabled Wolves to snatch a late equaliser.

TEN SPRING COLLAPSES

With Spurs in a good position as the days get longer, a collapse is still more likely than glory. Here are ten examples of Spurs throwing away strong League positions through a collapse that begins around the start of March.

1 **1956/57:** Only one win in eight in the League after the FA Cup fifth-round shocker at Bournemouth sees Jimmy Anderson's team drop the title pace, before rallying to finish runners-up.

2 **1959/60:** Only one win in seven, including four defeats from the middle of March, sees Spurs give up a three-point lead in

the title race. The season was still sufficient warm-up for the double the following year, though that also had its only consecutive defeats at the start of March.

3 **1961/62:** Five games without a win from the end of February, including the infamous 1-3 home defeat to eventual champions Ipswich Town, put an end to a double double as the title passes from Nicholson to Ramsey, former teammates in the 'push and run' championship.

4 **1962/63:** Four games without a win from the end of March see Spurs blow a three-point lead at the top of the table before eventually finishing runners-up to Everton.

5 **1963/64:** Three consecutive home defeats and four defeats in five from the start of March see Spurs blow a four-point lead at the top of the table to go fourth and five points adrift by the start of April under Bill Nicholson.

6 **1977/78:** Only two 1-0 wins from the last eight games cost Spurs the Second Division title, but fortunately not promotion.

7 **1984/85:** Four consecutive home defeats starting in March quash Spurs' title hopes under Shreeves.

8 **1999/2000:** Four defeats in five from mid-March to mid-April ended hopes of UEFA qualification under Graham.

9 **2010/11:** On 22 February, Spurs lost 1-3 to soon-to-be-relegated Blackpool, a week after beating AC Milan in the San Siro. This started a slump of one win in 10, and missing out on Champions League requalification.

10 **2011/12:** From 2-0 up after 40 minutes at Highbury on 25 February, Spurs' season went into reverse, with five defeats in nine to end League title and ultimately Champions League hopes under Redknapp.

Eleven opponents with strange names

1 *Nondescripts (1887); 6-1 (unknown scorers)*
2 *Robin Hood (1890); 1-0 (unknown scorer)*
3 *Vulcan (1890); 2-1(Buckle, Bassett)*
4 *Orion Gymnasium (1891); 7-1 (unknown scorers)*
5 *Vampires (1895); 2-1 (Hunter, Pryor)*
6 *The Kaffirs (1899); 6-4 (Kirwan (2), Melia, Raby
    (2), Stormont)*
7 *Testgyakorborora (1905); 12-1 (Bull, Stansfield,
    Cameron, Woodward (4), Glen (2), O'Hagan (3))*
8 *Music Hall Artists (1914); 3-2 (Banks, Cantrell,
    Bliss)*
9 *Syrian Police (1981); 4-0 (Holmes, Falco, Taylor (2))*
10 *Stjørdals (1984); 9-0 (Kempes (3), Falco, Galvin,
    Hoddle, Ardiles, Crooks, og)*
11 *Arsenal . . . no stranger name than that of a team
    named after an orifice.*

CAN WE PLAY YOU EVERY WEEK?
SIX OF THE BEST OPPONENTS

Despite Spurs' own legendary inconsistency, they have a positive record against most sides. But there are always some teams who make the Lilywhites shine.

1. MILLWALL

While the fans have a fearsome reputation, its a pity Spurs don't play Millwall more often in competitive fixtures as they have a spectacularly good record against them. In Millwall's last flirtation with the top flight, Spurs won home and away both seasons, including a 5-0 win at the old Den. You have to go back to 1939 for Millwall's last win, which preceded a run of seven straight Spurs wins.

Spurs v Millwall

Games	P	W	D	L	F	A
Total	26	20	4	2	59	26
Home	14	12	2	0	32	12
Away	12	8	2	2	27	14

2. FULHAM

Across London, Spurs have a similarly impressive record against Fulham, who share with Stoke the distinction of being the side against whom Spurs have the greatest ratio of wins to defeats. Spurs' doldrums in the early noughties weakened this record, but Fulham are usually very welcome opponents when a win is needed, including when rolling over 4-0 in the FA Cup to save Martin Jol's job in 2007 and on the final day of the season in 2012 when the big Dutchman was in the other dug-out.

Spurs v Fulham

Games	P	W	D	L	F	A
Total	76	38	26	12	126	80
Home	37	23	12	2	67	28
Away	39	15	14	10	59	52

3. MANCHESTER CITY

In all competitions since the start of the Premier League in 1992, Spurs have won 23 of their 36 games against Man City, up to and including the Champions League play-off encounter in 2010. The perfect season was 1992/93 where Spurs won home and away in the League and also dumped City out of both cups at Maine Road.

Spurs v Manchester City

Premier League-era games	P	W	D	L	F	A
Total	36	23	6	7	57	39
Home	17	11	3	3	28	20
Away	19	12	3	4	29	19

Given the 5-1 reverse at the start of the 2011/12 season and all the new money, things may be about to change for the worse in this relationship, but it was fantastic while it lasted.

4. EVERTON

Everton are another favourite from the Premier League era. However, the pattern here is more one of home wins and away draws, but seven defeats in 41 matches tell their own story of Spurs' modern dominance.

Spurs v Everton

Premier League-era games	P	W	D	L	F	A
Total	41	20	14	7	62	44
Home	21	13	5	3	41	24
Away	19	7	9	3	20	16
Neutral	1	0	0	1	1	4

The impressive record makes it all the more baffling that Spurs played so badly and lost 4-1 to Everton in a FA Cup semi-final in 1995, when the stage had been set for Jürgen Klinsmann to reach Wembley and pick up some silverware.

5. SOUTHAMPTON

Spurs v Southampton

Games	P	W	D	L	F	A
Total	109	45	28	36	187	137
Home	53	32	11	10	130	58
Away	55	13	17	25	56	77

Spurs' overall record against Southampton is pretty decent: when it comes to handing out a hammering the Saints are top of the list. Spurs have scored five or more on 12 occasions against Southampton over the years, including in the last home game back in 2004 (see box below).

Saints Spankings

1 Div 2, Sept 1931; **Spurs 5-2 Southampton**
   (Meades (2), Brain, O'Callaghan, Bellamy)

2 Div 2, Oct 1932; **Spurs 5-0 Southampton**
   (O'Callaghan (3), Hunt GS, Evans W)

3 Div 2, Mar 1936; **Spurs 8-0 Southampton**
   (Meek (3), Hunt GS (3, 1pen), Evans W (2))

4 Div 2, Apr 1938; **Spurs 5-0 Southampton**
   (Ward (pen), Sargent, Morrison (3))

5 Div 1, Nov 1966; **Spurs 5-3 Southampton**
   (Mullery, Mackay, Greaves (pen), Jones (2))

6 Div 1, Apr 1968; **Spurs 6-1 Southampton**
   *(Mullery, Greaves (2, 1pen), Chivers, Jones,
   Hollywood og)*

7 Div 1, Sept 1982; **Spurs 6-0 Southampton**
   (Brooke (pen), Perryman, Galvin (2), Villa, Crooks)

8 Div 1, Mar 1985; **Spurs 5-1 Southampton**
   (Ardiles, Falco, Hoddle, Crooks, Brooke)

9 Div 1, May 1986; **Spurs 5-3 Southampton**
   (Galvin (3), Allen C, Waddle)

10 FA Cup fifth round replay, Mar 1995;
   Southampton 2-6 Spurs (aet) *(Rosenthal (3),
   Sheringham, Barmby, Anderton)*

11 Premier League, Mar 2000; **Spurs 7-2
   Southampton** *(Richards og, Anderton, Armstrong (2),
   Iversen (3))*

12 Premier League, Dec 2004; **Spurs 5-1
   Southampton** *(Defoe (3), Kanoute, Keane)*

6. NOTTS FOREST

Spurs have struggled a bit against Forest in the Premier League
era, but overall it's been a very good fixture for Tottenham.
During the Bill Nick era, Spurs won 19 of the 28 games
between the teams, including 9-2 and 6-1 home wins and a
successful FA Cup semi-final.

Spurs v Notts Forest

Games	P	W	D	L	F	A
Total	119	54	30	35	196	157
Home	59	32	9	18	114	77
Away	58	20	21	17	78	78
Neutral	2	2	0	0	4	2

THE SPURS BOGEYMEN

1. THE 'SKY 4'

Spurs don't really have a bogey team but a bogey alliance. The teams that have dominated the Premier League era – Arsenal, Manchester United and Chelsea, along with modern-day also-rans Liverpool, collectively known as 'the Sky 4' – have made Spurs' life a misery since the inception of the new competition in 1992. To some extent, Redknapp stemmed the tide with wins against all bar United, but from 1992 to 2008, the numbers make horrific reading, especially away from home.

Spurs v 'Sky 4' away, 1992/93–2007/08

Spurs away at ...	P	W	D	L	F	A	Average points per game
Arsenal	16	1	6	9	11	24	0.563
Chelsea	16	0	5	11	10	31	0.313
Liverpool	16	1	5	10	14	33	0.500
Man United	16	0	3	13	5	29	0.188
Total	64	2	19	43	40	117	0.391

A sum total of two wins in 64 fixtures away from White Hart Lane over this period is little short of pathetic, especially as both victories were back in 1993 and one of them was against an Arsenal team who, like Spurs, had rested several key players for an FA Cup final they fluked their way into at Spurs' expense. When your team only scores five goals in 16 visits to Old Trafford, it is even perplexing that one of them is actually booed by a large number of Spurs supporters. The goal in question was Sir Les' opener in 1999, which momentarily put Arsenal ahead of United in the table on the last day of the Premier

League season. They may as well have enjoyed it, as Spurs meekly gave way afterwards for the usual defeat.

Spurs' miserable run against Chelsea since the start of the Premier League is all the more startling given what went before. In the old Division One, Spurs achieved 19 away wins to Chelsea's 17 home wins at the old Stamford Bridge. However, Tottenham's away record at Liverpool has always been dreadful. In a sequence that started just before the *Titanic* sank and spanned two world wars, Spurs failed to win in 43 matches, with two of the 28 defeats being record losses at the time, with seven goals conceded. The irony is that Spurs had won the previous two games up there before 1912.

The White Hart Lane results are nothing to write home about either.

Spurs v 'Sky 4' home, 1992/93–2007/08

Spurs home v ...	P	W	D	L	F	A	Average points per game
Arsenal	16	4	8	4	21	23	1.250
Chelsea	16	1	6	9	15	31	0.563
Liverpool	16	6	5	5	20	21	1.438
Man Utd	16	3	3	10	20	29	0.750
Total	64	14	22	28	76	104	1.000

2. MIDDLESBROUGH

Spurs have a positive record against most clubs outside the elite, so it is surprising that they have such poor form against a side that have just one League Cup to show for 100-plus years of football.

Spurs v Middlesbrough

Games	P	W	D	L	F	A
Total	80	27	20	33	124	137
Home	40	21	9	10	83	60
Away	40	6	11	23	41	77

194 • THE GLORY OF SPURS

The poor record is fairly consistent over time and especially bad away from home, with only six wins in 40 games. This would lend some weight to the 'southern softies' cliché if it weren't for Spurs relatively decent record at both Sunderland and Newcastle over the years, and must just be one of life's mysteries.

3. HOME SLIP-UPS

One of the great fascinations with Spurs is how they can be brilliant one week and rubbish the next. How many times has a brilliant away win been followed by a home draw (or worse) against some rubbish outfit? The classic teams to carry this off are little clubs which the Spurs supporters, and all too often the players, assume are just there to make up the numbers. While Coventry and Palace have had their moments, Leicester and Charlton are the classic examples of this phenomenon.

Spurs v Leicester City

Games	P	W	D	L	F	A
Total	88	41	17	30	166	149
Home	44	19	11	14	90	66
Away	44	22	6	16	76	83

Even in the double season, Spurs followed up an away win at Filbert Street with a 2-3 home defeat later in the glorious season. The same thing happened the subsequent season and again on a regular basis up to 1999/2000, when a Ginola winner up there compensated for another 2-3 home defeat. It also happened to the 'push and run' team while winning Division Two in 1950, when an early season away win was followed by a home defeat. It is the classic Leicester pattern, and Spurs teams from every era seem to repeat it.

Spurs v Charlton Athletic

Games	P	W	D	L	F	A
Total	50	25	9	16	96	62
Home	25	12	5	8	51	30
Away	25	13	4	8	45	32

It's always quite easy to underestimate a side whose fans applaud the other team, and after winning 3-0 at the Valley on Christmas Day in 1951, it was very Spurs to lose 3-2 at home the very next day to the same side. For good measure, Spurs repeated the pattern in consecutive seasons between 1954 and 1956, and after an absence in fixtures, again in 2003/04.

SIXTY CELEBRITY SPURS

Here are some celebrities, who may or may not be Spurs fans:

1 Neil Pearson, star of *Drop the Dead Donkey*

2 Matthew Horne, *Gavin and Stacey* star

3 Trigger from *Only Fools and Horses*, also known as Roger Lloyd-Pack

4 Norman Jay, cool DJ

5 Simon Mayo, not so cool DJ

6 Chas 'n' Dave, rockney musicians

7 Jude Law, actor

8 Warren Mitchell, actor

9 Phil Cornwell, *Stella Street* comedian

10 Peter Cook, wit

11 Paul Whitehouse, comedian

12 The other Dean Martin, Capital Gold DJ

13 Bennie from *Grange Hill*

14 Mark Billingham, crime author

15 Richard Littlejohn, unreconstructed media type

16 Chris Acland, drummer in Lush/Lillies

17 Becky Anderson, CNN presenter

18 Adele, Tottenham-born singing sensation

19 Charlie Whelan, Labour chap

20 Derek 'Do they mean us?' Jameson

21 Linda Lusardi, 1980s glamour star

22 Tony Butler, Big Country bass player

23 Rachel Stevens, pop singer

24 Stephen Mangan, actor

25 Stelios Haji-Ioannou, founder of EasyJet

26 David Nobbs, author of *Reggie Perrin*

27 Natasha, 1980s pop sensation

28 Shaznay Lewis, the talented one in All Saints

29 Baby Spice, from the Spice Girls

30 Brandon Block, celebrated DJ

31 David Aaronovitch, journalist

32 Captain Mark Phillips, royalty

33 Paul Young, 1980s crooner

34 Kenneth Branagh, actor and former Mr Helena Bonham-Carter

35 Jo Whiley, Radio One DJ and presenter

36 Bob Marley, reggae legend

37 A.J. Ayer, logical positivist philosopher

38 Bernie Winters and Schnorbitz, comedian and dog

39 Frankie Vaughan, entertainer

40 Salman Rushdie, author

41 Bernard Bresslaw, *Carry On* star

42 Barry Dennis, bookie and pundit

43 Gary Olsen, actor

44 Luke Donald, golfer

45 Rikki Clarke, cricketer

46 Steven Severin, Siouxsie & the Banshees' bassist

47 Paul Hawksby, Talksport bloke

48 Darren Day, former popular entertainer

49 Colin Buchanan, actor

50 Henry Kelly, *Going for Gold* frontman

51 Wiley, rapper

52 Barry Norman, film guru

53 Andrew Ridgeley, the underrated one from Wham!

54 Dave Clark, of the Dave Clark Five

55 Iain Duncan-Smith, former Tory leader

56 Patsy Kensit, actress/singer

57 Julie Harris, singer with 1980s one-hit wonders Tight Fit

58 Ray Liotta, *Goodfellas* actor

59 Dave Barbarossa, drummer with 1980s band Bow Wow Wow

60 And finally . . . Trevor MacDonald, newsreader

ELEVEN SPURS MANAGERS WHO LEFT AFTER A WIN

1. JOHN CAMERON

Southern League, 16 Mar 1907; **Spurs 2-0 New Brompton** *(Walton, Reid)*

Like fellow Scot George Graham, Cameron's resignation meant he left the club on 16 March; but unlike Graham, Cameron's reign is remembered fondly, including Spurs' first championship in the Southern League in 1900 and the famous FA Cup win as a non-League side a season later.

2. PETER MCWILLIAM

War League, 2 May 1942; **Spurs 7-1 Fulham** *(Broadis, Gibbons (2), Stevens (2), Ludford (2))*

McWilliam's second spell concluded after this wide-margin win when he announced his retirement over the subsequent summer, having managed Spurs in over 750 matches in major competitions.

3. ARTHUR TURNER

League South, 26 Jan 1946; **Spurs 2-0 Coventry City** *(Burgess, Whitchurch)*

Although never officially acknowledged as Spurs manager, Turner was a club stalwart who performed a variety of roles during his 50-year stint at Tottenham, which included looking after the first team during World War II after Peter McWilliam's retirement. It was fitting that this ended in a win before Joe Hulme was appointed at the resumption of the Football League.

4. KEITH BURKINSHAW

UEFA Cup final second leg, 25 May 1984; **Spurs 1-1 Anderlecht** *(Roberts)*. **Spurs won 4-3 on penalties.**

Although technically a draw, Burkinshaw's decision earlier in the year to quit the club at the end of the season meant that he bowed out on a night of European glory.

5. PETER SHREEVE

Div 1, 26 Apr 1986; **Queens Park Rangers 2-5 Spurs** *(Falco (2), Allen C (2), Hoddle)*

Div 1, 3 May 1986; **Spurs 4-2 Aston Villa** *(Falco (2), Allen C (2))*

Div 1, 5 May 1986; **Spurs 5-3 Southampton** *(Galvin (3), Allen C, Waddle)*

Fourteen goals scored in three wins, part of a run of eight wins in 12 games, tell one story; but crowds of 14,854 and 13,036 in the last two home games tell another, and the cabbie had to flick up his 'for hire' sign at the end of the season as Spurs appointed David Pleat.

6. DOUG LIVERMORE AND RAY CLEMENCE

Premier League, 11 May 1993; **Arsenal 1-3 Spurs** *(Sheringham, Hendry (2))*

Considering this was one of only four away wins at Arsenal in the 34 years since promotion, the front-seat passengers to Venables' back-seat driving can consider themselves a bit unlucky. However, boardroom changes meant managerial changes were inevitable.

7. OSSIE ARDILES

Premier League, 29 Oct 1994; **Spurs 3-1 West Ham United** *(Klinsmann, Sheringham, Barmby)*

Sugar bided his time after bad defeats to Watford, Manchester City and Notts County to wait until Spurs were back on track against West Ham before he pulled the plug on Ossie. The soon to be rescinded 12-point deduction and FA Cup ban made things look worse than they actually were for the fledgling 'famous five' side.

8. CHRISTIAN GROSS

Premier League, 29 Aug 1998; **Everton 0-1 Spurs** *(Ferdinand)*

The man with a train ticket started and ended his Spurs career with away wins at Everton.

9. DAVID PLEAT

Premier League, 3 Oct 1998; **Derby County 0-1 Spurs** *(Campbell)*

Premier League, 15 May 2004; **Wolves 0-2 Spurs** *(Keane, Defoe)*

Pleat recorded wins in the last games in two of the three care-taker spells he got in his role as director of football, but it was never enough for him to be considered for the main job again.

10. GEORGE GRAHAM

FA Cup sixth round, 11 Mar 2001; **West Ham United 2-3 Spurs** *(Rebrov (2), Doherty)*

The fantastic cup win at West Ham turned out to be Gunner Graham's last game in charge, which would have made it a double celebration had the fans known at the time.

11. HARRY REDKNAPP

Premier League, 13 May 2012; **Spurs 2-0 Fulham** *(Adebayor, Defoe)*

Fourth place is a sackable offence for Spurs managers these days.

NINE PEOPLE NOT ON HARRY REDKNAPP'S CHRISTMAS CARD LIST

1 **Mario Gómez:** Redknapp could have wished Gómez had played as he did for Germany in Euro 2012 in the Champions League final for Bayern Munich to beat Chelsea.

2 **Robin van Persie:** If only van Persie's atrocious finishing for the Dutch in Euro 2012 had been the same while carrying the rest of the Arsenal team in the Premier League in 2011/12.

3 **Marton Fulop:** A very strange late replacement for normal WBA keeper had a total shocker against Arsenal, gifting the visitors three decisive goals to upset Spurs' Champions League push.

4 **Martin Atkinson:** Managed to award Chelsea a goal in the FA Cup semi-final that was nowhere near the line.

5 **The FA:** If they had no intention of appointing Redknapp, Brooking *et al.* could have announced it in February rather than April and not led the Spurs manager on.

6 **Rob Palmer:** Sky Sports interviewer who now knows that Redknapp is not a 'wheeler-dealer' but a successful football manager.

7 **Heurelho Gomes:** A shocker in the Bernabéu ended Spurs' thrilling Champions League campaign in 2011.

8 **Jermain Defoe:** With the score at 2-2 in the last minute against eventual champions Manchester City, all Defoe needed to do was slide in for the winning goal for Spurs. He failed, as did Tottenham.

9 **Daniel Levy:** Redknapp rescued Spurs from a start that had seen them earn two points in eight games under Levy's man Ramos, only to be bounced out of the club after nearly four years of constant high achievement.

TWELVE CHINESE YEARS OF THE COCKEREL

1 **1885:** Hotspur FC is renamed Tottenham Hotspur and they win their first competitive match 5-2 against St Albans in the London Association Cup.

2 **1897:** Spurs reach their first cup final, albeit only the Wellingborough Charity Cup, and lose the final 2-0 to the eponymous hosts.

3 **1909:** A draw in the last game of the 1908/09 season is enough to get Spurs promoted to the top flight at the end of their first season in the Football League.

4 **1921:** Spurs beat Wolves 1-0 in the 'Jinking Jimmy Dimmock' FA Cup final to win the first major trophy as a League club.

5 **1933:** The golden year of the Percy Smith reign, with promotion in 1932/33 and a third-place finish in 1933/34. The magic of the cockerel soon wore off, however, and Spurs were relegated the following season.

6 **1945:** Ten consecutive Southern League victories from the start of 1945 see Spurs crowned champions three days before VE day.

7 **1957:** Spurs push the star-studded pre-Munich Manchester United side all the way, and eventually finish runners up in League Division One.

8 **1969:** Club legend Steve Perryman makes his debut. As does John Pratt.

9 **1981:** Spurs win the 100th FA Cup final with the greatest goal in the greatest final in the history of the greatest cup competition in the world, cementing their place as 'Cup Kings'.

10 **1993:** Alan Sugar wrestles sole control of the club from Terry Venables and Spurs were assured a bright future under his visionary and talented leadership.

11 **2005:** Martin Jol completes his first full year as manager with Spurs sitting in fourth at the end of 2005, and about to push on to qualify for Europe via the League for the first time in a generation.

12 **2017:** Spurs complete Premier League and Champions League double for the third consecutive season, and round it off by winning the World Club Cup . . .

NINE EPISODES IN THE SECRET HISTORY OF THE WOOLWICH WANDERERS

1 As Dial Square, the formative Arsenal reportedly played their first game with an open sewer running through the middle of the pitch. The stench remains an integral part of their brand to this day.

2 With Spurs cantering to a 2-1 hammering of their opponents when the two clubs first met in 1887, Arsenal somehow managed to get the game abandoned with 15 minutes to play to avoid defeat. The first of many sneaky tricks played on the footballing connoisseurs of Spurs.

3 Under the snide guidance of Henry Norris, and despite the protests, Arsenal rocked up from South-East London in 1913 to sit uncomfortably close to proper North London sides Spurs and Orient.

4 When football was suspended because of World War I in 1915, Chelsea and Spurs had finished in the bottom two of the First Division, with Arsenal a modest sixth in Division Two. As the League planned to expand by two teams, precedent dictated that there would be no relegation and the top two teams of Division Two would be added to the top flight to create the expanded division. Henry Norris had other ideas and engendered some funny goings-on at the Football League meeting in March 1919, which saw Arsenal take Spurs' place in the enlarged Division One. To this day, Arsenal have never won an honest promotion.

5 Spurs had toured Argentina and Uruguay in 1909, and on the boat journey back, the parrot used by some of the players in a fancy dress competition was presented as a gift to the club by the captain. The bird lived a long and happy life in N17 until it fell off its perch and died on the very day of Arsenal's 'promotion' and Spurs' relegation in 1919. It has been suggested in some quarters that this was the origin of the phrase 'as sick as a parrot'.

6 The murky arts of Henry Norris were at work yet again as one of the three consecutive 'Road' stations on the Piccadilly Line was inexplicably renamed from 'Gillespie Road' to 'Arsenal' less than 10 years after their unwelcome intrusion north of the river. Chaos ensues for generations to come as most of the tiled signs retain the old name and people seeking the Woolwich Armoury end up drinking skinny lattes in Islington.

7 It has been alleged that lilywhite was introduced to the Arsenal kit on the sleeves and collars during the managerial reign of ex-Spurs player Herbert Chapman in the 1920s, to appease his conscience for having to work with such rotters.

8 Over the years, generations of Arsenal players have engaged in all sorts of dodgy activity and it was a pity that some of these did not make it on to the recently redesigned club crest, along with the Latin word for 'offside'.

9 While Spurs attract a wide range of cool and savvy celebrities, Arsenal can count on Jamie Oliver, Reg Hollis from *The Bill* and Sonia from *EastEnders* among their band of glory-hunters in the sponsored silence of the Emirates stadium.

The Spurs hit parade: top twenty

1 *'Ossie's Dream': Chas 'n' Dave and Spurs cup final squad (1981)*

2 *'And David Seaman will be very disappointed about that': The Lillies (1991)*

3 *'McNamara's Band': The Evergreens (1960s)*

4 *'Nice One Cyril': Cockerel Chorus (1973)*

5 *'The Victory Song': Chas 'n' Dave (1991)*

6 *'Can't Smile Without You': Barry Manilow (1978)*

7 *'Tip Top Tottenham Hotspur': The Totnamites (1961)*

8 *'Stand by me': Andros Townsend and the younger squad (2011/12)*

9 'What do you want to make those eyes at me for?': Terry
   Venables (1974)
10 'Tottenham Tottenham': Chas 'n' Dave and Spurs cup
   final squad (1982)
11 'Inspurations': uncredited (1990s)
12 'Hot Shot Tottenham': Chas 'n' Dave and Spurs cup
   final squad (1987)
13 'Glory Glory Hallelujah': 1967 squad
14 'Tribute to Ardiles and Villa': Amigos O'Lane
15 'It's lucky when the year ends in "one"': Chas 'n' Dave
   and Spurs cup final squad (1991)
16 'Hotspurs Boogie': Spurs squad (1973)
17 'Strolling': Jimmy Greaves (1967)
18 'Diamond Lights': Glenn and Chris (1987)
19 'Up the Spurs': The Cheers (1970s)
20 'Ooh Gary Gary': Her (early 1990s)

And not forgetting the 1981 Christmas stocking-filler The
Tottenham Hotspur Party Album.

SIX OF THE BEST SPURS READS IN OLD AND NEW MEDIA

THE BOOKS

1 *Spurs: Day-to-Day Life at White Hart Lane*, Graham Betts

2 *The Boys From White Hart Lane*, Martin Cloake and Adam
   Powley

3 *The Glory Game*, Hunter Davies

4 *The Great Divide*, Alex Fynn and Olivia Blair

5 *Spurs – A Complete Record*, Bob Goodwin

6 *The Official Encyclopedia of Tottenham Hotspur Football Club*,
   Tony Matthews

THE FANZINES AND INTERNET

1 *The Spur* — early 1990s fanzine

2 *CaDD: Cock-a-doodle-do* — late 1990s/2000s fanzine

3 *My Eyes Have Seen the Glory* — fanzine and later leading website (www.mehstg.com)

4 The Spurs-List — email list

5 www.fromthelane.co.uk — messageboard/forum

6 www.topspurs.com — moany old Spurs website

IF ALL ELSE FAILS: FIFTEEN PLAYERS WITH ALTERNATIVE CAREERS

Some start their business careers early, as Paul Miller and Chris Hughton did when they appeared regularly in Spurs programmes of the 1980s advertising dapper sheepskin coats. However, most ex-footballers drift into owning a pub, do a bit of cabbing, or (if they have a bit of faux charisma), become overseas estate agents. Here are some of the post-Spurs career options:

1 Cliff Jones (butcher)

2 Ramon Vega (Romford jeweller/fashion model)

3 Terry Naylor (market porter/postman)

4 Chris Hughton (lift engineer)

5 John Gorman (artist, specialty being large heads on small bodies)

6 Jimmy Holmes (West Midlands Old Bill)

7 Ted Ditchburn (grocer)

8 Ossie Ardiles (lawyer)

9 Tony Galvin (Russian translator)

10 Steve Perryman (travel agency founder and sports outfitters)

11 Gundi Bergsson (lawyer)

12 John Lacy (double-glazing sales manager)

13 Maurice Norman (florist)

14 Espen Baardsen (hedge fund analyst)

15 John Pratt (window cleaner).

SPURS' SONGSHEET: TWENTY TERRACE FAVOURITES

1. 'OH WHEN THE SPURS GO MARCHING IN'

This has become the classic Spurs song of the modern era. Sung slowly for several rounds, with arms outstretched and hands shimmering, before building into a heart-lifting crescendo that can rock any stadium. Admired by others, and yet to be nicked by anyone.

2. 'WE ARE TOTTENHAM'

To the tune of Rod Stewart's 'Sailing', the simple 'We are Tottenham, we are Tottenham, super Tottenham, from the Lane' is a timeless Spurs classic.

3. 'COME ON YOU SPURS/WE LOVE YOU TOTTENHAM, WE DO'

When it's not going well for Spurs, these simple chants have been a proper team-lifter for years.

4. 'GLORY, GLORY TOTTENHAM HOTSPUR'

The battle hymn of the republic, and Spurs-related versions thereupon, was a classic Tottenham chant from the double era in the 1960s onwards, but has gradually tarnished after Manchester United nicked it for one of their lame cup final songs.

5. HOME PRIDE

Unless you are one of the cardboard cut-outs in the West Stand, one of these is yours:

> *We're the Paxton, we're the Paxton, we're the Paxton Tottenham*
> *We're the Shelfside, we're the Shelfside, we're the Shelfside Tottenham*

or,

> *We're the Park Lane, we're the Park Lane, we're the Park Lane Tottenham'.*

6. OLD SKOOL CLASSICS

'Nice one, Cyril, nice one son, nice one Cyril, let's have another one,' went beyond the terraces to be a household phrase in the 1970s. The British Caledonian advert of the time inspired the 1980s classic 'We'll take more care of you Archibald, Archibald', while 'Oh Stevie Stevie, Stevie Stevie Perryman' to the tune of Chicory Tip's 'Son of my Father' has remained the skipper's song to this day. Depending on your vintage, Hoddle or Gilzean '. . . is the king of White Hart Lane' and Taylor or Galvin is '. . . on the wing'.

7. THE LEDLEY KING SONG

It was in the Fernhurst pub before the Blackburn game, a few weeks after Sol Campbell's defection to Arsenal in 2001, that the 'You can stick your Sol Campbell up your Arse, cos we've got Ledley at the back' song was first heard. It made its way on to the terraces later that day and has stuck with Ledley ever since, with rumours that the players used to sing it to him in training.

8. FROM THE PROPER OLD DAYS

Shared with Everton and Celtic, 'It's a grand old team . . .' including such lines as 'And if you know your history, it's enough to make your heart go whoo-oh-oh . . . For we only know that there's gonna be a show, and the Tottenham Hotspur will be there', is a proper great that can trace its lineage back to the 1960s. Another share with Everton from that era is the 'You are my Tottenham, my only Tottenham, you make me happy when skies are grey'. Chants to the tune of 'Guantanamera' have gradually died away, but 'There's only one team in London' sometimes gets a welcome airing.

9. ARSENAL SONGS

There have been some great anti-Arsenal songs over the years, but nothing really tops 'My old man'. Others try to adapt it but it doesn't really work away from the Spurs/Arsenal relationship. It is by us, for them.

10. 'BY FAR THE GREATEST TEAM THE WORLD HAS EVER SEEN'

'And it's Tottenham Hotspur, Tottenham Hotspur FC, by far the greatest team the world has ever seen.' Spiritually uplifting and factually correct. As was 'We all agree, Hoddle is better than Rixy.'

11. OBSCURE HITS

The cheesy 'Can't Smile Without You' by Barry Manilow is an unlikely terrace hit, but a group of lads who travel everywhere with Spurs took it from their coach to the terraces and it became widely adopted, along with the iconic picture of them singing it above their flag at the 2001 FA Cup semi-final. From the early 1990s, an old Venables cover of Emile Ford's 'What do you want to make those eyes at me for?' was the anthem of the football terrace love vibe generation.

12. BOVVER BOYS

'Hark now hear, the Tottenham sing, the Arsenal run away, and we will fight for ever more because of Boxing Day,' and 'Hello, hello, we are the Tottenham boys, hello, hello, we are the Tottenham boys, and if you are an Arsenal fan, surrender or you'll die, 'cos we will follow the Tottenham,' have both been hoolie mainstays for many generations.

13. YOU DON'T HAVE TO BE A GREAT PLAYER TO HAVE A GREAT SONG

'My name is Nicola Berti, aged around 30 . . .' is probably the most unlikely and wonderful of all player songs. From the same era, Ramon Vega was fortunate to have a Christian name that rhymed with the foot-stomping 'Come on, come on', by the now-disgraced Gary Glitter. Sometimes, if sung loud enough on top of a long session in the pub beforehand, it could almost make watching the poor Spurs side of the era bearable. Almost.

Ronnie Rosenthal had more good songs than good games for Spurs. 'Ronnie, Ronnie' worked perfectly with the Hebrew folk tune 'Hava Nagila', and he was also around at the time of Oasis' 'Wonderwall', which produced the following ode sung to his memory

> *All the runs that Ronnie does are winding*
> *And all the goals that Ronnie scores are blinding*
> *There are many things that I would like to say to you, but*
> *I don't know how*
> *But maybe, are you gonna be the one that saves me?*
> *And after all, you're my Rosenthal.*

Another limited player who was blessed with a good tune was Noé Pamarot, who easily fitted into 2 Unlimited's 'No Limit': 'Noé Noé, Noé Noé Noé Noé, Noé Noé Noé Noé, Noé Pamarot.'

14. GALLOWS HUMOUR

When it comes to gallows humour, singing 'We've got Andy Booth, we've got Andy Booth . . .' on a cold night at West Ham in the middle of four consecutive 0-0 draws takes some beating.

15. AWAY DAYS

The classic 'We will follow the Tottenham, over land and sea (and Leicester), We will follow the Tottenham, on to victory' is with luck followed by Jingle Bells, '. . . Oh how fun it is to see

Tottenham win away' towards the end, or after the final whistle if you are a proper pessimist.

16. 'WHO ARE THE BEST?'

F**k 'em all, f**k 'em all, United, West Ham, Liverpool
'Cos we are the Tottenham, and we are the best,
We are the Tottenham, so f**k all the rest.

17. WEMBLEY SONGS

'Ossie's Dream' always gets everyone in the mood for the FA Cup. When Spurs are struggling in a cup game, it's 'Score Tottenham, score! When you get one, you'll get more,' and when Spurs are winning, 'Wem-ber-ley, Wem-ber-ley, we're the famous Tottenham Hotspur, and we're going to Wem-ber-ley.'

18. PLAYER OF THE YEAR

Back in 1999, Beckham may have won the treble but Ginola won the player of the year and had this little ditty, first heard away at Derby: 'Posh Spice is a slapper, she wears a Wonderbra, and when she's shagging Beckham, she thinks of Ginola.'

19. ODE TO FORMER GREATS

Just when it looked like Arsenal were going to fluke a European trophy:

Nayiiiiiiiiiiiiiiiiiim, from the halfway line,
Nayiiiiiiiiiiiiiiiiiim, from the halfway line,
Nayiiiiiiiiiiiiiiiiiim, from the halfway line.

And another one for Popescu's winning penalty for Galatasaray five years later:

Chim-chimeny, chim-chimeny, chim, chim, cheroo,
First it was Nayim, and now Popescu.
Chim-chimeny, Chim-chimeny, chim, chim, cheree,
Gica from 12 yards, Nayim from fifty.

20. AND LASTLY

An Arsenal song that it's fair to say quite a few Spurs joined in with:

> *Oooh Tim Sherwood, oooh, oooh Tim Sherwood, oooh*
> *He comes from Borehamwood, he's not very f**king good,*
> *Oooh Tim Sherwood, oooh . . .*

THE CLUB WHERE THE SUN NEVER SETS: TOTTENHAM AROUND THE WORLD

Just as the British Empire turned the map red, so the spread of Spurs supporters clubs around the world has turned it lilywhite.

BRITISH ISLES

- Republic of Ireland: www.corkspurs.com
- Northern Ireland: www.southbelfastspurs.piczo.com
- Scotland: www.facebook.com/pages/Tottenham-Aberdeen-Fc-Stand-Free
- Wales: www.angleseyspurs.com

SCANDINAVIA

- Denmark: www.spurs.dk
- Finland: www.spurs.fi
- Iceland: www.spurs.is
- Norway: www.tottenhamhotspur.no
- Sweden: www.tottenhamhotspur.se

NORTHERN EUROPE

- Belgium: www.flemish-spurs.be and www.cockerel.chez.com
- Holland: www.rob-online.nl/spurs

- Germany: www.myspurs.de
- Jersey: www.jerseyspurs.co.uk
- Poland: www.spursmania.org
- Switzerland: www.spurs.ch

SOUTHERN EUROPE

- Bulgaria: www.bulgariaspurs.com
- Cyprus: www.spurs.com.cy or www.cyprusspurs.com
- Greece: www.facebook.com/groups/20926842648
- Malta: www.spursmalta.blogspot.co.uk
- Spain: www.spurssupportersspain.com

MIDDLE EAST/SUBCONTINENT AND AFRICA

- Dubai: www.facebook.com/group.php?gid=4240682031& v=wall
- Israel: www.facebook.com/group.php?gid=384305001146
- Mauritius: www.facebook.com/pages/Tottenham-Hotspur-Mauritius
- Pakistan: www.facebook.com/pages/Spurs-Fan-Club-Pakistan
- South Africa: www.spursfans.co.za

FAR EAST

- Hong Kong: www.spursinhongkong.com
- Indonesia: www.indospurs.com
- Japan: www.spurs.sc
- Malaysia: www.myspurs.org
- Singapore: www.spurs-sg.org
- Thailand: www.spursthailand.net

OCEANIA

- Australia: www.ozspurs.com
- New Zealand: www.thfcnz.co.nz

NORTH AMERICA

- Canada: www.spurscanada.ca
- USA (Central): www.chicagospurs.org
- USA (East): www.nyspurs.com
- USA (West): www.laspurs.com

SOUTH AMERICA

- Brazil: www.tottenhambrasil.com.br

Thespian Hotspur: thirteen Spurs on the screen

1 *Teddy Sheringham: wooden cameo in* Footballers Wives.
2 *Graeme Souness: meets Yosser Hughes in* Boys from the Blackstuff.
3 *Danny Blanchflower: as himself in the* Those Glory Glory Days.
4 *Ossie Ardiles: part of Michael Caine's team in* Escape to Victory.
5 *Northern Spurs youth: another pro-United referee against Spurs in the movie* Kes.
6 *Gary Mabbutt: a cameo in CBBC's* The Queen's Nose.
7 *Chris Waddle: pizza advert penance for missing a World Cup penalty.*
8 *Gary Lineker: as himself in* An Evening with Gary Lineker.
9 *David Ginola: appeared in the first episode of* At Home with the Braithwaites.
10 *Lineker and Gazza: in a classic crisp advert after the 1990 World Cup.*
11 *Carrick, Crouch and Postiga: in straight-to-DVD* Goal! III.

THE GREATEST SPURS GAME

OO–15 MINUTES: SPURS 3-1 ARSENAL (1991)

Boy's Own stuff as a tactically astute and pumped-up Spurs race into a 2-0 lead after 10 minutes. The famous Gazza free kick and the Lineker toe-poke after a dazzling move down the right providing the goal reward the overall play.

15–30 MINUTES: SPURS 8-1 GORNIK ZABRZE (1961)

With a 4-2 deficit to overcome from the first leg in their first ever crack at Europe's premier competition, Spurs settled the tie with a flurry of goals midway through the first half, including a hat-trick for Cliff Jones that set the tone for the 'Glory, Glory' nights at White Hart Lane.

30–45 MINUTES: SPURS 4-2 FEYENOORD (1983)

Probably one of the most complete first halves in Spurs' history reached a crescendo as Hoddle pulled the strings to set up Archie and Galvin for a couple each, taking Spurs into a 4-0 half-time lead. Glenn's man-marker Johan Cruyff was forced to look on in awe from a respectable distance.

45–55 MINUTES: SPURS 5-1 CHELSEA (2001)

Having worried away a 3-0 half-time lead against United earlier in the season, Spurs thankfully came out with positive intent for the second half of this semi-final. Even if the game did not feel won when Sheringham's volley put Spurs 4-2 up on aggregate, it was beyond Chelsea when tormentor-in-chief Hasselbaink was the victim of mistaken identity and sent off on 55 minutes.

55–60 MINUTES: SPURS 4-2
SOUTHAMPTON (1993)

On 55 minutes, Sheringham nodded Spurs level, and soon after Barmby put them ahead. Anderton fired in Spurs' third goal from distance and Sheringham scored the fourth after Spurs got the ball back from the restart. Not a bad four minutes 44 seconds in Spurs' history.

60–75 MINUTES: CHELSEA 2-3
SPURS (1982)

Resplendent in an all-white kit with yellow socks, Spurs swept Chelsea away with some of the most breathtaking football of the 1980s team. In between Archibald tapping in and Hazard sweeping home a third, a fine move culminated with a flick from Archie, a lay-off from Hazard for and a pinpoint half-volley from Hoddle from 30 yards that rates as one of the great Spurs goals.

75–90 MINUTES: SPURS 9-0 BRISTOL
ROVERS (1977)

Coming into the final 15 minutes, Spurs were 'only' 4-0 up, but what looked like being a good victory turned into a record-breaking one. Debutant Colin Lee nodded his hat-trick on 75 minutes, followed swiftly by a couple for the much-maligned Ian Moores to seal his own hat-trick. Lee scored his fourth and Spurs' eighth before Hoddle appeared on his own at the far post to score the fifth goal in fifteen minutes to round off Spurs' biggest League win, and the majority of the goal difference by which Spurs eventually got promoted.

INJURY TIME: WEST HAM 3-4
SPURS (2007)

As Berbatov lined up a free kick going into the 90th minute West Ham, inspired by a first goal from talismanic Carlos Tevez, were on the brink of pulling off a shock and much-needed win in one of their many relegation scraps. Berbatov made no mistake from 20 yards to pull Spurs level at 3-3, to the delight of the travelling fans. But it was not over. Spurs withstood a bit of pressure from West Ham before managing to nick the ball away and set up a quick counter-attack with Defoe. The former Hammer got his shot away, which Green parried only for a Spurs player to pounce on it and slot home the winner. When the celebrations had died down, no-one could quite believe that it was mild-mannered Canadian fullback Paul Stalteri who'd somehow sprinted out of defence to be the furthest up the pitch in the last minute of stoppage time. He was the most unlikely and wonderful hero as he never did anything as spontaneous before or since.

EXTRA TIME: SOUTHAMPTON 2-6 SPURS (1995)

Extra time had seemed unlikely before Ronnie Rosenthal's two second-half corkers had dragged Spurs back into the game, but the charismatic Israeli was not finished there. In the first period of extra time, Rocket Ronnie drove towards the Southampton goal and let fly with a 30-yarder that arced away from Grobbelaar's modest attempt at a save. As the Saints pressed for an equaliser, Klinsmann and Sheringham combined so the latter could score, Barmby broke the offside trap to make it five and Anderton drilled home for the final goal in a joyful finale.

PENALTIES: SPURS 4-3 ANDERLECHT (1984)

Robbo scored and Parks saved. Bilko, Shakey and Archie all scored, only for Danny Thomas' fifth and final effort to be saved. As 'There's only One Danny Thomas' rang round the stadium, Parks saved again to win the UEFA Cup for Spurs in General Burkinshaw's final game. Virtual perfection.

5

THE SEASONS

MEMORABLE SPURS SEASON
NO. 1: 1981/82

The marathon 1981/82 season had almost everything, with Spurs challenging on four fronts for most of the season and finally delivering some silverware in the last of the 66 matches.

The season got off to an inauspicious start with consecutive home defeats to the claret-and-blues of West Ham 0-4 and Aston Villa 1-3, but Spurs soon recaptured the form that had seen them to FA Cup glory the previous May. The next 10 games produced nine victories in all competitions, including home and away wins against European giants Ajax on Spurs' return to Europe.

With typical Spurs inconsistency, however, the run came to an end with a home defeat to lowly Brighton, but there were signs that the cup team of 1981 were gelling into potential title contenders in 1982. The chief reason for this was the summer acquisition of Ray Clemence from Liverpool, who after a sticky start in the Charity Shield added some genuine class between the sticks for the first time since Jennings. His influence on the quality back four of Hughton, Roberts, Miller and Perryman dropping in at right back was evident. Spurs chalked up six consecutive clean sheets in October and only conceded 19 goals in the 37 matches up to the League Cup final in March. It was a very different Spurs for whom the first rather than the third or fourth goal was often the one for victory.

Spurs' reward for beating Ajax was what should have been a straightforward tie against Irish part-timers Dundalk, but Spurs only scraped through 2-1 on aggregate. As with the European campaign, Spurs overcame the most difficult League Cup opponents, Manchester United in the opening round with home and away wins, before putting away more straightforward opposition to take the cup interest into the new year.

Things were also going well in the League, and after beating United for the third time in three months that season (depressingly the same number of wins Spurs have notched up against the Red Devils in 40 Premier League matches over 20 years up to 2012), Spurs stood in second place, two points off the top with two games in hand, and yet remarkably they had lost as many home games as the bottom side, Sunderland. Another home loss was in prospect in the game against Coventry.

By the turn of the year, Spurs had more home defeats than wins but still remained five points off the top with three games in hand. They then embarked on a run of four 1-0 wins, including victories over Arsenal, with an assist from Big Pat in the Arsenal goal, and over Leeds in the FA Cup. A thrice-taken missed penalty from Hoddle did not stop Spurs progressing past Forest into the League Cup semi-finals.

A Ricky Villa-inspired Spurs opened the 'new' West Stand with a 6-1 win over Wolves at the start of February, and later that week a Micky Hazard goal was enough for a 1-0 aggregate win over West Brom in a niggly League Cup semi-final, where Galvin and subsequent Spurs manager Martin Jol had seen red in the first leg.

As March approached, the big games were coming thick and fast. A midweek European Cup Winners' Cup win over Eintracht Frankfurt was followed by a memorable 3-2 win over Second Division Chelsea in the sixth round of the FA Cup at the weekend. This was in turn followed by an away win at Brighton the following midweek, before the trip to Wembley in the League Cup final. It was an exciting time to be a Spurs fan.

The final at Wembley against Liverpool, the dominant team of the era, was always going to be difficult. Spurs held their early lead from an Archibald goal right up to the final minutes when Liverpool presented a soft equaliser after Archie had missed a great chance to put Tottenham two up. Liverpool went on to win the game in extra time against a leg weary Spurs side who had given their all. It was a choker to come so close, but Spurs fans responded with 'Sing, sing wherever you may be, we lost the Milk Cup at Wem-ber-ley. But we'll be back to win the other three, and we'll go down in history,' to keep the good vibe going.

The big games kept coming, and an away goal in Frankfurt was enough to see Spurs into the Cup Winners' Cup semi-final. The following weekend, Spurs entertained table-toppers Southampton nine points adrift but with a massive seven games in hand. Roberts moving into midfield had a dream match against his home-town club – who had rejected him as a schoolboy – and scored his only Spurs at-trick in a 3-2 win, the final goal memorably looping up and into the Paxton net after being hit into the ground.

The emerging Falklands crisis put more strain on a side with two star Argentinian players, and Spurs' League form began to suffer. Despite that, there was still time for a tremendous win at Highbury on Easter Monday when a contingent of Spurs fans made themselves at home on the North Bank.

Spurs eased past Leicester in the FA Cup semi-final but the draw for the Cup Winners' Cup semi had not been so kind in pairing Spurs with Barcelona. In a violent first leg, Barcelona were gifted an away goal when a long-range shot somehow drifted past Clemence, and Spurs needed a late Roberts equaliser to preserve their unbeaten home record in Europe. Spurs lost to the only goal in the Nou Camp, though, as the long battle on four fronts was starting to take its toll.

At the start of May, Spurs had to fit eight League games into 17 days, which included playing League-leaders Liverpool home and away. Spurs gave the title challenge a good go, and after a 2-2 draw at White Hart Lane took the lead at Anfield when Hoddle's brilliant 35-yard shot flew in. But once again,

Liverpool came back to win the game 3-1, and once the title was out of reach Spurs eventually settled for a credible fourth place in Division One as attention shifted to the FA Cup final – the last chance of a trophy that the season's efforts deserved.

Spurs lined up against QPR, a third consecutive Second Division side they faced in the competition, who were managed by Tottenham old boy Terry Venables. A long-range shot from Hoddle in extra time looked to be enough to win a forgettable final before Terry Fenwick popped up to force a replay with only two minutes remaining. In a typically bucca-neering run, Roberts earned a penalty that Hoddle put away early in the replay, but again a tired Spurs failed to close the game out. They eventually hung on for 66-game ever-present Steve Perryman to lift the cup. The final did not have the same glory of the year before, but it was a just reward for a fantastic season.

THE CLASSIC CUP RUN NO. 1: FA CUP 1990/91

After starting the League season well on the back of the positive World Cup 1990 vibe, Spurs were once again out of the run-ning for the Division One title by the time the FA Cup third round draw sent Spurs up to Blackpool. The game was mostly memorable for the windy weather, but a goal from Tangerine old boy Paul Stewart in his newly acquired midfield role was enough for a slightly fortunate Spurs. Oxford United put up a bit of fight in the next round, but goals from Spurs' three best players of the time – Mabbutt, a couple from Gazza and Lineker – saw the Lilywhites home with a 4-2 scoreline.

There was drama before the fifth round tie at Fratton Park with Terry Fenwick breaking a leg in the warm-up, although it would be difficult to think of a less sympathetically received injury. With the game being played amid rising financial worries, things also looked a bit bleak on the pitch for a while as Pompey took the lead approaching half time. With the wind behind Spurs in the second half, though, it was a different story, and as in the previous round Gazza once again stole the show. His first was a rare headed goal that levelled things up, before a more familiar run and shot won the game for Spurs to the delight of the packed away end behind the goal.

Once again, lower-tier opposition threatened to spoil the party when Notts County took the lead at White Hart Lane in the sixth round. With the sense of destiny and the year ending in one, Spurs were not to be denied, and Nayim equalised before Gazza curled home the winner after a series of one-twos, to ensure Spurs were not embarrassed in front of the live TV audience.

Gazza was the most famous footballer in the country after his World Cup exploits, and was rapidly becoming the hero of the cup run, with match-winning performances in the previous three rounds.

However, immediately after the Notts County game, he required an operation that gave everyone a nervous month waiting to see whether he would be back in time for the semi-final.

That match paired Spurs with Arsenal, and the scale of the occasion meant the game was the first semi-final moved to Wembley and played on a Sunday lunchtime. Venables got everything just right for the game: he replaced Nayim with the more reliable Samways to give Spurs a much stronger midfield, and turned out a highly motivated and tactically aware side who were far superior to Arsenal. Gazza made it to the starting line-up but had played only 30 minutes reserve team football since the quarter-final. However, he proved to be Spurs' cup talisman once again. After five minutes, he scored the now-legendary free kick to put Spurs ahead, made even more special by Barry Davies' superb commentary: 'Is Gascoigne going to have a crack? He is, you know . . . Oh I say . . . that's . . . that's schoolboy's own stuff.'

The second goal is often forgotten, but if anything it captures perfectly how Spurs took Arsenal apart from the start of the game. Superb build-up play down the right involving Ollie and

Gazza saw Spurs players turning and finding each other with the ball while Gunners chased shadows and fell over. The goal itself was only a toe-poke by Lineker, and the first to celebrate was centre back Gary Mabbutt, who'd somehow found himself standing next to Lineker in the Arsenal six-yard box from open play after 10 minutes, which typified the inspired performance.

Arsenal pulled one back before half time and Spurs lost a little momentum after Gazza was replaced after managing an hour on his comeback, but what has become St Hotspur Day in Spurs folklore was capped by Lineker, who squeezed a shot past David Seaman to give Spurs an unassailable lead. Once again, Barry Davies' memorable commentary is very much part of the goal, and fans of a certain age can repeat it like sad Monty Python devotees – 'Mabbutt, fed it well . . . Nayim to the left . . . Samways ahead, and Lineker uses him by not using him . . . Good try, he's scored . . . and David Seaman will be very disappointed about that, it seemed to go through his fingers!'.

The outpouring of joy at the win was enormous, but all the time in the background, the dark clouds of the financial threat to Spurs' very existence tainted the build-up to the final. Chas 'n' Dave had to produce two cup final songs: the brilliant first effort 'The Victory Song', that contained the lines 'We're off to Wembley 'cos we beat the Arsenal, in the North London cup, they was only runners-up, now they can't do the double down the Arsenal', had captured the post semi-final mood perfectly, but was replaced with the more sedate 'It's lucky for Spurs when the year ends in one', comprising a few Spurs phrases thrown over the tune of 'London Girls'.

Forest hammered the Hammers in the other semi and went into the final in great form, starting slight favourites. Unfortunately, the occasion got to Gazza and a reckless opening few minutes ended with him being stretchered off, after Stuart Pearce had put Forest ahead from the free kick awarded for the foul that caused Gazza's injury. Having done so much to get Spurs to the final, it was a cruel blow to the player who brought so much joy to so many at that time.

Spurs could have been forgiven for thinking they'd used up all their luck in the semi, as Lineker had a goal disallowed and then had a penalty saved, and they trailed at the break with their best player already in hospital. However, despite the scoreline, Spurs were playing the better football and had come together as a team in the absence of the star. A deserved equaliser arrived from a low shot from man of the match Paul Stewart just before the hour, but Spurs could not find a winner in normal time. With the score level after 90 minutes, the increasingly erratic Brian Clough did not get off the bench and the momentum was very much with Spurs. From a corner, after a looping header from Paul Walsh had hit the bar, what proved to be the winner came via the head of Forest's Des Walker, who fittingly was being pressured by Gary Mabbutt who four years earlier scored the decisive own goal in the cup final in the same net for Coventry City.

There was still time for the goading of a very young Roy Keane by Steve Sedgley and Justin Edinburgh, caught perfectly by the cameras to round things off for the TV audience. Mabbutt lifted the cup in front of Princess Diana to exorcise his Coventry ghosts, and all was well with the world as Spurs had another trophy in a year ending in one.

After lifting the cup, the players went to visit Gazza in hospital, while the Spurs board sweated over the extent of his injury as they needed to sell him fit to help pay off the debts. The cup win helped save Spurs – but at a price, as the off-field problems weakened the club, and meant it was the last dash of glory for a while.

MEMORABLE SPURS SEASON NO. 2: 2001/02

After a decade in the doldrums, new owners and the return of Glenn Hoddle as manager raised hopes that 2001/02 was going to be the year Spurs bounced back to the big time. Not even the departure of Sol Campbell in the summer upset the feel-good factor among the fans, who felt they'd got their Tottenham back.

Early expectations were dampened with just one point from the first three games, rescued at Goodison when the team went down to nine men after the Ginger Pelé and Poyet were dismissed against Everton, but things were back on track just before the 9/11 attacks, with the emerging Simon Davies and the gifted new signing Christian Ziege setting Spurs on their way to a 2-0 win against Hoddle's previous club Southampton.

Spurs' form was better than bare results with new signings Sheringham, Ziege and Poyet bedding in well with the emerging young players in Hoddle's favoured 3-5-2 formation. Hoddle also signed Dean Richards to steady up the defence in time for the visit of Manchester United, who had already been beaten by Spurs under Hoddle at the end of the previous season. Things looked to be going well again as Richards flicked home the opening goal from a corner, Sir Les drilled in the second, and Ziege flashed in a spectacular diving header to put Spurs 3-0 up just before half time. Hoddle's Spurs seemed to have properly arrived, but it felt like a long 15-minute break. An air of foreboding fell over the stadium when Cole pulled one back in the opening minute of the second half, and sure enough Spurs folded to lose 3-5. The joke 'Have you heard about Dean Richards' new house? It's a three up, five down,' had to be endured for quite a while afterwards.

Spurs bounced back in tremendous fashion with a superb display against Derby. The 3-1 scoreline hardly reflected the manner of the victory, and another Ziege goal was a fine example of the fluent football Hoddle was getting from a side that had played out four consecutive 0-0s under Graham earlier in the calendar year. From the United reverse, Spurs won six of the next nine, including a classy away win at top-of-the-table Newcastle on a very wet Sunday, and at West Ham where Poyet knocked himself out setting up Ferdinand's winner then appealed to the referee for a corner not realising Spurs had scored.

Sir Les scored the Premier League's 10,000th goal to set Spurs up for an easy 4-0 over Fulham in early December. This put Spurs level on points with Manchester United and six points off the summit. With bottom-of-the-table Ipswich due to be the last game before Christmas, things were looking very good for Spurs. Too good, in fact! The easier the game, the bigger the mess Spurs can make of it, and despite taking the lead against the Tractor Boys, Spurs slid to a 2-1 defeat and went on a run of one win in seven that ended any faint hopes of a podium finish.

The season was far from over, though, as a superb League Cup run had seen Spurs score at an average of four a game before being paired with bogey team Chelsea in a two-legged semi-final. Spurs had not beaten Chelsea in 26 matches – over 10 years – at that stage, and had lost 10 of the last 11 going into the first leg at Stamford Bridge. Spurs equalised midway through the second half through Sherwood, who reserved his two best Spurs performances for this tie, but Hasselbaink was once again our nemesis, and by the end Spurs did well to lose 1-2.

On what was to become one of the greatest 'Glory, Glory' nights under the lights at White Hart Lane, the second leg got off to the perfect start when the mostly useless Iversen seized upon a John Terry mistake to level the tie after two minutes to set the mood for the rest of the night. Spurs skipper Sheringham ironed out Zenden to reaffirm Spurs' intent, and when Sherwood scored a magnificent goal from a 'Sheringham corner routine', the fantastic atmosphere took confidence in their passion. There were no half-time collywobbles this time, and within a few minutes of the restart, Sheringham's volley from Poyet's chest-trap curved its way into the Paxton net. Spurs were two goals clear but no-one dared to dream just yet. Down the other end, a fracas in the Spurs penalty area saw chief goal threat Hasselbaink sent off instead of the real culprit Melchiot. Chelsea soon ran out of ideas, and emerging star Davies made it four – safe for even the most pessimistic fan – with 20 minutes to go, and Rebrov nipped in to dink home the fifth just to make sure. Chelsea got a late consolation but it was a great night for Spurs, and the fans sang the song after which the game has become known: 'Who put the ball in the Chelsea net? Arfa, arfa, half of Tottenham.'

With the prospect of a final against moderate Blackburn, who were suffering injury and suspension worries, everything looked set for Spurs to land a trophy in Hoddle's first season. On a wet afternoon in Cardiff, however, nothing went right for Tottenham, who despite not playing well missed a host of chances, especially Sir Les, who found Brad Friedel in inspired form. Even then, after Poyet had rattled the bar when he should have scored, Spurs were doubly denied in the last minute, first not getting a penalty for a trip on Sheringham and then Sir Les picked out Friedel once again rather than the net with a close-range header when he really should have scored. Spurs eventually lost 1-2, and it was in some ways a very Spurs defeat, things going wrong when they seemed almost too much in our favour.

The defeat tore a huge hole in the Hoddle project, and almost immediately afterwards Spurs lost three games 0-4, two of them to Chelsea who extracted a painful revenge. Spurs eventually lifted themselves in the League and had a decent end-of-season run, culminating in a 1-0 win over title-chasing Liverpool that put them in seventh place: the first UEFA qualification via the League for a generation was within Spurs' grasp going into the final round of matches. However, an anaemic display at Leicester saw them relinquish any chance to salvage the season, and they slipped to ninth.

In many respects, 2001/02 was 'Spurs in a season'. Moments of brilliance, a great cup run, but slipping up when it all looked too good, some catastrophic collapses, all wrapped in a mid-table League finish. At times the football was great, but not enough people at Spurs believed in Hoddle's way, and it would ultimately represent another false dawn.

THE CLASSIC CUP RUN NO. 2:
UEFA CUP 1983/84

The strong finish to the 1982/83 season, which included a glorious 5-0 victory over Arsenal, propelled the club into fourth place, and entry into the following year's UEFA Cup. Spurs' first opponents in Europe were Irish side Drogheda

United, who put up little resistance over the two legs, and Spurs emerged with a record-equalling aggregate win of 14-0.

Cup draws free from the rigged outcomes of seeding had a great habit of throwing up dramatic ties at any stage of the competition. The balls from the velvet bag presented Spurs with a rematch against Dutch side Feyenoord, exactly 10 seasons after the UEFA Cup final between the two sides that had been marred by violence. Further spice was added to the tie with past master Johan Cruyff paired against the current master Glenn Hoddle. In the first leg at White Hart Lane, Cruyff chose to man-mark Hoddle. It was a terrible misjudgment, and 45 minutes of chasing Hoddle's shadow later, Spurs were 4-0 ahead with Hoddle instrumental in all four goals. Feyenoord grabbed a couple of away goals in the second half to keep the tie alive, but a consummate display by Spurs in the second leg, with goals from the left-side pairing of Galvin and Hughton, erased the negative memories of 1974.

Spurs' reward was an even more difficult tie against German giants Bayern Munich, who'd ended Spurs' previous European campaign in the Munich fog the season before. This time the first leg was away, and Spurs held out until near the end when a late Rummenigge goal gave the Bavarians a slender lead. In another of the great 'Glory, Glory' nights at White Hart Lane, Spurs were superb throughout, but going into the final minutes only had an Archibald goal to show for it to level the tie on aggregate. As extra time loomed, the ball fell to Hoddle, who conjured a chipped pass into the box. Falco lunged to get on the end of it and got away a weakish-looking shot that managed to elude Belgian keeper Pfaff and crept into the corner to send Spurs through.

In the quarter-final, Spurs faced Austria Vienna, who'd done Spurs a favour by beating Inter Milan in the previous round. In a tense first leg at White Hart Lane, Spurs did enough to come away with a 2-0 lead, and an early goal in the away leg all but settled things in Tottenham's favour, although the Viennese fought back to 2-2 on the night.

At the semi-final stage, Spurs were paired with Yugoslavian out-fit Hadjuk Split, while fellow English representatives Notts Forest had the misfortune to meet Anderlecht who it later emerged had bribed the officials to secure their path to the final. The first leg behind the Iron Curtain was a tense affair until Falco gave Spurs a precious away goal on the hour in the aftermath of a missed penalty. Split fought back, and although Spurs were disappointed to concede two late goals, they were still favourites to progress with the away goal. A rocking White Hart Lane saw Micky Hazard's early free kick put Spurs ahead on away goals after six minutes. But like Hazard, who lost a contact lens in the goal celebrations, Spurs lacked the focus to increase the lead against a high-quality side, and needed a heroic goal-line clearance by the great Graham Roberts to preserve their advantage as the Yugoslavs pressed in vain for a goal.

The first leg of the final was marred by tragedy when Spurs fan Brian Flanagan was shot dead in Brussels before the game. Spurs again opened the scoring from the unlikely source of Paul Miller, but a late equaliser and the booking of captain Perryman, and his subsequent suspension for the second leg, took the gloss off the result. The Belgians were a much better side at White Hart Lane, and took the lead on the hour. Spurs kept pressing but were devoid of luck. With six minutes to go, substitute Ardiles hit the bar from a yard out, and it looked even more like it was not going to be Spurs' day. But in moments of crisis, legends are created. From the Ardiles miss, Danny Thomas returned a high ball to the box and captain-for-the-night Roberts came charging through the Anderlecht defence. In a moment of inspiration, he chested the ball down rather than heading it for goal from distance, and with Anderlecht defenders bouncing off him he tore through the heart of their defence to roll the ball in for the equaliser. It was a fantastic combination of vision, courage and skill, and in context is one of the great goals the old stadium has witnessed, often overlooked in the light of what was to come.

Archie nearly won it for Spurs before the 90 minutes were up, but the game went to extra time and eventually penalties. Once again, Roberts led by example in putting away the first penalty, and when young keeper Tony Parks saved from Olsen, Spurs had destiny in their own hands. Falco, the much-maligned Stevens and Archie all scored, meaning it was all down to Danny Thomas, who had never scored for Spurs, to take the final penalty and win the cup. His weak penalty was saved, but in one of the greatest moments of Spurs history, the fans put aside the possible magnitude of the miss and immediately sang 'There's only one Danny Thomas!' as he trudged back to the centre circle. Thomas' agony was short-lived, as Parks saved Guðjohnsen's penalty and the ground erupted in European glory once again. It was a great story for local lad Parks, who had initially got his first-team chance a few months earlier through an injury to regular keeper Clemence, and who ended up being Spurs' European trophy-winning hero on the night.

Among the joy there was some sadness, as manager Keith Burkinshaw had decided this was to be his last game in charge and club legend Steve Perryman, who had played in the 1972 and 1974 finals, stood respectfully in the background, having been denied a place in the team through suspension. But the over-riding memory was of a great win, perhaps the greatest in terms of opponents played in the competition, and a win that grows greater year by year in the absence of subsequent achievements.

MEMORABLE SPURS SEASON NO. 3: 1984/85

As the memories of the UEFA Cup final win began to fade, Spurs went into the new season with a new manager, the unassuming Peter Shreeves chosen as Keith Burkinshaw's replacement with John Pratt as his assistant.

The season could not have got off to a better start, with a 4-1 win up at Goodison seeing goals from new signings Clive Allen and John Chiedozie on their debut. In time-honoured Tottenham tradition, a fine away win was followed up by disappointment, as Spurs only drew the next game against Leicester at White Hart Lane. When away defeats followed at Sheffield Wednesday and Sunderland, with both Clive Allen and Graham Roberts being sent off at Roker Park, it looked like anything but a special season.

Spurs bounced back in impressive fashion with two wins against current Division One champions Liverpool in the League and League Cup, then put five past QPR, four past Pleaty's Luton and hit nine without reply over two legs against Sporting Braga in the UEFA Cup. John Chiedozie's Spurs star did not burn for long but it burned very brightly over that golden autumn, and Micky Hazard emerged from the shadow of the injured Glenn Hoddle as the star midfield man, with the display against QPR one of his finest moments.

Away form was still a bit shaky, and when Spurs slipped to a fourth away defeat of the season at Old Trafford, it seemed inconceivable that this would be the last loss on the road all season. Equally, with four wins and a draw at home in the first five matches, there was no hint that Spurs would lose more than they would win at White Hart Lane for the remainder of that season.

The return of Hoddle in early November saw Spurs embark on a 14-match unbeaten run, and by the time Newcastle visited in December, Spurs were second in the League and firmly established as title contenders. A first glimpse of the magic of Chris Waddle, bamboozling Maxi Miller for the visitors' opening goal, threatened to upset Spurs, but a couple from Mark Falco helped Tottenham to a comfortable 3-1 win. Like Hazard, this was the season Falco stepped from the shadows of Crooks and the recently sold Archibald and was ever present, with 22 League goals.

Spurs travelled to Highbury on New Year's Day, leading Division One on goal difference. With the wind behind them, second-half goals from Crooks and Falco saw Spurs home, with Graham Roberts giving a salute made famous by Harvey Smith to remind the Arsenal fans of the score. It's not a championship challenge without the obligatory toughed-out 1-0 away wins, which came in consecutive games at West Brom and Stoke, and Spurs seemed to be in good shape as the season stepped up a gear going into March.

Meanwhile, Spurs had quietly progressed to the quarter-finals in defence of the UEFA Cup, but the draw had not been kind, pitting them against Real Madrid, the last remaining serious opponents. Spurs' famous unbeaten home record in Europe went down to an early goal deflected off Steve Perryman, and worse was to follow at the weekend with a home League defeat to Manchester United and, courtesy of Norman Whiteside, a season-ending injury for Gary Stevens, another unheralded star of the unheralded season.

Spurs bounced back with a famous win away at Liverpool, where a Garth Crooks goal ended a winless run at Anfield going back 73 years, and when Spurs won the first of three consecutive home games against Southampton, they were level on points at the top of the League with Everton.

That was as good as it got. A dodgy offside goal saw Villa leave with the points, and the following Wednesday, Spurs entertained Everton in an epic top-of-the-table clash that seemed likely to determine the League title. Andy Gray silenced the home crowd with a tremendous volley early in the game, whose brilliance even garnered a polite ripple of applause from some sections of the Spurs crowd, despite the magnitude of the game. Spurs battled back well, but were undone again in the second half when Trevor Steven pounced on a Mark Bowen mistake to put the visitors two up. The heroic figure of Graham Roberts pulled one back for Spurs with another long-range effort to match Gray's, and Spurs pressed non-stop to the final whistle for an equaliser. The deciding point of the match and perhaps the title race came when Neville Southall pulled off a superb save from a Falco header in the dying minutes. It was not to be for Spurs.

The demoralising defeat was compounded by further injury woe with Crooks joining Stevens and Mabbutt (who had broken his leg at West Brom) on the long-term sick list. With the team in a slump, another set of successive home defeats against Arsenal and Ipswich, in which Crooks was replaced in shirt but not class by recent non-Leaguer Dave Leeworthy, sealed Spurs' fate.

Four wins from the last five games ensured Spurs finished level on points with second-place Liverpool, but there was still time for the seventh and most humiliating home defeat of the season, 1-5 to Watford. The unforgiving crowd, many sporting the trendy Spurs/Celtic or Spurs/Rangers woolly hats, gave a torrent of abuse to the side putting up the best championship challenge since 1962.

So near and yet so far; and so easily forgotten by so many fans. In some ways a bit like the 2011/12 season, where a title challenge and a high League finish were largely overshadowed by a spring collapse on the back of injury-hit or tired players.

THE CLASSIC CUP RUN NO. 3: LEAGUE CUP 1998/99

The League Cup is very much the poor relation of the major domestic trophies, but it nonetheless provided one of the great Wembley finishes for Spurs back in 1999.

Spurs started their campaign without a manager after the sacking of Christian Gross three games into the new season. Caretaker manager David Pleat managed to guide Spurs beyond Brentford with 3-2 away and home wins, most notable for Stephen Carr's first goal for Tottenham and a goal just after half time at White Hart Lane by Campbell that large sections of the crowd missed. George Graham was at the helm by the time a couple of Chris Armstrong goals set Spurs up for a comfortable win at Northampton.

The competition came alive when Spurs were drawn to play away at Liverpool in the next round. The famous FA Cup-tie-winner from Klinsmann up there in 1995 was still fresh in the mind, but Spurs had not beaten Liverpool since and had a desperate overall record at Anfield with only three wins in nearly a century.

The Lilywhites got off to a dream start when a looping header from Iversen found its way in beyond Brad Friedel. Soon after, former Liverpool player John Scales scored what proved to be the only goal of his mostly miserable Spurs career to give Tottenham the giddy sensation of being 2-0 up at Anfield. Liverpool fought back and were pressing for a way back into the game midway through the second half when Allan Nielsen broke away to put the tie beyond doubt, helping him achieve the unique distinction of being the only Spurs player ever to score a third goal at Anfield.

The draw was again unkind to Spurs with a home tie against Manchester United. While the United line-up was missing a few familiar faces, it was full of internationals and headed by both goal scorers from their Champions League triumph later that season. Spurs and in particular Ginola were irresistible, though, and had two Chris Armstrong goals to show for it midway through the second half. The returning Sheringham pulled one back for United to set up a tense final 20 minutes, but any frayed nerves were settled when Ginola ran along the majority of the United defence before whipping home a stunning third goal to settle a memorable tie. Spurs were the only team to beat Manchester United in any competition that season as they later went on to win the treble.

With United out of the way, only a few lesser teams stood between Spurs and one last visit to the Empire Stadium before its scheduled renovation in 2000. In a quirk of fate, Spurs were paired with Wimbledon in the semi-final, who'd also come out of the hat in the fourth round of the FA Cup, and both ties coincided with the scheduled League fixture. This meant that, with a replay in the FA Cup match, Spurs played the Wombles five times in the 31 days between 16 January and 16 February 1999. Both the League game and the first leg of the League Cup at White Hart Lane ended level. The tide turned for Spurs in the fourth game, with an emphatic FA Cup replay win. The second leg of the League Cup semi-final at Selhurst was not a classic, but an early Iversen goal, nonchalantly chipped into the net over Spurs-keeper-to-be Sullivan, always looked likely to be enough for Tottenham, who celebrated with what will probably be one of the last pitch invasions at the end.

The final paired the teams who had contested the FA Cup final in 1961, but this time it was Martin O'Neill's Leicester team, which had tasted competition glory in 1997, who started favourites. Ginola was at his peak and about to be crowned player of the year. Leicester's game plan consisted of triple marking him and hoping for the best, and this resulted in a pretty ordinary game for the spectators. With 20 minutes to go, some play-acting from Robbie Savage saw Justin Edinburgh sent off, and things looked tough for the 10 men. Spurs managed to hang on until the final minute, when Iversen broke away and, looking for once like a Champions League quality forward, bore down on the Leicester goal. He managed to get his shot away, and Kasey Keller could only push it out to Allan Nielsen, who dived in to head home.

A last-minute diving header to win a game when down to 10 men at the famous old Wembley stadium is Roy of the Rovers stuff, and this remains a much underrated triumph in a difficult era for the club.

MEMORABLE SPURS SEASON NO. 4: 1977/78

The plan was simple: a year in the lower reaches to recharge the team's batteries, and the chance for the fans to tear up a load of new away grounds before returning to the top flight as Manchester United had done the season before.

A new match-day programme complete with a colour action photograph proved a good omen as Spurs won their first seven home games, including a 9-0 hammering of Bristol Rovers, a margin of victory that would prove crucial as the season reached its climax. It was refreshing for the fans to see Spurs win so often after the struggle of the relegation season the previous year, and everything seemed to be going to plan.

The first reality check came in November when Spurs failed to score in three consecutive matches against what were emerging as our promotion rivals in the form of Brighton and Hove Albion, Bolton and Southampton, but Spurs were still well placed in second as Christmas approached.

Black-and-white images of fans in flares with scarfs tied round their wrists heading south over London Bridge into the lions' Den to watch Tottenham win 3-1 on Boxing Day is stuff of Spurs folklore. Not quite so memorable was the home draw with Mansfield Town a couple of days later, which is typical of the inconsistency that defines the essence of the old club.

One thing that was consistent during this season was team selection, in which six players played in at least 41 of the 42 matches. Even now the team is easy to recall: Daines, Naylor, Holmes, Hoddle, McAllister, Perryman, Pratt, McNab, Duncan, Lee and Taylor, give or take a few changes up-front and McAllister replacing Osgood at the back halfway through the season. This was also the season Perryman dropped from midfield to centre back to allow a 4-3-3 formation, with Hoddle running the show in the middle.

From the Bolton away defeat in November, Spurs put together an impressive 19-game unbeaten run to after Easter, but too often drew games which they should have won. A figure of ridicule for much of his Spurs career, John Pratt had one of his great moments when rescuing a point with a late double at Notts County. Peter Taylor fell over in the mud after rounding the keeper with an open goal beckoning at Fulham, which cost Spurs another point. He may have looked like a hairdresser, but Don McAllister played like an assassin and quickly filled the void at the back following Osgood's mid-season departure. He popped up with important goals such as beating the offside trap for the equaliser against Blackpool and later in the season the diving header that won the crucial top-of-the-table clash against his former club Bolton.

In consecutive away games in March, Barry Daines had the rare distinction of creating two 'What happened next?' moments for *A Question of Sport*. The first was an overhead own goal at Bristol Rovers in a 3-2 Spurs win, and the second saw him charging out of his goal on a muddy pitch at Field Mill to spectacularly miskick, allowing Dave Syrett to score his hat-trick and put Mansfield 3-2 up going into the closing stages. Fortunately, the class of a Hoddle free kick secured a draw for Spurs in the final minute, but once again, in the era of two points for win, it was a point dropped against a team Spurs should have been beating.

Millwall smashed up White Hart Lane on Easter Monday, and Spurs dropped yet another point in a 3-3 draw – their third in a season that saw them concede as many goals as relegated Orient. Despite this, Spurs travelled to Burnley for the next game as Division Two leaders with six games to play. However, the wobbles set in properly at Turf Moor with a 1-2 defeat and further reverses against promotion rivals Brighton and unexpectedly at home against Sunderland saw Spurs drop to third, only a point ahead of Brighton going into the final week of the season.

Talk of championships had rapidly changed to talk of promotion, and Spurs needed at least a win and a draw in the last two matches against Hull and away at League-leaders Southampton to ensure promotion. A tense midweek evening game saw Spurs leave it late before skipper Perryman forced home a controversial late goal to beat Hull City – a great time for him to score his first of the season. As every Brighton fan knows, Spurs and Southampton would both be promoted if they drew, and despite the Saints rattling the woodwork, a final score of 0-0 saw Bolton end up as champions, Southampton in second and Spurs promoted in third place, ahead of Brighton only on goal difference. Thankfully, this was before the era of the play-offs.

It ended up being an undignified scramble, but the mission was accomplished and with many epic matches and memorable experiences along the way, the season remains a firm favourite for some of the more senior members of the Spurs brethren.

BIBLIOGRAPHY

BOOKS

- *Spurs: Day-to-Day Life at White Hart Lane*, Graham Betts
- *The Spurs Miscellany*, Martin Cloake and Adam Powley
- *Spurs – A Complete Record*, Bob Goodwin
- *The Spurs Alphabet*, Bob Goodwin
- *Tottenham Hotspur The Essential History of*, Bob Goodwin
- *The Official Encyclopaedia of Tottenham Hotspur Football Club*, Tony Matthews
- *Tottenham Hotspur, Player by Player*, Ivan Ponting
- *Spurs: the 25-Year Record (1972–1997)*, Michael Robinson
- *Tottenham Hotspur: The Official Illustrated History 1882–1996*, Phil Soar

OTHER PUBLICATIONS

- Back issues of *CaDD/The Spur* fanzines
- Various Spurs programmes and official handbooks

INTERNET

- www.fromthelane.co.uk (Spurs forum)
- www.mehstg.com (My Eyes have seen the Glory)
- www.topspurs.com (including the associated Facebook and Twitter pages)
- www.tottenhamhotspur.com (official Tottenham Hotspur club website)
- www.tottenhamhotspurmad.co.uk

THE GLORY OF SPURS
SPONSORS LIST

Keith Preston; 'Keith Preston: hooked since 1964.'

David Hayes

Matthew Leonidas Kyriakides; 'I've spent some of the best moments of my life with Spurs.'

Betty Stevens

Frank Wyse; 'In the late sixties when everything was in black and white, I discovered the colour, the vibrancy, the life, of that which is Tottenham Hotspur F.C.'

Thomas 'Langis' Langoergen; 'My best memory of spurs was when we beat Chelsea in the Carling Cup final, and celebrating with my best friend Øystein Haugen!'

Greg Meyer; 'Sure to be a good read from the legend that is Topspurs that is Jim Duggan. From Greg Meyer and all at the Kent Pub.'

Vidar Edell; 'Vidar Edell, President of Tottenhams Venner (Spurs Norway), and also proud owner of the Norwegian company Topspur AS.'

Penttti Pesonen

Steve Edmunds; 'To Jim, for enabling those far detached from UK shores to keep up with and participate in all that is Spurs through your dedication to inform. Saludos from Mexico!'

Iain McMahon

Dave Newcomb; 'In loving memory of Alan Newcomb, my very much missed Dad.'

Darren Willis; 'for Darren Willis, a Spurs fan.'

Morten Hauge Brakstad; 'It is better to fail aiming high than to succeed aiming low. And we of Spurs have set our sights very high, so high in fact that even failure will have in it an echo of glory.'

Mark Carmichael

Øystein Haugen

Davy Williams

Steffan Chirazi

Tamsyn Woodman; 'Glory.'

Bruce Woodman; 'Glory.'

Will and Sue Dyson; 'One night in the Brickies …'

Eddie Bradbrook

Colin Ashby; 'Jim Duggan, a Top Spur. Best wishes with the book and having a right riveting read. Keep me focused on my favourite team while living in France.'

Lauren Crader; 'Lilywhite & Blue. Always & Forever. COYS.'

Andy 'Geordie' Hall

Partha Sengupta

Martin Lawther

Julian House

Lee Dumont; 'It's easy to list the many past greats and rightly so but closest to my heart are those I have spent many hours enjoying and enduring Spurs alongside in the Paxton. Jon, Will, Jason, Colin, Mel, Thom, Simon, Jamie, Mum, Pete and Tom. You're Spurs and you know you are. Here's to my beautiful daughter Georgia being added to that list sometime soon.'

Scooby Brown; 'What better choice of author than Jim "The Memory" Duggan. His knowledge of Spurs history is only surpassed by his knowledge of equine winners & blood lines. About time he got a job anyway! COYS.'

Clint Rance; 'Moved away from London area over 20 years ago, Topspurs and FTL have made it possible for me to feel part of the "Spurs family" from nearly 200 miles away … wouldn't change it for the world, wouldn't have met Lisa or had my two lovely girls Amy and Christie, if I'd stayed … COYS.'

Mark Astaire

Ben Astaire

Max Astaire

Steven Timson; 'Being a Spurs fan can be interesting as you are never guaranteed an easy life. The team can make you cheer with pride, cry with frustration but I'd never be anything but a YID. COYS and look forward to reading the book.'

Paul Dandy (CumbrianSpur); 'My eyes have seen the glory.'

JimmyG2; 'Fame is the Spur', JimmyG2 at Spurs Musings.

David Jacobs

Katie Jacobs and Chris Jacobs; 'Lifelong Spurs supporter – it's all my dad's fault!'

Philip Cross; 'to my Dad (Peter Cross), lilywhite's through and through, Tottenham 'til we die. The FA Cup run of 91 sticks in my mind, Gazza's late goal vs Notts County, Paul Stewart's equliser in the final. Come on you Spurs, Love Pip x.'

Nick 'Bizness' Higgs

Hans Meekers; 'Topspurs, world famous internet home of the Spurs. Always a great read, a well of knowledge on the glorious past of the club. Dating back to a time when a stamp-sized pic would take ages to load on your PC. And through its message board I've met plenty of fellow Spurs fans who've become mates. Long may it continue and I've really looked forward to this book. COYS.'

'Spidofspurs' and Bridget Rider

JonH1964; 'To absent Yids – gone but never forgotten.'

Eric Mallia; 'Topspurs has always been my first port of call online when seeking my daily dose of Spurs related news, stats and engaging opinions. Living overseas for so many years it's an invaluable resource and window into everything Tottenham. Topspurs is deserving of a place in the Tottenham Hall of Fame in its own right.'

David Etere

Logan Holmes

Carl Feehan; 'Plenty more downs than ups but wouldn't change it for the world. Not always a joy supporting THFC but always a pleasure. COME ON YOU SPURS.'

Colin Rowland

Chris 'Tottenham Hotspur Forever' Ion; 'I love spurs more than life itself.'

Anthony Ronan

Daniel Wynne; 'This book is a must for all Spurs fans. Who better than Jim Duggan to lead us through this light hearted look at our club's rich history.'

Samantha Johnson; 'Grateful to my sister for having the good sense to marry a Tottenham supporter.'

Mally Armstrong; 'We are TOTTENHAM from the NORTH, Cumbrian Spurs.'

Bazzer

Grahame Howells

Annamarie Howells

Simon Hayes/Clives49; 'Simon Hayes – My Wife Is A Gimp.'

Lynford

Mark Anthony

Thom Martini

Dan Johnson

Robert Sumner

Richard Ceeney

Simon Ittig aka Stockport Si; 'Expect the unexpected.'

Richard Pymont; 'Good to see another quality book about the Club.'

Matt Wright; 'This is why your Dad made you Spurs. Enjoy the ride son!'

Andy Varley; 'To Baby Varley, sorry for the lifetime of disappointment I have bestowed on you with Spurs.'

David McKean

Colston Vear; 'It's a grand ole team to cheer for ...'

Glen Sapsford

James Mariner

Danny Keene

Michael O'Sullivan

Adam Powley

Chris Hardie

Sean Connolly

Chris Morgan

James Morgan

Andrew Bryce

Carsie – East Belfast Spurs; 'Good luck Jim, glad to see Topspurs go from strength to strength, from your friends over in East Belfast.'

Leigh Richards; 'I can't think of any other club for whom the style of football we play is as important – and maybe more important – than winning. That's one of the things that makes Spurs special. Tottenham till I die.'

Sigvaldi Torfason; 'I have supported Spurs since 1969. Got to know them through a friend who has now passed away. The first Spurs game I saw was in Reykjavik against Keflavík. There was no turning back after that. COYS.'

Graham Carpenter; 'With thanks to my late Dad for passing on his love for THFC to me ... also big thanks (I think!) to Jim for introducing me to the big, bad world of Spurs message boards. COYS.'

Gary Briggs; 'Who set up Ricky Villa in '81 ... Tony Galvin on the wing!'